© copyright 1995
Idea Books
Via Vigevano, 41
20144 Milan

All rights reserved.
No part of this book may be reproduced in any form without written permission from the publisher.

ISBN 88-7017-121-3

Printed in Italy

Front cover:
CROSSBOW, Mega-Communication Center
Renato Severino, Architect

FOREWORD

I began planning this book in the early Seventies when, literally "midway on the path of life that man pursues I found myself in darkling wood astray, for the direct way had been lost to view". This happened at the time when the global dominance of the Modern Movement in architecture was coming to an end. I had been brought up within the limits and principles of this ideology and had found inspiration in it for more than twenty years.

At that point in life, without a meaningful perspective, I had to search for a new direction through a catharsis and I felt that the writing process would be the right way to achieve this. It was not clear to me then whether the book would be a means or an end, since it could be considered either an autobiography or a manifesto. I have, in fact, asked myself if it would be more meaningful for a reader, in this period of confusion in the visual arts, to have direct testimony of a historical period that is ending, or whether it would be more helpful for those who want to look at the future.

Torn between these two alternatives, I have produced various versions of the manuscript in English and in Italian, alternatively giving more space to one or the other of these two possibilities.

Many friends have helped me by reading and evaluating my manuscripts. Considering the long period elapsing between the start of the work and its completion, I may unfortunately forget to mention some of them. I wish above all to thank my wife Mimma, for her concrete aid in the English language version and for having sustained me in my long personal torment.

I am indebted to Barbara Loos for her precise research and to Mario Salvadori and Ana Daniel for their constructive criticism. Adriano Mastelloni, Paolo Riani, Piero Pescarolo and Nicoletta Gentile, Renato Polidori and Michael Fantacci have been of great help in the conclusive phase of the work.

Filippo and Angela Passigli, the publishers of Idea Books, have followed this book from its birth to the final stage. Catherine Frost has been responsible for the final editing.

I would like to express special thanks to James Ziskin, director of the Italian house, Zerilli Marimo' of New York University, for having organized the first exhibition of my works published here and the presentation of this book.

Florence, february 1995

INTRODUCTION
AND AUTOBIOGRAPHICAL OUTLINE

At times one needs to build as much as possible, while at others one should stand back to look at the past and evaluate the present in order to make crucial decisions for the future. In the mid-Nineties, this would seem the most logical attitude to take in a world that is changing faster than ever before.

In the writer's own case the posing of philosophical, or even existential, problems comes implicitly from the certainty that, on both the personal and the professional level, architecture derives from ideas and the influence of society. This can be seen particularly when the planning and construction of large-scale projects becomes a complex activity, taking place over several years and involving the political, administrative, technical and legislative aspects of any organized community.

This book is published at a time when people in the western world are wondering what will become of their cities and their culture in view of the peaceful but relentless invasion of people from the poorer nations. Such a world-wide significant event is particularly noticeable during a period of difficult readjustment of western nations, which are trying to retain their traditions while embracing the innovations of technology in the midst of a major global economic change.

My reflections are an attempt to find a new direction or at least to participate in clarifying the situation in a world that has produced architectural solutions often unacceptable inasmuch as they have sprung from disorder and contradiction. It was, in fact, the continuous feeling of insecurity caused by the many conflicting demands of society that convinced me of the need for a critical method to evaluate the logic of my thoughts and actions. The process of analyzing contemporary phenomena became essentially a real psychological self-analysis to see if my vision of the world was completely realistic or ideologically slanted. This opened up new perspectives and determined the need to study, examine and weigh all factors that determine architecture.

My long analysis thus began in 1973 when I realized that my mode of thought, deriving from the Modern Movement, was no longer adequate to the expectations of the new society emerging at that time. Not merely by chance, I was then teaching at Yale University, which was more steeped in American tradition than the liberal, often radical, Europe-oriented Columbia University where I had taught for five years starting in 1967. In my teaching, I tackled the problem facing society on two levels: the first was that of social consensus due to the acknowledged need of architects to communicate with a wider public; the second was related to a purely personal intellectual need to conceive and produce architecture of a significance that could be widely shared.

I felt strongly about the problem of social consensus because I had experienced all of its aspects. Growing up in the Italy of the 1930s I had been confronted with a dual-natured truth: an official one taught by my Fascist schooling and a liberal one, free of dogmas, imparted by my family. My adolescent mind was divided between the attraction of promises of a great future for Italy offered by the then powerful regime and my father's predictions of the failure and collapse of Fascism, which dampened my enthusiasm. The dilemma was soon resolved, as within a few years Fascism began to disintegrate showing its ineptitude and fatuousness, while the persecution of my father, anti-fascist but not left wing, continued until the end of the war. I had therefore experienced the power of social consensus and conformity, which emerge in all societies when an ideology becomes the overriding influence. At the same time I valued the importance of sharing ideas in a large group for the results that can be obtained by directing collective will-power and action towards the same goal. But above all, I had begun to understand how consensus must be based on solid, well-tested truths rather than on an ideology which is inherently self-limiting.

When I entered the School of Architecture of the University of Florence in 1948 I found myself growing along with the Modern Movement, which was rapidly becoming the dominant philosophy in all schools of architecture and in the profession. I participated, therefore, in a situation of general consensus, to which I adhered not out of opportunism or conformity but out of deep conviction, for I sincerely believed then in the possibilities offered by Modernism. In the following two decades I dedicated myself with innovatory spirit to the construction of that society known today as the Third World but which was then for young moderns their own new world.

By the age of thirty-two I had begun to travel to Africa to fulfill my dreams and offer my help. I was personally given the task of building two new universities and many other public and private buildings. Although these were certainly not easy undertakings for my group, given the environmental and cultural difficulties we had to overcome, the projects were successfully completed.

In the following years my Modernism became even more radical with a philosophy of industrial mass-production associated with a moralism that heralded technology as the means of overcoming poverty and backwardness. My first book, "Equipotential Space", was the expression of my credo in its search for a new perspective for the ideology of the Modern Movement which was beginning to show its limitations. Fortunately I came through this ideological storm, with all that it meant in terms of post-war reconstruction, to realize that I had not been responsible for destroying country or urban landscapes since I had always refused to support speculation in building and the hurried realization of superficially conceived projects.

In the 1960s, Marxist ideology dominated the universities and schools of architecture in Italy. In the understandable anxiety for a just renewal of society it seemed that one could no longer be capable and intelligent without being Marxist. Those like myself who believed in the values of the Western Tradition were crushed on one side by the power of Marxism, arbiter of the majority of innovative forces, and on the other by Catholic traditionalism, dedicated to the defense of its past. Here again the achievement of consensus within ideological movements appeared to be a necessary prerequisite for the popular flow of ideas. Inevitably, however, conformity limited the freedom of those who did not accept either of the two ideologies which were slowly pushing Italy toward the margins of Europe. This was one of the reasons why, in 1968, I decided to leave Italy for the United States, where a more open-minded attitude toward new ideas gave me the necessary psychological freedom and protection from political extremism. It was there that I began the period of reflection that was to lead to the deprogramming of my way of thought, conditioned by the orthodox ideology of the Modern Movement. But it was only when I came to write the final version of this book, which was begun as a means of helping me to organize my thoughts and make them accessible to others, that I realized that I had been witness to as well as participant in the evolution of ideas in architecture for four decades. The years since World War II have seen many changes in philosophical approaches which I have tried to analyze, often through my own experience. In studying how the ideas of those years have been translated into architecture, I have tried to understand the relationship between changes in society's modes of thought and architectural concepts. To do this I have had to dive back into the past, for like all Modernists, I had for years made the error of looking only to the future.

While researching and analyzing the history of civilizations, I found myself wondering what would be the result of the growing economic and cultural differences between western nations and the rest of the world. I also began to consider that there are a great many poor people in the west, who are becoming increasingly isolated from their own countrymen by their inferior living conditions and expectations. This was the theme of my first book which was rejected by many traditionalists, not so much for the proposed solutions of a technological nature but rather because it dealt with a difficult problem that has now become even more urgent and thus even more difficult to face.

A number of historians have commented on the fact that many civilizations of the past were defeated or weakened from within as the result of a continuous wave of immigration which slowly submerged and obliterated them. Many great cities whose quality of life attracted people from without have perished in this way. Their conquerors built new towns over the ruins, calling them by the same name, but these were in no way comparable in terms of culture. Rome itself died out, smothered by its own ashes, when the new culture emerging from the catacombs brought the Western Tradition to a halt for almost a thousand years. Historians and social scientists refer to this phenomenon when speaking of the millions of people living below the poverty line in western countries, the United States in particular. These men, women and children live in the tunnels of the subways, under bridges and in abandoned houses: are these the new catacombs?

In this book I have included part of my own work, built on three continents, as demonstration of my very direct personal involvement in the recent short-lived historical cycles that mirror the rapidly changing socio-economic reality. These changes have become a materialization of the main philosophical orientations of western society over a period of forty years, from the Modern through the Post-Modern to the solutions of the Nineties. As the works which demonstrate my interpretation of each phase have been documented in major American and European magazines and in several books, they can, I believe, be considered representative of the times they describe. But the main function of these examples is to make explicit and comprehensible, particularly to young architects, the relationship existing between thought and action. The responsibility of an architect lies in his or her capacity to be faithful to his or her own ideals while responding to the needs of society. My research into the history of realism in architecture and in the visual arts is based on just that conviction, in its attempt to analyze those periods in which architects were able to offer a lasting contribution to their own and future communities.

CONTENTS

Part One   9
THE RELATIONSHIP BETWEEN ARCHITECTURE, THE CITY
AND SOCIAL CONSENSUS

1 - The Spirit of the Leader-City
2 - The Relationship between Architecture and Society
3 - Social Consensus
4 - Artistic Synthesis

Part Two   19
NON-CONSENSUS IN SOCIETY, IN THE VISUAL ARTS AND IN ARCHITECTURE
AT THE CLOSE OF THE XX CENTURY

1 - Division and Polarization in Western Society
2 - Division in the Country and in the City
3 - The Crisis of Technologically Inspired Ideologies
4 - Non-Consensus in Painting and Sculpture
5 - Non-Consensus in Architecture
6 - The Crisis of the Modern Movement and the Return to Traditionalism
7 - Post-Modernism Conquers the Scene
8 - Confrontation between the Modern Movement and Post-Modernism
9 - From Ambivalence to Neo-Surrealism
10 - Deconstructivism and Neo-Surrealism
11 - Contemporary Architecture Is on Trial

Part Three   57
THE INFLUENCE OF MENTAL PROCESSES ON ARCHITECTURE

1 - The Significance of Tradition and Innovation in History
2 - The Two Creative Modes of Thought
   a) The Analogical Process: Tradition
   b) The Analytical Process: Innovation and Science
3 - Two Concepts of History
4 -. The Linear Concept of History in Modern Art and Architecture

Part Four 68
THE BALANCE BETWEEN THE TWO MENTAL PROCESSES IN HISTORY:
REALISM AND META-REALISM

1 - From the Balance between the Two Processes:
    the Birth of Realism in Art
2 - Meta-Realism in Art and Architecture
3 - The Levels of Expression of Realism
4 - The History of Realism

Part Five 105
META-REALISM IN THE FUTURE OF ARCHITECTURE AND URBAN PLANNING

1 - Utopia and Meta-realism
2 - The Three Variables Determining Architecture
    in a Meta-Realistic Perspective:
    a) The First Variable: Consensus in Urban Planning
    b) The Second Variable: the Relationship between
       Traditional Influence and Innovation
    c) The Third Variable: the Language
3 - The Meta-realistic City
    a) The Multi-Racial and Mono-Cultural City
    b) Permanence in the Urban Environment

Appendix
 115

1 - Preface
2 - Restoring the Broken Links: Reality - Dream - Pure Thought
3 - Cartesia: the Concept of a Traditional City Seen in the Present
4 - A Possible Aesthetics for Meta-realism in a Future Projection
5 - Town and City in the XXI Century

Part One

THE RELATIONSHIP BETWEEN ARCHITECTURE, THE CITY AND SOCIAL CONSENSUS

1 - The Spirit of the Leader-City

There is a growing hope among young people in the Western world for a new city that incorporates the best traditions of the past while looking towards the future with enthusiasm and optimism. The desire to participate in the building of this ideal city is apparent not only in schools of architecture where bold, inspired projects experiment with new forms and situations, but also in disciplines concerned with human relations in the society of the future. With systematic progress based on new access to information and the establishment of criteria for development, the young of the Nineties will have to determine the parameters of a society that finds in cities the fulcrum of ideas. Planning a city, in fact, implies contributing to its immediate development in all aspects, economic, ethical and intellectual. The urban space has always been the scene of social and cultural exchange when the flux of relationships and activities is nourished by dreams of a better life.

The spirit of a city lies in the kind of future it is capable of imagining and putting into practice. If it is not fed by this vital, dynamic spirit, any urban community falters and is inexorably pushed towards decadence. The early Seventies saw a rapid change of scene as a result of the spread of urbanization after World War II. Cities all over the world which had represented poles of attraction for centuries soon became virtually unlivable. An alarm has been sounded world-wide warning of the possible self-destruction of the largest cities, tormented by so many problems of physical and social origin.

Why then have the cities of the world lost their proverbial magnetism? The process of architectural change, with its shift in philosophical direction and blatant U-turns, which took place in the post-war period in a climate of contradiction has given rise to an urban life no longer acceptable to its inhabitants. With its illogical planning the city, no longer on a human scale, is unpleasant and hard to live in. It has been publicly defined as a collection of large boxes untidily jumbled together around the few still attractive areas built in the last centuries.

No modern synthesis has been able to produce an urban environment derived from a creative dream. By contrast, all of the great leader-cities of the past were thought out in every detail by the people of the community and the architects who built them. An architect has always had to dream in order to envisage an urban space capable of developing coherently over time, handing down his vision to those who come after him. Thus a city like Venice has, over a period of five hundred years, developed a pattern of urban space among the canals, squares and alleyways, that has always followed the original concept. The visitor who discovers the city for the first time sees a truly three-dimensional theatrical show, coherent in its script, which is constantly changing but faithful to the original intent of its creators.

Cities built in earlier centuries were able to absorb gradual change without having to accept radical transformation or transfiguration of the existing fabric. It was only after World War II that large-scale projects, necessary for medium and long-term planning, brought about the collapse of the classic urban structure. The charm, the continuity and the intimacy of old cities were lost along with the functionality that should have been created.

The reason for this global disaster lies in the erroneous conception of new cities and new parts of existing cities, built to outdated, inefficient XIX century patterns camouflaged by modern aesthetics.

The classic city, built on one level where people and vehicles live and move, even with subways built underground and huge highways above, no longer seems able to respond to the demands of the XXI century. A truly innovative conception is needed, able to solve the catastrophic problems of traffic and pollution, providing all of the elements required for a city in the year 2000 and beyond.

Admittedly then, the XX century has not yet been able to build a city that will go down in history with a formal conception and comprehensive design of its own. Only in the late XIX century and the first few years of the twentieth did the American city seem able to suggest new solutions, while the metropolises of Europe stayed firmly anchored to traditional planning. New York and Chicago offered at that time an exciting new dimension, attracting people from all over the world driven by ambition and the desire to participate in the building of a better future. The canyons created by the avenues of New York with their towering buildings and distant perspectives seemed finally to have achieved that large-scale third dimension sought by Modernism(*) to embody its ideas in a representative urban space. This dream, however, was not to be fully realized.

The immutable laws and principles of the leader-cities assured their survival throughout the centuries. It is this capacity to communicate a sense of security which has been their major appeal, making these urban centers of the past so highly admired. The equation:

LEADER-CITY = CELEBRATED ARCHITECTURE = HISTORICAL ENDURANCE has shown itself to be the best guarantee for the continuity of a city's life.

It is conceivable that in the process of planning, the new three-dimensional and spatial conception can be adopted without limiting it to a functional, abstract and mechanistic idea, as in the modern urban fabric where a narrowly defined systematic engineering has predominated. The restoration of artistic composition to the architectural process, as an integral part of the design of the city, may provide the impetus which will again attract and stimulate the best creative forces. But above all, a new relationship of direct communication between the architectural process and society seems necessary, to obtain comprehensive solutions deriving from logic, feeling and contemporary intuition.

2 - The Relationship between Architecture and Society

The most distinctive features of the celebrated architecture which is forever valid have always been authenticity and formal balance. Authenticity, seen as a temporal and environmental expression of originality and identity, passes on to the future the truth of the initial creation, which is comprehensible to all. Formal equilibrium comes from acceptance of the stable aesthetic values which have guaranteed the

---

(*) In speaking of the modern period we are referring specifically to the years from the Twenties to the early Seventies. After this period, a philosophical change occurred on the level of both society and architecture. A parallel development was that of criticism which evaluated the influence of modernity in a new light.

In art and literature the last few years are commonly referred to as the Post-Modern period, without qualifying it precisely. Modernism can be described as a philosophy whose values are based predominantly on economic and scientific progress. Among the general public, the term "modern" is frequently used as opposed to "ancient", and not in a strictly philosophical sense. In referring to the world of today, the term "contemporary" should be used in place of "modern".

The failure of modern cities

An obsessive order, perceivable in each building conceived only as a container of functions, has produced with its tormenting and repetitious rhythms a physical and social disorder in the new cities.

The patterns of modern facades in New York and in the new areas of Florence use the same language that expresses the same sense of renunciation of an artistically accomplished architecture.

Social consensus gives shape to the city

Lasting stability and receptive architectural forms attract all sorts of activities and offer emotional identification to the future generations of inhabitants.

Florence, Piazza Signoria (left) and New York, Rockefeller Center (right).

spiritual continuity of humanity, inasmuch as they have always been universally recognized. This balance is a direct reflection of the moral tension present in the architectural synthesis. Every past and present society has believed in these values, which provide reassurance from one century to the next, although the emphasis is shifted according to the different philosophical tendencies of each period. Values must be based on a perfect balance of the highest qualities such as sincerity, honesty, the ability to transform ideas into reality, and feelings. But over and above these principles is the ability to invent and to dare, to achieve with courage and wisdom new goals in architecture. When these qualities are shared by intellectuals and artists as well as the public at large, they determine the cultural level of a society, making it possible to reach the highest levels of civilization. Great architecture, painting and sculpture have defended these values over the centuries, providing a continuity that is manifest in their works, and thus conferring on the civilizations that have produced them the necessary physical and spiritual stability. The ethical-aesthetic relationship here again proves to be indissoluble.

The state of grace is represented by the leader-city, reflecting the self-determination of a society perfectly able to construct the space it requires. Moreover, authenticity results from a balance between acquired experience that has become immutable tradition and innovation represented by the spatial, functional and technical concepts characteristic of each period. Loss of authenticity, on the other hand, derives from imbalance between these two factors, when one outweighs the other. For example, a preponderance of traditional values results in a poor copy of the past, while the dominance of utilitarian and dehumanized innovative solutions produces only sterility.

The spiritual continuity required for the moral stability of every society through the ages is provided by the natural tendency toward equilibrium of the human mind. The characteristics of this equilibrium have remained unchanged since the beginning of history; scientific research has shown that the structure of the human skull and brain has been basically the same for thousands of years. Human aspirations and qualities have not changed, nor have ethical and aesthetic parameters. For this reason human terms of judgement remain the same, enabling us to evaluate today with the same logical parameters Egyptian architecture of the Old Kingdom and Sumerian writings dealing with the problems of organized society. In like manner, the message of the Greek philosophers of the V and IV centuries B.C. reaches us loud and clear.

It was finally realised in the Eighties that the ever changing conditions of life have not altered our basic mental and spiritual equilibrium. Appalling errors have been made in recent history in the attempt to modify the human psyche according to the precepts of modern ideologies hypothesizing an entirely new mental equilibrium. Architecture has faithfully mirrored these ideologies, proposing projects that put these theories into practice, particularly on an urban scale. But if we look to history we see that, on the contrary, the leader-city is born of a stable equilibrium, based on respect for the principles that transcend short-lived philosophies. Proof of this can be seen in the elaborate and well-proportioned spatial sequences of the cities built up to the end of the XVIII century. Their continuity provides a a comforting sense of security, while the overstated "modern logic" surrounding us produces discontent and psychological detachment.

Any present or future society that aspires to go down in history must pass on to future generations an architecture based on principles and values understood and shared by the many, yet fully representative of its own time. Architecture has always been the true mirror of society, faithfully reflecting the standard of living as well as the achievements, ambitions, dreams and contradictions of every period. In its visible substance, architecture has been the vehicle for transferring a society's aspirations from the mental level to the concrete. The most impressive testimony of past civilizations is represented by what remains of their edifices.

3 - Social Consensus

Celebrated architecture has always come out of a society where consensus among its citizens, seen as unity of purpose and similar interpretation of reality, has become clearly stabilized, even if for a limited period. Social consensus is thus the most important factor in architecture. The most significant quality of consensus is its very authenticity.

In analyzing the architectural and artistic production of each historical period, it becomes apparent that, when a society possesses unity of purpose, there is almost unanimous consensus of its citizens as to resolving problems and shaping a common image of the future. This phenomenon has always resulted in the creation of a leader-city capable of stimulating new and more rapid development.

False consensus, on the other hand, comes from the social imbalance produced by a dictatorship which limits freedom and creativity. Imposed by force or through psychological subjection, false consensus has never contributed to civilization or produced an art form expressing the highest humanistic values. The ability and will of individuals in a community to debate problems constitutes the intellectual and political element that offers humanity the chance to attain new heights. Neither imposition nor intimidation have ever created outstanding artistic achievements to be handed down to future generations.

Certain cultures have produced, under the dominance of a political power, a form of architecture that can be appreciated more for its impressive physical presence than for its absolute value. The distinction between architecture whose value is limited to the moment of its production and great architecture achieved through true social consensus is a fundamental one.

Consensus with active participation develops in stages, since time is needed to sift information, analyse it and finally implement it. This process takes place on three different levels:

— On the first level public assent is generated.

— On the second level the contributions of critics, schools and the Élite who are directly interested in the process are evaluated.

— On the third level the opinions of the artists and individuals directly responsible for the creation of architecture are appraised.

Obviously, the larger the majority, the more effective is the consensus. Thus when majority consensus exists within each level, the process moves towards interaction among the three levels. At this stage difficulties may appear due to the possible differences in judgement among the three groups, deriving from their intellectual, philosophical and social dissimilarity.

While a majority decision for each problem may be easily reached within each level, a clear consensus of the three levels is more difficult to achieve. Although a new trend may quickly find favor with artists, critics and the intellectual élite, it will be harder to conquer public opinion, since the mass public does not share the ideas of the professionals in the field, much more susceptible to the influence of the new and avant-garde.

If the lack of consensus among the three levels lasts for a long period, indicating a state of continuous opposition and tension between groups of individuals within the same society, the situation becomes very negative. When the positive forces within a society are not moving in the same direction, history teaches that there is a loss of precious energy impeding any kind of progress. The state of decadence of that society soon becomes manifest and is inevitably reflected in its architectural production.

CONSENSUS = PROGRESS = LEADER CITY = CELEBRATED ARCHITECTURE

In the alternation of societies throughout history, this sequence has unfailingly brought about an architectural state of grace.

When consensus appears in the social fabric of a balanced culture, economic, social and moral progress soon follow. In this context it is necessary first of all to define what is meant by progress. Orthodox and religious traditionalists attribute it at least in good part to divine providence, while scientific and materialistic thought sees it essentially as a product of economic origin.

Progress can be seen as a state of relative improvement acquired by the majority of individuals in a given society. For this society to make a positive, enduring contribution to other communities throughout the world, the level of its achievements must be high. This occurs when in some area of the world the highest levels of art, scientific discovery, architecture and general culture are attained, representing the greatest intellectual achievements of that time. Humanity has made lasting progress only when knowledge transmitted from one society to another has proved to be of use to other peoples, in a different context but in a realistic situation.

Only a limited number of cultures have attained this goal. Presumably other future cultures will also do so. The pendulum of history has frequently changed the rhythm of its oscillations at intervals of centuries. In certain geographical areas progress has only come about in recent times, while in others the pendulum, after swinging rhythmically for centuries, seems to have slowed down or stopped.

To achieve balance and thus contribute to a lasting civilization, progress must be simultaneously economic, social and moral. There must be economic progress to ensure wealth to future generations. There must be social progress guaranteeing freedom and defense of human rights to all members of society who choose to work for their own welfare and that of the community. Above all, there must be moral progress since the cohesive force of a society comes from the spirit of sacrifice necessary to attain the highest ethical results.

When progress becomes mainly economic, dangerous social imbalance ensues. The consequent tendency to hedonism leads eventually to decadence. On the other hand, the predominance of a moralistic tendency leads to the overwhelming power of religion, bringing with it economic and social imbalance.

In societies where social consensus and progress have been exceptional, we see active pluralism or democracy with diverse cultural elements which produce enthusiasm and competition but also create controversy and tension.

During the period when the Modern Movement held sway, a number of critics believed in the deterministic power of architecture, seen as an autonomous process capable of influencing its own development. In reality, self-determination in art and architecture as regards ideas and their development over a period of time has never existed. Artistic expression, and architecture even more, have always followed the leadership of the society in which they developed. The circumstances and theory determining any kind of artistic development have always been outside of art per se, which should be seen as a commentary rather than an end in itself. Although the artist is responsible for the quality of the commentary, the work has always and only been a reflection of the aspirations and level of the society in which it was produced. In every period and every geographical context, artistic capacity has always had a direct relationship with the quality of other achievements. Every society is thus self-defined by its production, consisting of thought and works of art which are handed down to later generations in the typical style of the times. The great architecture of the Greek temples was born along with the illustrious philosophy, literature and theatre of the time, because the semiotic origin of every form and every concept which was physically transposed into architecture was inevitably common to all of the other disciplines of the time.

Sienese painting of the early Renaissance provides us with another example. The message of society was received by local artists in a precise and linear manner. The responses of the artists were remarkable in their continuity and quality. Through personal interpretations, they speak a common language describing a felicitous reality shared by all Sienese citizens. Expressed in "courtly language" these paintings describe a community able to project its image of the future, communicating through expressions as simple and clear as their serene landscapes.

To achieve outstanding architecture it is vitally important that the architect have complete freedom in producing his or her artistic composition. Society's influence on the architectural process, when it derives from a genuine consensus on three levels, imposes no restraint on the architect. On the contrary, this influence provides him with psychological security and moral assistance, as he feels not only supported by society but also entrusted with a mandate to create.

4 - Artistic synthesis

After social consensus, artistic synthesis is the second determinant element for architecture, linked to the capacity of the human mind for elaborating data deriving from different origins and spheres, placing each element within a system where each has its own role to play, in order to arrive at the final result. In this synthesis all the qualities of the human mind have a precise function. Intuition and emotion fuse with the capacity for logical processing to produce continuity and fluidity. Over and above these capacities are other specific talents acting as catalysts in this complex process.

In personality, the artist who achieves the most perfect synthesis is always a child of his or her time, although employing a personal symbolism, language, subject and technique. This interpretation only emphasizes the effect of the historical context in encouraging or limiting artists, in determining the direction of their thinking, while not diminishing in any way the significance of their personal contributions.

The design process in any field is always basically an artistic synthesis, even as regards projects where the technological element is predominant, as for example a car or a supersonic airplane. At first sight, this may appear illogical to those accustomed to mentally separating art from science or technology. Particularly in this century, the general tendency is to refer to artistic production only in representational terms of traditional derivation and aesthetic nature. In architecture of high quality, however, the difference between art and science cannot be found, simply because it has never existed. All great works come from a synthesis in which artistic and scientific components are fused. In Brunelleschi's dome for the Cathedral of S.Maria del Fiore in Florence, how could the aesthetic criteria be separated from the technological? Brunelleschi created a total synthesis in which all the elements necessary to build the perfect dome, statically balanced and constructed in the most logical way, came into play simultaneously. Such a communion was possible because the persona of architect and engineer were one and the same, and not separate as is the case today due to the specialization which tends to differentiate between the expertise of each individual.

Contrary to true artistic synthesis is the essentially mechanistic constructive process of assembly typical of modern architecture, which uses compositional elements in set, repetitive schemes. Modern cities have been built mainly through this process, with the result that spaces on a human scale have been destroyed by the assemblage of huge, monotonous buildings constructed for the atomic age. Artistic synthesis, on the other hand, comes from a total vision that is always unique: a "work of art" which uses real and existing elements but uses them in a metaphysical relationship where intuition and freedom of expression coalesce in a real context. The difference between a "product of assemblage" and a "work of art" is like the difference between bread commercially produced in large quantities and the fragrant hand-kneaded loaves of the local baker.

In architecture too, a product can be easily assembled by technically minded architects who are uninterested in or incapable of producing a sublime artistic synthesis.

All great architects, up through the XVIII century, were always acclaimed artists, possessing talent, instinct and sensitivity along with the capacity to use the most sophisticated techniques. In addition to works of architecture, they have handed down to us paintings and sculpture of the same high quality. All of the great architecture that won universal acclaim was produced solely by architect-artists. They were not only artists but also builders, since in order to give meaning to their projects they had to see them constructed.

During the Renaissance, painting, sculpture, architecture and three-dimensional urban planning were all parts of a single activity nurtured by the same dream. Accordingly, the concept of the city was thought out on many different levels down to the last detail. For example, the painting "The ideal city", attributed to the school of Piero della Francesca, is direct testimony of a synthesis which aims to provide a total vision of a unique entity. Such a work not only proposed artistic-urbanistic synthesis on a purely conceptual level, but also provided the means for planning, using a technically perfected method of perspective.

The direct relationship between artistic synthesis and matter was clear to all architects of the past. Renaissance architects not only designed buildings, but in their youth worked in stone with their own hands in the same way as did sculptors. The transposition of the design into physical materialization of the building was, in fact, essential for the artist to communicate clearly with society. In this century, on the contrary, technological progress substitutes for the communion of artistic intuition-matter a synthesis-system. This approach is only rarely able to offer a complete artistic solution.

Before the XIX century and the split between art and science, many architects had contributed to various fields of knowledge. The first of these was the Egyptian Imhotep, who lived 27 centuries before Christ and was an artist, engineer, builder and scientist. Known for having designed the Pyramid of King Zoser as well as for having invented advanced techniques of construction, he was the forerunner of that classical tradition which has produced the greatest architectural treasures.

This tradition continued during the Greek and Roman periods when new technologies were developed and applied to architecture. But it was Leonardo da Vinci, more than any other artist-scientist, who captured the imagination with his discoveries and designs for machines of the future. Yet the designs of Leonardo did not really serve the cause of architecture. Although fascinating from a technological point of view, they proved to be inconclusive; too futuristic for the times they failed to reflect the ideas of the society in which they were produced. The architectural process of the time would undoubtedly have benefited more if Leonardo had designed avant-garde structures within a conceptually realistic context instead of exemplifying the first major split between architecture and engineering.

As a pure engineer, Leonardo certainly did

**The great architects of the past
were also renowned painters and sculptors**

Left - Sepulchre of Giuliano de' Medici by Michelangelo.
New Sacristy of San Lorenzo, Florence.

Right - "Creation of Adam" by Michelangelo.
Vault of the Sistine Chapel.

**Art and Science are an indivisible part
of celebrated artistic synthesi**

Left - Brunelleschi was the architect, engineer and builder of the Dome of Florence.

Upper right - The "Ideal City", detail, school of Piero della Francesca, well exemplifies a XV century comprehensive vision of the urban fabric.

Lower right - An airplane is also derived from an artistic synthesis. Even when the technological design component is very visible, the process of invention is the same as in the design of a building.

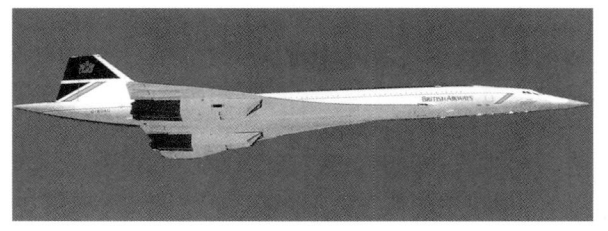

not achieve successful results. His structural studies led to mistaken conclusions because his research into the strength of materials could only be based on intuition, which was in this case erroneous. The basic principles of structural stress analysis are not intuitive. The ability to put forward an abstract idea based on para-scientific studies, in which Leonardo excelled, also proved to be different from the ability needed to contribute to an artistic synthesis with concrete possibilities of realization.

Language, the third determinant factor in the architectural process, is a systematic means of communicating ideas and feelings using conventional signs and symbols. It can also express abstractions, which are fully comprehensible within a cultural context where the same values and guiding principles are shared by all. Every artistic synthesis or work of art communicates with society via a language that has developed in parallel to those of other disciplines. Such a means of communication must be considered original when created by an authentic synthesis within a specific physical environment. This produces its own aesthetics, which evolve to reach an apogee while finding affirmation in the cultural stability generated by their repetitive use. At this point, however, their communicative power begins to wane, the language becoming a series of safe, well-tested axioms no longer capable of conferring originality on a work of architecture.

From the beginning of history, authentic architectural languages have been created in different parts of the world, achieving traditional status only when re-introduced in later centuries in a different environmental and historical context, reproposing the recognizable features of the artistic synthesis of the past, as with the Greek styles. Parallel to this, the development of construction techniques and new ideas on the use of space have resulted in the development, from the late XVIII century onwards, of a language of purely technological origin. In its continual transformation, this language has produced a divorce between function and aesthetics, a split that has had deleterious effects on the architectural process. Over the last two centuries load-bearing structures in particular have tended to become lighter, with the lessening of the specific weight of the building, to the point that new buildings are often only schematic and utilitarian spatial containers. No true artistic level is expressed here, because such a language does not itself derive from a complete artistic synthesis but only from an unbalanced process, dominated by the logic of the load-bearing function.

Language defines the aesthetics of synthesis and is the element immediately available to the observer. Thus the most immediate communication of architecture, not only with the society that produces it but also with future societies, takes place via its aesthetic message. It is for this reason that its language, rather than any other aspect of architecture, tends to become the main theme of historical study.

Part Two

NON-CONSENSUS IN SOCIETY, IN THE VISUAL ARTS AND IN ARCHITECTURE AT THE CLOSE OF THE XX CENTURY

1 - Division and Polarization in Western Society

The latent non-consensus existing in contemporary society has been the subject of debate since the 1980s. This non-consensus derives from the continuing presence of conflicting ideas not only in the individual mind but in all aspects of everyday reality, in every field of knowledge, in the theory and practice of all activities, on both the moral and the utilitarian level.

The philosophical incompatibility leading to this state of malaise, without precedent in its extent and range, displays the same characteristics everywhere. The direct and indirect consequences of this situation are alarming, since the achievement of consensus within society is one of the key elements determining its satisfactory development and thus influencing architectural synthesis. This is true particularly of western society at the close of the XX century, where large strata of population coming from different cultural backgrounds and up to now uninterested in the democratic process are now emerging.

The obvious non-consensus has been blamed mainly on technological development, which in all fields offers an alternative to traditional logic, providing new solutions in every sector and giving rise to uncertainty and bitter disagreement by destabilizing the existing equilibrium. In western countries, which may be defined as European nations, including some of the former Communist countries, and North America, there is a similar socio-economic formation despite obvious historically defined cultural differences. In the post-war period when its hegemony over the free world was clear and undisputed, the United States took the lead in offering the world a wide spectrum of new ideas, particularly visible in architecture. During this period, technological progress began to change the pre-existing world, still largely based on humanistic principles. This was accomplished by superimposing on the traditional environment a stratum of new constructions and communication networks, in which modern engineering dominated every aspect, imposing a new scale of ethical values on the world community. A different way of life was thus dictated to society, which began to move about on the planet more rapidly, producing a new dimension of material prosperity but at the same time pollution and incalculable damage to the natural environment.

To understand the prevailing psychology of the Sixties and the triumph of technology we must look at some of the international architectural projects published at the time, proposing the superimposition of megastructures on cities like Paris, London and Florence. Although such proposals were clearly utopian and pure intellectual speculation, it was clear that a new techno-world was working towards total substitution of the old one. It was obviously not the first time in history that such an undertaking had been attempted, although on a smaller scale. Baroque Rome was built by demolishing part of the pre-existing urban fabric, just as the building of Renaissance Florence destroyed part of the medieval city. A striking difference in the type of cultural change can, however, be seen in the extent and depth of this phenomenon. Technology and Modernism attempted to bring about a radical, irreversible transformation in every physical, economic and moral aspect of world society on an unprecedented scale. A state of unease was created by the unrestrained growth of science, often accused of respecting no pre-existing tradition or custom, accepted form or acquired symbol, nor the codes derived from ancient ceremonies and rites. The new progress also affected human relationships, encouraging the emotional, psychological and financial independence of the individual from the traditional family nucleus and giving people of both sexes an incentive toward self-direction. In the Eighties all religions and the Pope in particular repeatedly and explicitly denounced technology as the greatest evil in our society. A number of intellectuals expressed the opinion that if technology continued to progress at this speed it would lead to the destruction of the human psyche and the environment and the eventual annihilation of humanity.

The destabilization of the pre-existing balance has certainly influenced all aspects of world society, altering the time-established positions, roles and functions of individuals and institutions. Above all, the positive effect of the new role of women in contemporary society and in the work force in particular has aroused continuing debate due to the opposition of orthodox traditionalists. At the same time the question of global management and protection of the environment creates tensions between those who aim for zero growth and those who indiscriminately exploit natural resources for their own profit and thus advocate increased consumption.

The new technology of today means isolation and obsolescence for the unskilled and uneducated. The use of expensive, technically refined equipment makes it hard for the poorer nations to compete. The growing cost of every task and every manhour generates relentless economic pressure in every field, leading to a frenetic productivity syndrome.

In this situation non-consensus implies a growing polarization between the two extremes. On the one hand, traditionalists tend to defend the equilibrium of the past. On the other, the technologically-oriented accept a rapid transformation of society with all the risks inherent in constant change. These two philosophical positions, in opposition on every aspect of life and human psychology, tend to create two separate and mutually exclusive worlds.

2 - Division in the Country and in the City

Protests against the excessive influence of Modernism and technology, so conspicuous in cities all over the world, come from all sides. Only now has it been realised that modern cities have grown in surface size and volume using almost exclusively technical means such as motorways and functional containers, repetitive look-alike high-rise buildings and rows of identical houses, while the human values and sense of proportion which contribute to social interaction have been almost entirely forgotten. One cause of this imbalance may be seen in the actual separation of the various parts of the city, which now lacks continuity and communication because the growing population has not been integrated gradually into a well-planned living space. The newly arrived inhabitants are alienated in a modern city that no longer enjoys a degree of consensus among its inhabitants, as was nearly always the case in the past, in spite of the fact that history has its fair share of internal struggles between factions in the urban environment. The classical city grew in a natural way as does a tree or a shell, developing as necessary and at intervals both its structural ribs and its connecting tissue, creating parts that came together to form a harmonious whole. It was just this episodic nature in its unique and diverse aspects that made the growth of the city interesting, allowing variety in its development. By contrast, the technological city which developed with the industrial revolution is the expression of a completely different concept,

Non consensus in the built environment and in architecture

The examples shown portray the situation of non consensus in the United States during the Eighties. In Europe there existed a similar climate of opposition between high-tech and traditional architecture.

High Tech

Top - IBM Headquarters on Madison Ave., New York, E. L. Barnes, Architects

Center - The techno-style of living: a trailer surmounted by a TV disk antenna and surrounded by parked trucks, cars and boats on carts.

Below - A small office building with full curtain wall facades, in Greenwich, Conn.

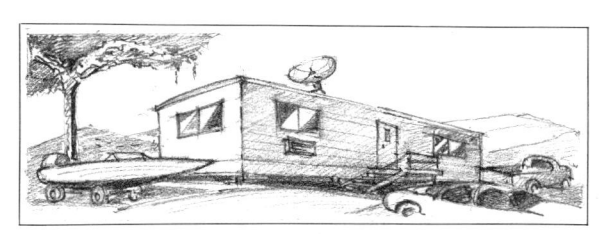

Traditional

Top - AT & T Headquarters on Madison Avenue, New York, Johnson and Burgee, Architects

Center - The typical traditional American house with pitched roof, shingle facades and chimney.

Bottom - A commercial structure built across the street from the office building shown in the opposite column.

deriving from a fundamentally mechanistic overall plan which divides and catalogues so as to rationalize its solutions. This method obviously tends to create a number of separate areas of similar characteristics with consequent stratification of people into distinct social groups.

The concept of implicit social division and separation of functions, so dear to the Modern Movement, derived not so much from practical necessity as from the erroneous application of a rigidly rational scheme of production to the much more complex phenomenon of the city. This philosophy expressed an attempt to escape from the complexity of systems deriving from different intellectual spheres and consequently from the elaborate geometry that produced the physical reality of the pre-industrial city.

Non-consensus is particularly evident in the United States, which offers a stunning example of the proliferation of zonal divisions created by barriers that are both visible and invisible. The exclusion of non-accepted groups is at times achieved by direct intimidation, as in the case of ghettoes and slums. In high-class residential areas, on the other hand, this exclusion is brought about by more complex and subtle means such as building regulations limiting uses and styles and thus representing a form of apartheid discriminating against new arrivals. To make the situation still more complicated, ultra-traditionalist groups such as the Amish in Pennsylvania do all they can to defend their areas, rejecting contemporary technology and remaining isolated from the rest of the nation. For this reason the houses of the Amish are still built as they were two centuries ago and they have no electricity.

Diametrically opposed to this is the life-style afforded by the mobile home parks, increasingly common throughout the United States. Here people live in pre-fabricated units resembling space modules with well-equipped kitchens and bathrooms. Thousands of these units are parked in vast areas, surrounded by cars, boat-trailers and work equipment. Often these accessories represent a greater volume than the dwelling-modules of the occupants. These communities are made up of millions of people, constantly on the move in search of a new job or a better climate. By contrast the traditionalists, whose number is increasing especially in the Europe of the Nineties, are returning more and more to the old city centres or to ancient country houses in the search for an atmosphere more in harmony with their way of life. The new is rejected since it offers neither equilibrium nor a credo worthy of being upheld and defended. Thus it is felt that only an old structure can offer the protection and balance that come from a pre-existing stability. Rejection of the new in favour of the antique or simply old has become a widespread trend, raising the prices of well-sited ruins that can be restored all over the world.

The fact is that the modern rarely achieves the dignified expression of volumes and proportions found in the old, where the predominant feeling is less logical and more poetic. In the modern, the search for a new design systematically acclaims short-lived inventive opportunism, whereas dignity comes instead from genuine feeling and immediacy of expression. In recent years, particularly in Italy, old town centers have become very desirable while local governments are endeavoring to correct the poorly planned suburban areas built in the 1950-80 period. Such costly large-scale programs are an indirect admission of the failure of modern urban planning and a total return to glorification of the antique.

The well-known rule of KISS, keep it simple stupid, quoted, approved and unconsciously widely applied in urban planning as well as in business during the last twenty years is often accused of having destroyed technological and industrial supremacy in many sectors of the United States economy. This doctrine, which rejects any kind of complexity in planning, has been criticized for emphasizing immediate profit with no regard to future consequences.

It is the rule of KISS that gave America its international supremacy in show business which, being only a temporary illusion, is the exact opposite of stability. Much of the gaudy architecture now to be seen in American cities seems follow the dictates of show-business in its brash, theatrical means of communication. During a long period of urban development American city planners abandoned all research into building types and transportation systems suitable to contemporary life, taking refuge instead in an obsolete evocation of the roaring Twenties. The development of experimental models for a new urban fabric, in harmony with the technological and humanistic requirements of society at the close of the XX century, has not been contemplated.

While the growing concern for protecting cities against crime is understandable, the overly defensive attitude which turns urban space into a series of impregnable fortresses is conceptually unacceptable. The American theory of "defensible spaces" was enthusiastically accepted everywhere in the Seventies as a positive, open proposal for redeeming the urban areas necessary for human interaction. However, both public and critics have become aware that the new cities of the western world cannot be built according to an urban planning theory based primarily on the concept of defense, and that there is no easy solution to a situation which has been deteriorating for decades.

3 - The Crisis of Technologically Inspired Ideologies

By the late Eighties the damage wreaked in both eastern and western society by a totally unbalanced period of accelerated technological development was finally acknowledged by the world community. The cities, or more specifically the new parts of cities built by the two political blocs, showed obvious symptoms of an advanced social crisis revealing the errors, and the horrors, of evaluation, planning and construction in the post-war programs.

It is symptomatic to see in this context how Marxism and capitalism, the two great socio-economic ideologies based on technology, enter into crisis at the same time, when the world population begins to impose new values on contemporary life. In the Seventies the absolute dominance of science, which for over half a century had been considered infallible, began to vacillate and the political systems based on scientific progress showed signs of breakdown. For the first time it was noted that science could be manipulated and used for purposes contrary to the interests of humanity and the expression "scientifically proven" assumed limited connotations, subject as it was to errors of interpretation and partiality.

The failure of Communist ideology had to be admitted in 1989, when it was clearly and emphatically rejected by the nations of the eastern bloc. Marxist science conceded that it was no longer able to solve the problems of the nations which had adopted its credo. State control over all citizens and their actions obtained through ideological pressure had destroyed any motivation for progress. Human individuality had been humiliated and conditioned by a system which aimed to solve all social problems by a restrictive and ruinous ideology of XIX century origin. The attempt to impose social equality is reflected in the terrible monotony of Communist architecture, distinguished by its oppressive dullness and repetition.

At the same time capitalist ideology with its promises of social and economic prosperity was showing signs of strain in the United States and the European countries where it had been wholeheartedly adopted. Capitalism in its extreme form proved to be the expression of a technological darwinian survival of the fittest, capable of destroying the weakest individuals who ultimately represent a large percentage of the population. The millions who live below the poverty line according to United States statistics and particularly the homeless sleeping in the streets of America are a tragic accusation of the capitalist system. The ghettoes and slums of big cities, covering tens of square miles, are the urban reflection of a part of this society, disoriented by its own moral collapse, by economic inequality and by social rejection.

The American Dream thus appears to waver, having lost its positive image of the future. With economic needs predominating over moral considerations, there has been great debate on all levels of American society in the attempt to achieve social consensus on the finding of an effective remedy.

Technology and economy are closely linked in the contemporary world, where they are mutually dependent on each other. Technology offers the economy the systems necessary for an ever wider world market, while the expansion of the economy affords great opportunities for ideas and action. Economic values take on an urgent, omnipresent role, subverting and too often diminishing ethical principles. What, it is asked, is the reason for the relentless rise of poverty and social alienation in the United States? Those who have studied the manifold aspects of this problem place the blame on the loss of psychological, moral and individual equilibrium, founded on pride in one's self and in the upholding of tradition. In the past, in every art and profession, the predominant guiding principles were a sense of responsibility for contributing to the well-being of society and the willingness to make sacrifices when necessary to maintain personal integrity. The architectural profession, with the high standards of its greatest figures, has always been pre-eminent in this moral covenant. In retaining traditional values, society was founded on the equilibrium resulting from the relationships between the roles played by individuals in a precise moral dimension. Thus in slowly changing the focus from moral to material values, the United States, the leader of the western world, has shifted the objectives of human activities almost exclusively to profit and hedonism. The essential pre-requisite for attaining these objectives is individual success based on aggressiveness and competition. With the faster pace life today, many individuals who cannot compete with the best begin to fall to lower socio-economic levels. In this harsh competition, stratification becomes inevitable. If material success, seen as the main goal in life, is not attained, the loser has no ideal or moral principle on which to fall back. Personal alienation, loss of self esteem and being forced to accept poor living conditions are the consequence. In the gladiatorial American society, the loser in the game is inevitably given thumbs down and, according to the rigid precepts of capitalism, he falls to the bottom of the social ladder.

4 - Non-Consensus in Painting and Sculpture

The climate of the Nineties has been faithfully reflected in painting and sculpture as well. The polarization of the opposing philosophies can be seen in the clear division of production into two distinct fields aimed at two separate sectors of the public. The first is the field of art inspired by traditional values; it is thus figurative and revisits classical themes. The other includes all non-figurative art, abstract or otherwise, always given new denominations, representing the latest artistic ideas and the most determined avant-garde proposals.

In every artistic cycle there has been an identifiable common denominator in the themes of leading artists. The arts of the 1950-90 period, however, show clear-cut division and polarity as well as fragmentation, resulting from a diversity of expressions so personal as to become totally non-communicative.

It is the first time in history that such diverse and opposing tendencies have been glorified by critics as true art. However, not only is there lack of consensus between the various groups in each field, but is even disagreement on the themes to be debated. Thus the discussions of the critics are incomprehensible to the public at large. In parallel, the schools no longer know what to teach their students, split as they are between figurative tradition, considered by some to be only an experience of the past, and the a myriad of new theories belonging to no precise, established philosophy. The episodic nature of contemporary is certainly not conducive to creating an organized course of study. Even more serious is the total incomprehension between critics who embrace the new theories and the general public. Consequently, the highest prices paid at international auctions are for the understandable, tendentially figurative art of the turn of the century: Monet, Manet and Van Gogh are the favourite painters.

In attempting to define the two opposing camps in Europe and the United States, we see evidence of traditional inspiration in the new landscape and still life painting, often marked by a gentle touch of realism. These works draw their inspiration mainly from French impressionism and late XVIII century English realism. This art appeals to those who believe in the defence of a stable world environment and thus in traditional values. The beauty of nature is the main theme of these works, accused by modernists of being déja vu and unoriginal. The figurative art of the Eighties took on many other aspects in both painting and sculpture, ranging from soft to photographic realism, and always attracted the attention of a large public.

At the other end of the spectrum, the contemporary art of modern derivation emphasizes the individualistic principles of the avant-garde and of new techniques. Everything is sacrificed to pursuit of the new, unseen and unproven, even when the price to be paid is the risk of total incomprehension. The world vision offered by abstractionists, conceptualists and the other currents that have appeared on the artistic scene in the last forty years is certainly not an optimistic one and well describes the anxiety and uncertainty of our times. The unusual and always new symbols proposed are not part of the so-called common reality understood by the general public. All too often an expert in each sphere of the avant-garde is needed to translate the artist's intended meaning. Traditionalists see this as a product of solitude, depression, alienation and even fear: the complete opposite of the image offered us by figurative artists. Contemporary art of traditional matrix, on the other hand, appears to withdraw from the tensions and pressures of the modern world when it creates atmospheres at times pastoral and rarefied, but too far removed from the incumbent reality (1).

The split between the two camps is becoming increasingly evident and communication in the art field ever more difficult and confused. From neither side do we get a successful and genuine representation of the situation of our time; one is too idyllic and often fatuous, the other too tragic and blurred. Traditional art certainly appears incapable of reaching the peaks of the past, while art of modern and post-modern derivation cannot offer a coherent, let alone positive, vision of the future.

While avant-garde and traditional art in Europe seem to exist in two separate non-communicative physical and psychological environments, in America hostility between traditionalists and modernists has been slowly building up for the last twenty years or so. Just as contemporary architecture was opposed by building regulations in the more affluent suburbs, avant-garde painting and sculpture have been ostracized by the traditionalists.

Typical examples of this situation were the removal by public demand of various sculptures by well-known modern artists from the town of East Hampton on Long Island and from the Federal Plaza in New York City (2). The sculptures, deemed "incomprehensible and unartistic" by a large sector of the local population, were widely discussed in the national press. These incidents, quite widely debated in artistic circles, seemed to mark the end of a period of reciprocal intellectual tolerance between modernists and traditionalists in the world capital of contemporary art, New York City.

5 - Non-Consensus in Architecture

If a rapid analysis of the situation in both city and country furnishes a clear example of non-consensus, the new architecture built in western countries, the United States in particular, during the Eighties gives at first glance an impression of dissension and polarization. The new buildings, rising one beside another in both large and small towns, display very different styles, reflecting various conflicting schools of thought. Again the geometrical forms of Modernism resemble more and more an industrial product of scientific origin when compared to traditional styles of local vernacular architecture attempting to recreate the symbolism of the past. The result is a clear materialization of the opposition between art and applied science existing in the popular culture of the last century.

These diametrically opposed philosophical positions deriving from the emerging socio-political equilibrium began to appear at the end of the XVIII century. In France, during the Revolution, the school of architecture was already split by the founding in 1794 of the Ecole Polytechnique, which made a sharp distinction between scientific and artistic education. A further separation between art and science took place in 1806 with the Napoleon's creation of the Ecole des Beaux Arts, a bastion of reactionary thought, established in opposition to the Ecole Polytechnique. During this period, for the first time in history, the possible solutions to a single architectural program were officially two: one of traditional matrix based on elitist principles, the other populistic and technologically oriented.

As regards social significance, the two schools were very different. The Ecole Polytechnique, created after the publication of the "Proclamation of the Right to Work" in France, was mainly directed towards the creation of a new rank and file in the construction industry. The Ecole des Beaux Arts, continuing its teaching of the arts and still boasting the protection of the ancien régime, addressed itself to the classes that could afford decorative, custom-built architecture. But above all, the diversity of the two schools on an intellectual level was portrayed on one side by a relaxed artistic vision, typical of a joyful or more contemplative life, on the other by a scientific and technological vision looking towards the practical world of production. The opposition between art and science grew out of just this situation, with a struggle for predominance developing, especially in Europe, between the classic architect and the engineer, destined to become a much deeper cultural conflict in the XX century (3).

The designers of buildings coming from the two schools were soon perceived by the public as very different in character. On the one hand was the artist, seen as a personality embued with genius and intemperance, on the other is the engineer who abides by rules and uses rational systems. The Renaissance concept of the art of building, centered on the architect's using his hands, head and heart, had changed as the result of an ideological dichotomy produced by assigning the various tasks to professionals mastering different skills.

The reason for the much discussed breach

can be attributed to specialization linked to the increased complexity of buildings from the XIX century onwards, when very sophisticated equipment and engineering began to be used. In reality, however, the separation between art and science represents a total incomprehension of the process of artistic synthesis, as a result of the dualism that marks contemporary thought. For this reason non-communication between scientists and humanists became the rule in all fields. Scientists and technologists felt bolstered by the support of industry, which used their talents, while the humanists, much less in demand, felt weakened and psychologically excluded.

C.P. Snow first defined "the two cultures" in the Forties, describing the separation and growing lack of communication between scientist and humanists. Lord Snow was speaking as an academic but with rare ability as both well-known scientist and successful humanist. In addition to his competence, his belonging to the British establishment assured that his analysis was not only listened to but also given serious consideration. While his theories were accepted by a large sector of the well-informed public however, they were not always understood by the active members of each of the two cultures. As C.P. Snow indirectly pointed out, these two cultures were unable to communicate and thus were incapable of fully understanding each other, and least of all were they able to evaluate the differences between their assumptions. Although Snow's theory had wide repercussions, the humanists of the time, interpreting culture in its strictly traditional sense, refused to recognize any cultural influence of science, due to its intrinsic lack of moral values. Moreover, they viewed local cultures in a restrictive sense, as separate entities that would not fit into a common matrix. In fact, identifying a common cultural matrix implies the recognition of a process of analysis capable of isolating common elements in the various traditions from all over the world, each linked to its own specific area. The pure humanists, who tend to confront each area of study deeply and thoroughly, consider this type of analysis as alien because the process is too scientific.

Scientists, on the other hand, already less inclined to abstract philosophizing, tend to divide science into specialized fields. This is certainly not conducive, except on rare occasions, to a comprehensive view of things or to understanding the relationship between ideas and social phenomena, and least of all to producing generalized definitions. Consequently the philosophical and methodological differences between humanists and scientists that were apparent in the post-war period tended to spread rapidly, except in a few specific cases, to all aspects of contemporary life, with the results that we have seen.

During the Twenties and Thirties the Modern Movement attempted to unite art and science, architecture and engineering in a common process, particularly through the contribution of the Bauhaus of Weimar directed by Walter Gropius. After this experience, if the work of the architect and that of the engineer did not exactly coincide they appeared at least to be parts of the same process. Initially, such an attempt seemed destined for success since it proposed an art form capable of using scientific elements in an industrial context for a larger society. In the years following the World War II, however, the Modern Movement failed to develop the artistic components provided by its more creative followers, favoring instead the technical-economic element increasingly more attuned to the logic of post-war reconstruction. This choice soon proved to be reductive however, and the Movement became the intellectual basis for the rapid industrialization of construction, but with a limited perspective. The sterile technical orientation produced by the continuing predominance of this aspect resulted in further lowering of standards for new buildings.

The rapid social and physical deterioration of these new constructions meant that serious damage to towns and cities was soon obvious to the public. The concept of the new in architecture, so attractive in the Fifties to those in search of new dwellings, became synonymous with cheap and undesirable, having lost its aura of cleanliness and true functionality. Modern planning based on the so-called rational and scientific process of the post-war period had failed.

1) In the summer of 1986, a new series of paintings and drawings by Andrew Wyeth attracted the attention of experts and the public. The subject of the works was a young woman, finely drawn in great detail. In the United States a bitter dispute ensued as to the artistic value of these paintings and the skill of the artist who produced them. Although internationally recognized as a painter of renown, Wyeth was judged by various noted critics of contemporary art to be merely a skilled illustrator. The reaction of the traditionalists was just as violent in accusing these critics, trained in the schools of thought of the Fifties and Sixties, of being totally incapable of understanding figurative art.

2) East Hampton in the state of New York, a city which boasts a large community of New York intellectuals and artists, was the scene of one such occurrence. In the summer of 1989 a number of large modern sculptures, exhibited in the centrally-located public gardens, were removed by order of the City Council. The local administration had voted to declare them unsuitable for exhibition within the context of the old, traditional buildings of the center, with which they were in formal contrast.

A similar event took place in March 1989 in Manhattan, in the heart of New York. A 40-meter long sculpture by Richard Serra, entitled "Tilted Arc", was removed by government decree from Federal Plaza, where it stood facing an office building. This sculpture, made of a curtain plate of steel, had been placed there in 1981, having been commissioned by the Federal Government. Its removal followed a lengthy and heated debate between the sculptor, one of the best known and respected American artists, and a large section of the New York public who opposed him, including a group of government workers from the offices overlooking the plaza. The decision was taken at a meeting of the City Council, where well-know personages in the cultural life of the city had spoken in favour of the sculpture. Serra's work, which expresses with great precision and skill a gigantic minimalism, had been described by many as "dehumanized", "strange and irritating" and had been the subject of dispute in both the United States and Europe.

In the Eighties Serra was acclaimed in Europe, where he was awarded many important commissions, including one for a statue in the Place de Choisy in Paris, for which he won the Chevalier de l'Ordre des Arts et Lettres, presented to him personally by President Mitterand. The case of Serra, who graduated from Yale and became established in the distinguished gallery of Leo Castelli, exemplifies the setting up of an alliance between the general American public and the traditionalist critics, marking the beginning of a new, stormy period in the field of art in the United States.

Another attack on modern art was made in 1989 by the "National Endowment for the Arts", in cutting finances for several avant garde exhibitions judged to be morally offensive. A large public had protested against these exhibitions, presenting art of a homosexual intonation. While critics were divided over the question of the interference of politics in affairs of art, it once again became clear that there was a negative reaction towards the contemporary avant garde, supported by a large sector of the American public.

3) In the Fifties and Sixties the split between architecture and engineering was quite clear in the USA. American architects jealously guarded their leadership in design, seeing structural engineering only as a tool, and denying any major influence of this activity on the design process. Engineers, even those whose artistic synthesis was acknowledged, were deemed incapable of designing a high-quality building, even when the structural element predominated. The following example is typical of this situation. In 1958 the New York Architectural League held an exhibition of the works of Pier Luigi Nervi, promoted by the association itself. The title proposed by the Nervi office was "Architecture in Concrete: The Work of Pier Luigi Nervi" but, before opening the exhibition, the Architectural League changed the title to "Engineering: The Work of Pier Luigi Nervi". The author of this book was the coordinator of the exhibition.

Although Nervi used a language of technological matrix with organic elements, he achieved a mature artistic synthesis that led to worldwide acclaim. However, the profession and critics of that time, seeing only the most obviously visible structural expressions, decreed that his works belonged only to engineering.

6 - The Crisis of the Modern Movement and the Return to Traditionalism

By the end of the Sixties it was clear that the Modern Movement was languishing. Not only critics but also the general public as well as many architects began to openly reject its principles and aesthetics. Its demise was paralleled by the growing philosophical crisis of the western world: a crisis deriving from loss of faith in the uncontested values of progress in a hypothetical mass society and abandonment of the principles of the industrial revolution. The Modern Movement thus lost the dominance over world architecture it had held for the 20 years following World War II.

Influenced by social doctrines and by the philosophy of technology, this movement had been embraced by nearly all schools of architecture in the world as well as by the profession. Its ideology, which spread as International Style, was animated by the same spirit, criteria and form in every country in the world, reigning supreme in Europe, the United States, Central and South America, Asia, Australia and Africa. Never before in the history of humanity had an architectural movement been so widely accepted.

It was generally believed at the time that every individual could achieve personal development and a place in a free community of man as a result of continual progress. A popular version of the Renaissance ideal of the universal man on a world scale seemed a tangible possibility. Just at this time, the Modern Movement with its simple lines and repetitive forms was making buildings of a sameness that freed them from the decorations representative of social status and from recognizable class symbols. Moreover, the aesthetic coordination and logic of its principles guaranteed the continuity of expression typical of a style which was stable, coherent and totally standardized. An ideal doctrine, perfect for a method of teaching which was structured at all levels, beyond any pre-existing traditional logic, for schools with international ambitions, with teachers and students coming from every country and culture.

These ideological developments were paralleled in psychology by the concept of the inborn equality of all: the mind as a "tabula rasa" to be developed by scientific progress, giving everyone the same chance for higher mental development. This was the basis for a general belief in the idea of one mind, one architecture and one science at the service of all people the world over.

The futuristic designs of the early modern period, the huge buildings conceived as schematic volumes linked by complex motorways, are certainly not attractive. Public opinion blamed the much vaunted vision of Le Corbusier and Mies Van der Rohe for this sad state of affairs. The bare simplicity of the architecture, which seemed a moral obligation in the '30s, was exploited by developers to make a quick profit and was later to become a symbol of housing for the poor.

By the Sixties the optimism of the post-war period was already starting to waver under the pressures of a new world socio-political situation. The advance of Communism in many third-world countries and the triumph of social democracy in Europe began to disrupt the balance of the existing social classes. At the same time it was commonly acknowledged that the so-called developing countries were not really developing at all. On the contrary, their economies were worsening day by day and capital invested at that time in third world countries afflicted by disease, debt and continual revolution bore very little fruit. (4)

By the late Seventies psychologists had abandoned the idea of a "tabula rasa" in favour of the theory of inherited genetic programming that determines mental development. New research indicated the predominance of nature over nurture. The message was clear; each adult is the sum of the mental characteristics he or she is born with, while the concept of all men being born equal was left to the American Constitution; obviously, however, the Constitution refers to the civic rights of all citizens.

Just as the myth of rapid development of third world countries was vanishing, the rest of the world was hit by the first great socio-economic crisis of the post-war period. The populist ideals which had often been put into practice were abandoned. The grandiose projects financed by international banks in third world countries came to a halt, as did housing projects for the poor in the cities of the western nations. In the United States, the abandonment of President Johnson's plan for slum reconstruction marked the end of his dream of a "Great Society". (5)

Economic pressures and racial tensions now meant that the world was viewed by the west not as a global entity, but as a series of detached areas, each with its own local reality. The return to tradition and localism, a minor phenomenon in the Fifties, was gaining popularity with both general public and social élite everywhere. The personal element was again in favour while the impersonal, believed by science to be a prerequisite for a successful mass society, was overwhelmingly rejected. The unique quality of hand-made objects was now preferred to assembly line products, reversing what had previously been seen as a positive aspect of industrialization.

Science, although it was being more extensively applied, seemed no longer desirable. This occurred at the very moment when electronics were taking over all sectors of business and knowledge, opening up new dimensions of freedom but also creating new limits. The term "post-industrial" was then being used in allusion to loss of faith in the massive manufacturing industry of western nations. The functional no longer appealed to the general public, who saw its intrinsic lack of beauty as a necessary but not sufficient condition for progress. The traditional also began to reappear in the psychology of marketing, in the revaluation of antique or merely old objects. This phenomenon, apparent in haute couture, furnishings, food, jewellery and all forms of design, was particularly noticeable in architecture, as columns and Palladian windows came back into fashion. The modern was now merely a style whereas in the Fifties it had been a philosophy dictating rules of aesthetics and techniques. The return to tradition was especially remarkable in town planning. While in Europe towns rigorously defended their historic centers, in the United States there was a growing respect for buildings constructed before the modern period, now considered historic monuments, along with a popular trend towards American folk architecture and shingle style.

On the political scene, the return to traditionalism has often been dramatic. In the west, the middle east and the third world, many nations have reassessed their past. This has proved fertile ground for the return of religious fervour. Iran is the obvious example of a country once well on the way to modernization, where a return to the fundamental principles of Islam has changed the course of its history in a few years. In Teheran the construction of buildings inspired by the International Style, as a symbol of western political influence, has been abandoned since this expression of the modern is considered immoral by the new Islamic regime. Traditional architecture is now the only acceptable one.

Within the profession itself, the Modern Movement was the target of increasing criticism. In *Complexity and Contradiction* in Architecture, Robert Venturi had already in 1966 addressed the architects of the Modern Movement calling for a return to classical architecture and the American tradition. The Philadelphia school, from which Venturi came, had already instigated a crisis in the Modern Movement in the early Sixties with the work of Louis Kahn, who used new forms of non-modern derivation. The malaise was becoming concurrently evident in many American architectural offices. Even the Architectural

Collaborative, headed by Walter Gropius, one of the undisputed heroes of the Modern Movement, presented a project for the University of Baghdad clearly influenced by Islamic folklore. In *Form Follows Fiasco* by Peter Blake and *The Failures of Modern Architecture* by Brolin, the principles of the Modern Movement are demolished one by one, through traditional logic which leaves no room for ideologies based on system and science. Published in 1982, Tom Wolfe's *From Bauhaus to Our House* was not only a great popular success but was highly appreciated by the cultural élite as well. He accuses Mies Van der Rohe and Gropius of having imported from Europe the evil influence of the modern, responsible for the glass boxes so prevalent on the American architectural scene. Wolfe, obviously no believer in historicism, claimed that a few strong-willed individuals could influence and manipulate a whole sector of art and knowledge. It was left to other critics to remind him that Modernism represented much more than a theory of design.

In changing its objective from a pledge to help the less fortunate to protecting the environment and conserving ancient monuments, the western élite had shifted its efforts to the preservation of an already existing stable society. The planning of new towns of the future was abandoned in favour of conservation and reinterpretation of the past. This phenomenon heralded the growth of a reactionary spirit. The demands of the new broader society, accused by traditionalists of claiming rights rather than fulfilling duties, made the stable middle-class yearn for the good old days when cities were not overflowing with foreigners and roads were not congested with traffic.

7 - Post-Modernism Conquers the Scene

In 1974 the Museum of Modern Art in New York, universally acclaimed as the temple of the Modern Movement, held a major exhibition on the Paris Ecole des Beaux Arts. In the psychological climate of the moment, the Belle Epoque attracted renewed attention. It should however be recalled that the western élite had always flirted with the opulent decoration and magnificent mise-en-scene of the Beaux Arts.

In the Seventies the traditional large house set in the open countryside, as reinterpreted by Robert Stern, brought back the old dream of individuality and privacy, in stark contrast to the apartment blocks designed and built by the architects of the Modern Movement.

This clear message of a total about-turn in architecture marked the beginning of Post-Modernism, which despite its formal heterogeneity had a common core in its humanistic approach and willingness to accept symbols of diverse cultural origin. It was consciously anti-rational in reaction to the ostentatious rationalism of the Modern Movement. Where the latter emphasizes the impersonal in its simple, bare forms, Post-Modern architecture is personalized by its use of decoration and color.

The new architecture covered a wide ideological spectrum, ranging from total evocation of the past, both in spirit and form, to the expression of individuality, subjectivity, élitism and a traditional concept of personalization. As it continued to incorporate modern and totally innovative elements, the return to traditionalism was only partial.

In tracing two different tendencies in this period we can measure the extent of polarization and contrast between the two philosophical trends in society. From a stylistic point of view the American Post-Modern ranges from the reconstruction of shingle style and the re-application of many elements from the past, to Californian informal architecture which, while rejecting International Style, always makes use of modern elements. In the United States, Michael Graves and Robert Stern are the undisputed

**The contributions of the Modern Movement
to the emerging world during the Sixties and Seventies**

Various buildings designed in this context by Renato Severino, Architect and Planner.

Top - Trade Center, Kampala, Uganda, 1970.
The two towers were prefabricated in Italy and erected on the site with local labor.

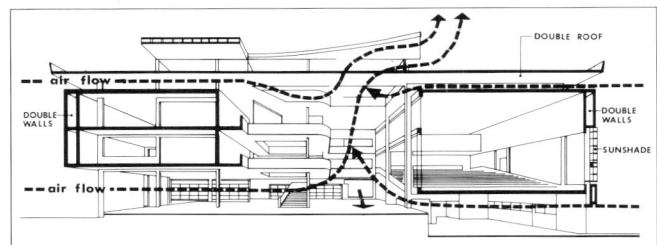

Center - The School of Administration, University of Ghana, Legon, Ghana, 1964.
The section drawing shows the natural flow of ventilation.

Bottom - The University of Cape Coast, Cape Coast, Ghana, 1966.

Prefabrication and industrialization in construction was seen at that time as the right medium for buildings of quality designed for a rapidly growing population.

Top - "Colonia Tepalcates", Mexico City, 1975. Self-help and teaching program for prefabrication.

The first factory-built apartment tower in the United States, Yonkers, New York, 1970.

A program to teach construction skills to African-Americans was financed by the U.S. Government.

leaders of this Movement, while Philip Johnson may be considered its high priest. While the evidence of Post-Modernism in Europe is less dramatic, at least in terms of the number of buildings constructed, its ideology has been publicized by a number of influential figures, especially in the schools of architecture more open to innovation. The main influences on the Venice school are, in fact, two post-modern architects: Aldo Rossi, whose teaching and ability in architectural composition are of undeniable importance, and Paolo Portoghesi via his direction of the Venice Biennale which has been the setting for highly successful exhibitions of post-modern architecture. Portoghesi, who had already produced classically inspired projects in the Fifties and Sixties, found an ideal opportunity in the Eighties to put into practice his ideas for various projects in a Post-Modern context. A man of great culture and a respected historian, he was attacked by the Moderns, who accused him of using classical motifs with which he was familiar to recreate intellectually worn-out themes. At that time Bruno Zevi, who had had a great influence on Italian and international architecture, was still the uncontested defender of the Modern Movement.

At Columbia University, Kenneth Frampton, in a similar philosophical position, was upholding the values of rationalism in his work as teacher, critic and architect. He has represented the stability and continuity of the most positive aspects of the Modern Movement while opposing the too rapid metamorphosis of the presently unbalanced world, a world that is facing unprepared its own disenchantment. Frampton writes in 1993:

"While the crisis of the neo-avant-garde derives directly from this spontaneous dissolution of the new, critical culture attempts to sustain itself through a dialectical play across a historically determined reality in every sense of the term. One may even claim that, critique aside, critical culture attempts to compensate in a fragmentary manner for the manifest disenchantment of the world. The transformed, transforming real is thus continued not only by the material circumstances obtaining at the moment of 'intervention' but also by a critical intersubjective deliberation upon or about these conditions both before and after the design and realization of the project.

Material constraints aside innovation is, in this sense, contingent upon a self-conscious, re-reading, re-making, re-collection of tradition (Andenken), including the tradition of the new, just as tradition can only be revitalized through innovation"

The Post-Modernists, entering the architectural field from historical and intellectual backgrounds and from posts as directors museums and art galleries, without previous professional experience, were often criticized for their inability to produce an authentic artistic synthesis. It was insinuated that in a period of artistic, social and political confusion, their knowledge of the past and their personal political ability could easily be converted into creative talent. Using their imagination they often tried to create a new ideological climate by a compilation of previously untested concepts or pre-formed ideas. The break with the classical concept of artistic synthesis was, in fact, responsible for this situation.

A number of stars in the architectural field in both the United States and Italy openly acknowledged their compliance with this trend by presenting ideas which were then translated, developed and implemented, as they themselves admitted, by other artists and technicians who transposed the products of their imagination into a real and communicable context. By contrast, Aldo Rossi's projects, using elements of the background architecture of Renaissance paintings, appeared to develop along the lines of classical artistic synthesis, although the details of his constructions did not follow traditional logic. Of interest in this regard are the writings of Giovanni Klaus Koenig, who used photographic evidence to denounce the rapid deterioration of architecture of Post-Modern inspiration, which striving for special effects rejected the use of tested construction details capable of withstanding atmospheric wear and tear.

It was in France in the late Seventies and early Eighties that the most imposing Post-Modernist works were constructed by an artist of Spanish origin, Riccardo Bofill. His projects, mainly for middle-class housing, were filled with traditional symbols and often very attractive, showing masterly design and precise intuition. However, they seemed inspired by the period of the Napoleonic Restoration, when dwellings were built for the officers and veterans of the regime, creating a style that was dignified but pompous and repetitive. Bofill's work represents in this case if not a clear step forward, at least a valid attempt to improve on the anonymity of large-scale housing projects in the wake of the negative effects of the Modernist experience.

By the late Eighties the active influence of Post-Modernism seemed to be declining in Europe, especially in France where the new Parisian quarter "La Defense", built for the celebration of the bicentennial of the French Revolution, shows an entirely different inspiration, following the rejection of a return to traditionalism by the critics and the Parisian public.

In the United States, "The Great Gatsby", the rich man of the Twenties depicted in F. Scott Fitzgerald's novel, personified the need of Post-Modernism to recreate the refinement and taste of a period that was perceived as happy and carefree. The driving forces of the Twenties, thirst for wealth and pleasure, were those of the Seventies and Eighties as well. In 1988, Robert Stern contributed to the official recognition of the Great Gatsby with unconditioned admiration expressed during his popular TV lecture series on the new Post-Modernist architecture. Just as the Gatsby era came to an end with the Great Depression following the Wall Street crash of 1929, its revival began to decline when the same stock market crashed again in 1987, giving rise to a major crisis in the financial and real estate markets of the United States and Europe. The early Nineties were in fact characterized by many of the same social and economic conditions that prevailed in 1929; hedonism and greed were the dominant forces of a Western society in deep moral confusion. The skyscrapers built in New York and Chicago in the Eighties emulated and even copied those of the Twenties. The buildings on Wall Street emanated the unnatural elegance and brilliance of a never ending celebration. The stylistic complexity of the buildings was matched only by the intricate financial dealings of the investment bankers who occupied them. Half a century after the 1920s, the same ethical and socio-economic factors produced identical architectural features.

8 - Confrontation between the Modern Movement and Post-Modernism

Throughout the Eighties, opposition between the Modern Movement and Post-Modernism continued to offer very different formal solutions for the same type of building, thus demonstrating the ideological uncertainty of our society. Good examples of this are the AT&T headquarters, designed by Johnson and Burgee, and the IBM building, designed by Edward Larraby Barnes, located on adjacent blocks on Madison Avenue, New York. The former is a typical example of Post-Modernist architecture, the latter of the Modern Movement. The two sixty-storey towers have almost the same volume, the same exposure, the same function, follow the same technical criteria and the same building regulations. Built mainly of granite, although of different colours, they present the image of two international companies in the field of high technology.

Their visibly grandiose structures assign these two buildings a prominent place in the history of

New York skyscrapers, although the images they present are quite different. The AT&T building makes use of detail and traditional design, its lobby reminiscent of the architecture of Graeco-Roman decadence, with black and white marble floors and a huge gilt statue in its center. Pink granite is used on the façades, while the top pediment suggests an XVIII century trumeau. By contrast, the bare volumetric surfaces of the IBM building use modernistic lines and elements while the polished dark green granite of the walls seems almost metallic.

These two opposing trends have at times resulted in open conflict as in the case of the project for the town hall of Portland, Oregon, completed in 1983. A group of Modernist architects in the State bitterly contested Michael Graves' winning project of Post-Modern inspiration, chosen by a jury chaired by Philip Johnson. The local architects preferred instead two competing projects of modernistic influence submitted by Mitchell-Giurgola and by Erickson Associates.

Thus the close of the XX century seems marked by growing conflict between the two opposing theories of architecture. Moreover, at the extremes of the vast and varied spectrum of proposals, two conflicting concepts of urban development are emerging. The first is represented by cities such as Houston and Dallas, Texas, and the Parisian quarter of "La Defense", defined by great volumes of reflecting surfaces linked by highways. In the other, buildings are grouped together in traditional spatial compositions, such as can be seen in Europe or on the Boston waterfront, where new and old form a harmonic blend, attempting to recreate the scale and atmosphere of cities of the past. These two concepts of architecture and urban development reflect two different philosophies of life which have become two distinct cultures, developing in the West and in Japan in particular. The motivating force of the first lies in technological development, in movement, and thus in impermanence and flexibility. Such a system works like an electrical circuit where energy is transferred from one volume to another via the movement of individuals along the roadway system to produce with their work goods and services. The second, in contrast, pursues humanistic values, and is thus open to the multiformity of personal interpretations and contributions. This conception of the traditional urban space is similar to that of the medieval city, with various scale juxtapositions; its aesthetics are of organic origin and, in contrast to the technological, offer variation in terms of culture and local color.

It is thus a difficult, if not an impossible task to judge one or the other of these two philosophies, as has been attempted by many critics, using the parameters of the opposite one without first evaluating the underlying principles of each. It is this situation which has led in the early Nineties to the malaise among architects.

The attempt was made earlier to define the two opposing schools of thought in order to judge their future influence. In 1983, during a seminar given at the Columbia University School of Architecture, Vincent Scully gave his definition of Tradition and Innovation. It was clear from Scully's formulation, which set out to define precisely American traditional architecture, that from a humanistic point of view total innovation is to be viewed as the breakdown of an existing balance. In this context, innovation and change must be seen as a negative phenomenon from a rigidly traditionalist point of view which seeks stability in forms from the past. On the other hand, James M. Fitch of the Department of Preservation of Harvard University, writing in 1983 when the dispute became more fervent, says of the Post-Modernists:

"Like the other stylistic revivalists of the past, they reject the contemporaneous norms of modern life in favor of disinterring those of the long dead. They refuse to attempt to distill from contemporary society, science and technology, new models of aesthetic expression. They return, instead, to the exotic, the esoteric, the deliberately idiosyncratic juxtapositions of flotsam and jetsam from the past."

Unlike Scully who tends to glorify the typical forms of American architecture of the past advocating their renewal, Ficht obviously rejects revivalism in favour of solutions derived from contemporary life.

It seems paradoxical that architecture should suffer a fundamental division between, at one extreme, a concept of traditional derivation and, at the other, an unbridled desire for innovation, although various combinations of the two also exist. Is it possible, we may ask, to confront the two ideologies as many architects have done, putting them together in the same context? Is it either logical or positive to unite in one composition symbols in opposition to each other, using irony as a catalyzer of form and meaning, as Charles Moore has done in Piazza d'Italia in New Orleans? Many critics and a part of the public see irony as resulting from insecurity and dissatisfaction, as a turning back to the past when the future appears uncertain. Piazza d'Italia, although designed with great skill, has been severely criticized by the inhabitants of New Orleans, who appear to accept the value of irony in literature and theatre but are adamant in their rejection of its possible application in architecture. Many, in fact, ask how long these ironic statements produced by the early Post-Modern and constructed on a grand scale will retain their validity, without becoming an absurdity for the city which houses them.

The negative reaction of the local population to a construction of modern inspiration is also comprehensible in a situation such as the Centre Pompidou in Paris, planned in the Seventies. This modern art museum-fair designed by Piano and Rogers has had enormous public success. Tens of thousands of visitors from all over the world spend an average of 90 minutes each in the building which has become as popular as the Eiffel Tower, with an added cultural and intellectual dimension. The museum functions superbly as a high-tech machine, capable of absorbing the attention of a vast public, who can enjoy a view of the surrounding city from the external escalators. But for the inhabitants of the old Paris quarter the sudden arrival of this technological object in their midst overwhelmed their traditional living space, now invaded by millions of people coming from outside every year.

In attempting to find a place within the community the two tendencies have dramatically revealed their differences. The Modern Movement, in placing within the pre-existing urban fabric structures which are totally different both aesthetically and structurally, has adopted a method which is direct and open, blatantly ignoring the local context. Post-Modernism, on the other hand, while claiming to respect the pre-existing environment, has been accused of becoming carried away with its own game, producing an ironic statement, too often on the borderline of the farcical. In their inability to achieve an acceptable ethical and functional balance, both tendencies reflect the insecurity of a society incapable of defining its own cultural and spatial environment.

9 - From Ambivalence to Neo-Surrealism

The moment of *redde rationem*, of personal psychological accounting, always comes when a situation which has been slowly maturing over the years becomes manifest in a wider reality, outside of the mind of the individual. In the early Seventies the architects of the post-war generation found themselves under dual psychological pressure. On the one hand their intellectual and professional training had made them followers of the Modern Movement, while on the other they had to confront the new historical situation

Last stage of the Modern Movement: Architecture for a "mass society"

Research on modular dwelling units typical of the Sixties.
Renato Severino, Architect.

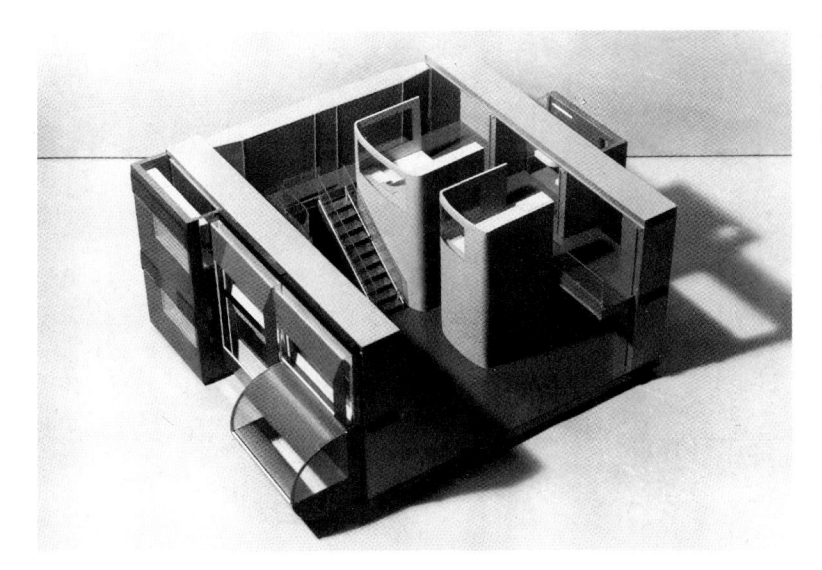

Top - Proposed dwelling units to be built with steel and plastic materials on assembly line. One of the winners of the C.E.C.A. (European Common Market) international competition, 1965.

Center and bottom - Research on prefabricated modular units. U.S.A. Proposed minimal unit with an internal tri-dimensional space. Full-scale model built by the students of Columbia University, New York, 1968.

Post-Modern conquers the scene

Top - Headquarters of Crown American Corporation, Johnston, Pennsylvania. Michael Graves, architect. A bold, very American solution produces new forms derived from conflictual aesthetics.

Center right - House in Delaware. Venturi & Rauch, Architects. The intellectual dimension of Post-Modern is fully represented by this emblematic approach.

Center left - Office building on Lexington Avenue, New York City. Helmut Jahn, Architect. A reference to the imagery of the 1920's skyscrapers.

Neue Staatsgalerie in Stuttgart. James Stirling, Michael Wilford & Associates, Architects. A new dimension of freedom in a European context.

created by the negative reaction of much of the public to their beliefs. Insecurity and anxiety were created by two kinds of pressure: one stemming from the impossibility of denying all of their formative training, the other deriving from the shift towards traditionalism of many young professionals and critics. Some post-war architects opted to stay with Modernism, defending it to the bitter end, feeling perhaps that their only intellectual choice was to remain attached to their roots. Others, however, gave in to the pressure of public opinion, already finding themselves critical of the Modern Movement, and thus accepting the new trend toward traditionalism and the Post-Modern. But a large group of professionals, in both Europe and America, were in an ambivalent situation, torn between the two opposing tendencies, intellectually interested in experimenting with the new ideas in order to clarify the situation. The traditionalist message, which now influenced their artistic synthesis, helped them to bring back the humanist elements they were aware of having lost. This group of architects, swept up by the rapid change, tried to deal with their conflicting feelings by adopting two solutions to the same problem, one Modernistic, the other traditionalist.

Architectural firms such as Skidmore, Owings & Merrill, which had produced the most famous works of the Modern Movement such as the Lever House in New York, demonstrated this split in various forms and accents. Another acclaimed Modernist, Cesar Pelli, also followed this trend but with clear leanings towards Post-Modernism, probably much encouraged by his younger associates. Philip Johnson, considered one of the fathers of this doctrine, for a number of years designed buildings like the AT&T skyscraper on Madison Avenue, alongside other projects of Modernist inspiration. The author himself was involved in this difficult situation; having achieved public and critical success with projects of traditionalist inspiration did not help to resolve his personal uncertainty. (6)

The ambivalence of the '80s is proof of the struggle of a whole generation of architects who felt carried away by the winds of rapid change. They sought a solution of compromise in a world in a state of fluctuation which no longer conceded time nor pardon.

Once again the influence of society and of American society in particular was instrumental in changing the direction of architecture and finding a new solution to the dilemma of traditional versus modern. Pluralism was now was now the dominant force in western society, which had become multi-racial as well as multi-national, having opened its doors to the influence of new cultures, and consumerism became the banner of economic growth. The need for integration on a social level as well as in architecture seemed to demand the rapid union of opposing tendencies and thus assimilation in a single process of the languages of traditionalism and techno-culture. The combination, in varying degrees and nuances, of the two languages is the keynote to the new architecture, which may be defined as neo-Surrealist. Although this definition should be taken in the broad sense and not with specific reference to the artistic movement of the Twenties, the influence of the latter is clear, on the psychological level, in the way in which a variety of elements are assimilated in the same artistic composition. Symbols of different origin and even classical elements such as columns and trabeations are put together in patterns of hi-tech systems to assume as sorts of configuration. These elements appear as in a dream, with real objects used in an unreal context. They are simplified or decorated to create special effects in a varied, non-consistent design. Although many of the original Surrealist works of art by such painters as P. Delvaux, Carrà, De Chirico and Magritte were so conceived, neo-Surrealism began producing in the late Eighties, particularly in America, such a great variety of examples that the original concept began to take

Modern Movement and Post-Modern in a conflictual situation of ambivalence

Center for the Elderly in Buia, Friuli, Italy. Renato Severino, Architect.
After many experiences within the Modern Movement, Severino confronts a new challenge in in the late Seventies, designing this center adopting a traditional architectural concept and details.

At right, the World Financial Center at Battery Park City, New York. At left, the Pacific Design Center in Los Angeles, California. Both projects were built during the late Eighties. Cesar Pelli and Associates, Architects.

School of Agriculture in Spilimbergo, Pordenone, Italy. A techno-agricultural solution

This proposal was first submitted to the client by Renato Severino in 1979.
On this page, a building with nurseries exposed to the sun and a walking path on the roof leading the students to the fields.

Opposite page, the School of Agriculture designed by Renato Severino, Architect, after his first solution was rejected by the client in favor of a traditional program voted by the local Board of Preservation.

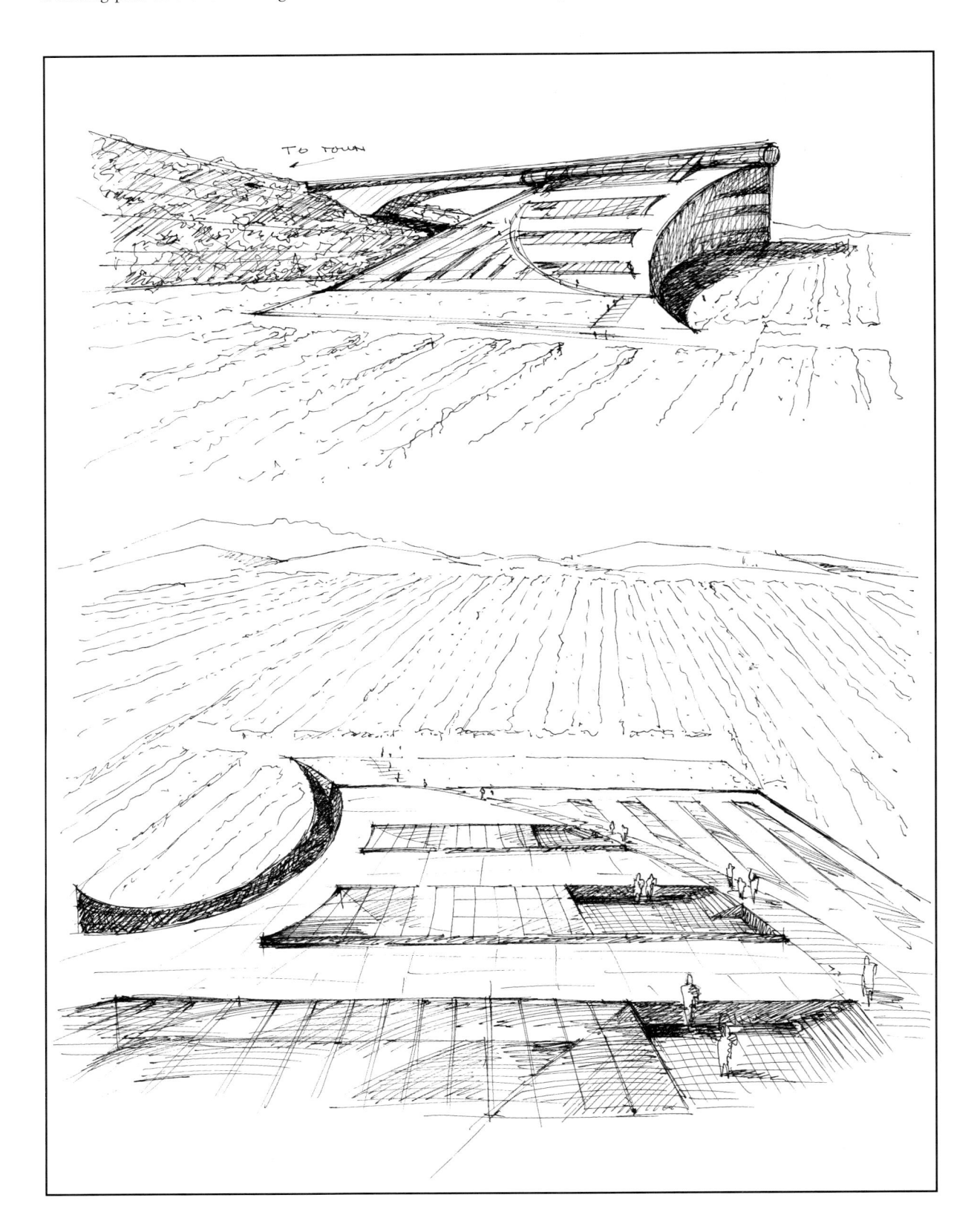

A traditional solution for the agricultural school of Spilimbergo. 1981

From the outside the building resembles a venetian villa surrounded by vineyards, while its interior is very contemporary in style.

The Tagliamento River and the Alps can be seen from the courtyard.

The interiors are traditional in concept but have contemporary detailing.

The exterior trim around the windows is of green and red marble. The stone sphere in the courtyard measures six feet in diameter.

Construction cost was funded by the U.S. AID Program after the 1976 earthquake in the Friuli area.

on a new phantasmagoric dimension of pure consumeristic origin. The coexistence of functionalism and an extravagant use of components gives rise to a great variety of intellectual exercises created by bold and unexpected combinations of shape, color and materials.

The first mild phase of neo-Surrealism, which initially addressed itself to tradition and adherence to context but with new forms of expression, can be considered Post-Modern. With time, however, the compositions became more and more complex, openly linking elements of contradictory inspiration from traditional and technological languages. The architectural and art magazines, in positively welcoming the new avant-garde, were naturally attracted to the sensationalism of neo-Surrealism and its capacity to transmit a message of shocking newness, its provoking forms and surprising hues which lent themselves to being photographed and published. But at the same time, from those sectors of the public and the general press which believed in the stable values of urban space, voices rose in protest against what was termed the too bold inspiration of the new brightly colored buildings now to be seen on the main streets of American cities. Disney World itself used the work of well-known architects to create a completely new environment, often with remarkable results, as in the Swan Hotel in Orlando, Florida, showing the talent and pictorial ability of an architect such as Michael Graves.

Many letters descended on the magazines that published these projects, denouncing the commercial fatuity of a product accused of being "grotesque", impermanent and cartoon-inspired. Brighton Pavillion, designed by John Nash in 1818-20 and London's Crystal Palace, built by Joseph Paxton in 1850, were cited as examples of architecture designed to attract a large public and celebrated for their success, which, without histrionics of any kind, had gone down in the history of architecture as masterpieces. Disneyian consumerism was thus seen by much of the educated public as a gigantic fairy tale, as another monster of advertising using its glitter to seduce and shock. Undoubtedly, however, these commercial undertakings were successful in influencing much of American architecture. This architecture seemed at last to have found that pop dimension sought with relentless intellectual ardour, but with only moderate success, by Venturi in the Seventies, when in his book "Learning from Las Vegas" he presented an image of this urban phenomenon as a possible future scenario for American cities.

With the spread its pop dimension, Surrealism began to appear more and more clearly as the opposite of classical art, seen instead as a lasting element of continuity, handing down through the centuries the essence of compositional balance to represent established human values. In a spectrum ranging from the traditional to the high-tech, Surrealism seeks to produce a sense of instability and mobility through the discontinuity and deliberate contradiction of its message.

An element of Surrealism on the psychological level has became increasingly noticeable in all aspects of life in the western nations, the United States in particular. It has appeared not only in the arts, the cinema and the theatre, but also in ceremonial affairs, both public and private, and in business. The surrealistic element seemed necessary to create a break of some kind with the boredom and pedantry of traditional ethics, which had become oppressive for the newly emerging society. The fact that the break-up of the conventional ethical balance could be acceptable is very important in the new socio-economic situation. The western world of the Nineties with its new enlarged community is once again in search of new solutions for the new, more complex and schizoid society. These solutions can only be achieved through a rapid, hurried and tortuous synthesis such as that of the neo-Surrealist response. The alternatives to this choice are few in the field of architecture. Pure traditionalism bored the public and even more the critics, appearing worn out and extraneous to the new social and economic reality. On the other hand, the high tech of average quality no longer made news except in the area of rear-guard modernism and real estate speculation. Neo-Surrealism, instead, expresses great energy, released by the clash of opposing ideas in search of a common platform. It is a forceful gesture, obtained with candour and direct dialogue with form. The genesis of this architecture lies in renunciation of creating a vision of the future for a society that expresses fundamental doubts about the equilibrium of its growth and the possibility of achieving a stable consensus among its participants.

The pluralism of the western nations, of which American democracy in particular had been the standard bearer, seems to have slipped out of the hands of the Establishment when, pressed by the need for cheaper labor, it began to accept a great number of immigrants from all parts of the world, who brought different habits and cultures, changing not only the socio-economic equilibrium but also the aesthetic balance of the Western Tradition. The great variety of inputs coming from all sides brought about a democratic and demographic opening up to many different ideas, with the need to descend to the lowest possible common denominator to represent all levels of society. A consequent theatricality is reflected in architecture, resulting from marketing pressure which demands the inclusion of all the components necessary to attract a public of varying origins and taste. At the same time, in a moral context, many conservatives judge that aesthetics derived from the acceptance of what they call the ephemeral and the simulated is the prelude to plagiarism and deceit as a way of life and to intellectual flight from reality through surrealist solutions.

In all western nations in recent years a superficial concept of history along with feelings of uncertainty about the present and the future has produced in many strata of society a deep nostalgia for the splendors of the past. The symbols of wealth and power of the Establishment of former years have become the object of desire, while the negative aspects and social limitations of those times seem forgotten. Emerging social groups fantasize a new state of nobility, and their dream becomes a new social horizon. Traditional ethical values, however, are incompatible with the hedonistic, exhibitionist values of consumer society, resulting in inevitable conflict. While the new social classes have lost their original cultural identity, of which they are frequently oblivious, they are still unable to make wise new choices. The evident ethical crisis in this society is demonstrated by its aesthetic tendencies. A form of decorativism irrespective of classical canons, attracting for the first time the emerging groups, has distorted all pre-existing principles of logic and authenticity. An ostentatious traditional type of decoration has become necessary as a symbol of wealth, and is consequently used in many buildings with a hybrid variety of styles never seen before, in an atmosphere of falsity and compromise. In the United States such schemes are even used in the interiors of mobile homes, often furnished and decorated in imitation classical style, both aesthetically and functionally inappropriate in these economical containers. The vulgarity of consumerism has thus proved to be a formidable means of communication in the emerging hedonistic society, where it always finds a positive response in a wide range of social strata.

It is thus logical and necessary to ask whether consumeristic architecture can be seen as positive for society, considering the continual change it tends to produce in the city and in the minds of its inhabitants. Consequently, we must then examine the question of how the architecture of future cities can follow the various stages of development of our society.

In this philosophical context, the experimentalism of neo-Surrealism seems to offer, if not

Two languages:
Comparing the two opposite philosophies when they adhere strictly to their principles

Top and bottom - The techno language: The Hong Kong Bank. Foster Associates, Architects. Interior and facade of the upper part of the building.

Top and bottom - The traditional language: Krier House, Seaside, Florida. Leon Krier, Architect. Overall view and detail of rooftop studio temple.

Neo-Surrealism appears in the Eighties

Top left - Western Region M & D Facility, Rocklin, California. Frank O. Gehry and Stanley Tigerman, Architects.

Top upper right - Antigone development in Montpellier, France. Ricardo Bofill, Architect.

Top lower right - Swan Hotel, Orlando, Florida. Michael Graves, Architect.

Bottom upper and lower left - The "Lipstick" office building on 3rd Avenue, New York. Overall view and detail of the entrance colonnade. Johnson and Burgee, Architects.

Bottom upper right - Schweitzer House in Joshua Tree, California. Josh Schweitzer, Architect.

Bottom lower right - Temporary landscape installation, Clarke County, Va. Tori Thomas, Landscape Architect.

a positive answer to the needs of a divided and tormented society, at least a description of the state of mind of many artists and architects. Neo-surrealist architecture derives from something inherent to its realization: it is a negation of the city as a stable entity, as it always has been, in both its physical organization and the psychological relationships among its inhabitants. This non-realistic aspect explains how the Surrealist avant-garde creates products which rapidly become obsolete in the same way as consumer products. As the market demands that they be produced rapidly, they are neither well evaluated nor well designed. A permanent work of art, by contrast, has a relatively long period of synthesis and an even longer period of materialization. The architect-artist needs incubation time for refining and filtering his ideas to produce work that can last, as both image of society and physically complete and permanent building.

10 - Deconstructivism and Neo-Surrealism

The Deconstructivist movement which appeared in architecture in the late Eighties can also be considered a clear Neo-Surrealist manifestation, of intellectual rather than pop derivation. The exploded buildings, appearing literally unfinished or already destroyed by an interior force, are, in fact, an affirmation of instability, recalling early Surrealist experiences. Deconstructivism is undoubtedly an image of a large portion of contemporary society: in a state of transition, problematic, unfulfilled and tending toward self-analysis and self-vivisection.

Some architectural schools of the American Ivy League had adopted this doctrine or tendency following the exhibition on Deconstructivism at the MOMA under the patronage of Philip Johnson, where this movement was given official recognition in the international architectural panorama. But the reaction of the press to Johnson's new philosophy was rather negative, rejecting this sudden about-turn of the so-called dean of American architecture, one of the founders and supporters of the Post-Modern of traditional derivation. At first glance Deconstructivism, in fact, appeared to be the philosophical antithesis of traditionalism, displaying elements of instability of Modernistic derivation. Such an apparent change of direction totally disorientated the critics. It should be recalled, however, that it was Johnson himself who promoted Neo-Surrealism with his so-called lipstick building on Third Avenue in New York, considered one of the most surprising buildings of the last half century, with its shocking silhouette of visual instability. It is undeniably a building of quality and as an avant-garde experiment, brilliantly executed down to the finest detail.

The fact that Philip Johnson had produced such diverse and multiform compositions in a brief space of time from the Sixties through the Eighties reveals a common matrix to all his works, certainly of neo-Surrealistic inspiration. The element common to all these buildings is the destabilizing concept, expressed as a negation of compositional firmitas. Added to this was the architect's apparent total freedom from any previous design schemes, rejecting both traditional and modern principles.

The difficulty experienced by critics in understanding neo-Surrealism derives initially from the overly abrupt changes in language used by its architects, in their anxiety to communicate with the public. This movement, in art and in architecture, developed with the growth of phenomenology as a vast philosophical trend, in the schools and among the intellectuals of the western world. This philosophy, founded by Edmund Husserl in the late XIX century, was not conceived as a closed system, founded on precise principles, but continued to develop and to change with the passage of time. It was developed as a method of uniting philosophy and science in a single process, to find an answer to all aspects of knowledge. It was a dimension of thought typical of that time, when the growing phenomenon of the industrial revolution called for an exhaustive answer to the problems posed by humanistic and scientific needs. The Modern Movement was also developing at that time, initially with the same principles, but as has been shown, rapidly opting for a rationalistic method based on XVIII century positivism. Phenomenology, on the other hand, adopted a predominantly humanistic approach in its investigation of the elements making up individual consciousness. In the Seventies this investigation took on the character of a revolt against the dominance of science, seen as oppressive by all those aware of the process of alienation affecting humanity and deriving from scientific progress and from elimination of the instinctive, emotional and non-rational elements from consciousness.

Phenomenology thus became a kind of counter-culture, a spiritual liberation movement opposed to the positivism and realism which form the basis of the thought of the Western Establishment. The clash between the two opposing philosophies is clearly defined in architectural terms in the buildings of European and American cities. The Post-Modern was the first visible sign of a counter-culture, although at times in a clearly reactionary vein, opposed to the systematic rationalism of the Western Tradition.

Still in the context of a counter-culture, in the early Eighties, "il pensiero debole", weak thought, developed as an alternative to systematic thought of pragmatic origin which in the west had tackled global problems with some presumption and little success. This "weak" way of thinking found particular favour with authors of Latin origin, suggesting to its Northern European critics a necessary choice deriving from genetic origin.

"Il pensiero debole" in refusing a global interpretation examines partial aspects of a problem, often only on a personal level. This is in evident contrast with the systematic analytic thinking of the Nineties which seeks clarification in the juxtaposition of ideas in a debate aimed at resolving global problems. It is certainly understandable that such a decidedly oriented mode of thought should be in crisis in the final years of the XX century, when the answers to the problems of life within a system of too many unknowns have become increasingly controversial. But "weak thought" seems to be an unconditional surrender, suggesting a loss of the courage and determination needed in the struggle to regain the ground lost by humanity in a defeat brought about by the unbalance in modern thought.

Now it must be asked whether "il pensiero debole", which has developed fundamentally along phenomenological lines, can provide a valid alternative to a mode of thought which can be put into practice on a global scale, or whether it is merely another form of anti-rational myth which, having no connotations common to all geographical regions, is applicable only to a small number of limited situations. Since communication would seem to be the crucial point in question, "il pensiero debole" reveals a spirit which is manifold, poetic, partial and personal, forever capable of appealing to the sentiments of all, and thereby able to achieve indirectly a new form of global platform.

It was left to Deconstructivism, in the wake of the success of the Post-Modern, to give substance at last to phenomenology, with a series of intellectually stimulating buildings. In these proposals, architecture, philosophy, literature and human behavior were put on the same level as never before. This same philosophical formulation had given rise in the Sixties to "happenings", which in art were a clear sign of revolt against the systematic scheduling and regimentation of the Modern.

Phenomenological buildings thus became a direct projection of human psychology in its most recondite thoughts and most open manifestations of emotion. The break with the past is clear, as there no longer exist the usual filters of established, traditional, professional practice placing all new relationships within a conceptual network of easy reference and possible limitations. Each piece of architecture inspired by Deconstructivism seems to be the result of a new and separate theory, produced by a personal mental conflagration, one of the possible outcomes of a chain reaction between preconceived ideas and momentary happenings.

Jacques Derrida, theoretician of the Anglo-American literary panorama of the Eighties, is the acknowledged philosopher of Deconstructivism. His work, considered by his supporters an incentive to continue the search, is instead difficult to evaluate for inspired by logic deriving from the Enlightenment. While the philosophy of Deconstructivism has a wide following, it has also been met with incomprehension and concealed anxiety, and this becomes increasingly apparent in the attempt to decipher and decode the new thought. Rodolphe Gasché provides a rapid critical synthesis and his own explanation of Deconstructivism. Referring in 1986 to Derrida's philosophical thought, he writes:

"Certainly the aspect of Deconstructivism, if it finds recognition, could be seen as the minimum coherence of a private and anarchic project, closer in its aberration to literature than to philosophy. Any adequate understanding of the nature and characteristics of Deconstruction is possible only on condition that we realize what Deconstruction can achieve. As long as we believe that its objective is to generate the aforesaid free and dissolute game, the nihilistic erasure of oppositions, the abolition of hierarchies and the demystification or ideologization of western philosophies, a definite and logical procedure of Deconstruction cannot be totally and specifically understood." (Translation from the Italian)

The question to be asked is: what is the objective of Deconstructivism in architecture, accused by some critics of pursuing contorted, nihilistic games? An example of this controversy can be seen in the works of a Deconstructivist matrix produced in the United States, where traditional references are associated with modern morphology. This clearly shows how the Deconstructivist movement is an integral part of neo-Surrealism although the two elements are read separately by many critics, perhaps still disorientated by the complexity and apparent contradiction of the phenomenon.

The architecture of Peter Eisenman in the eastern United States and of Frank Gehry in California represent the last stage in the search for a medium of expression to describe the Nineties three-dimensionally. In the compositions of these architects the imbalance of the form which breaks open to reveal the internal structure indicates the subversive tendency of a discontented society ready to explode to generate a new situation, even if this implicates self-destruction. The great international success of Frank Gehry lies in the materialization of this emotion. His architecture contains all of the ingredients of the artistic avant-garde of our time: the disintegration of form denying permanence, accentuated by the use of plain materials, and the novelty of untested compositions which, with their obvious freshness and immediacy, are the opposite of any kind of traditional expression.

In the work of Peter Eisenman the influence of a Modernist formation is felt more strongly. The emphasis is still on spatial and static balance, despite the playing down of structural and volumetric conception. On the other hand, in Gehry's work, every element of the composition seems to have fallen from heaven, caught in a tornado that sends whales and beams flying. Both the Deconstructivism of Eisenman and the élitist pop of Gehry follow to a great extent the same psychological lines.

Given the impermanence of unstable forms and structures that are perishable, we must ask the

Deconstructivism: an accurate portrait of the situation in the western nations at the close of this century?

Top 3 photos - Wexner Center for the Visual Arts. The Ohio State University, Columbus, Ohio. Eisenman/Trott, Architects.

Left center - Penthouse suite in Vienna. Coop Himmelblau, Architects.

Bottom left - Schnabe House, Los Angeles, California. Frank Gehry & Associates, Architects.

Bottom right - "Crystal Light" office and residence, Tokyo. Masaharu Takesaki, Architect.

question: is this really the urban architecture that we want, although it is undoubtedly an expression of the current widespread sense of insecurity? Will Eisenman's and Gehry's architecture not deal, perhaps, the final blow to the already fragile structure of our new urban fabric?

In November 1989 the Wexner Center for the Visual Arts at the University of Ohio in Columbus was officially inaugurated. Built according to the winning project in the competition held six years earlier, the Center immediately appears to be the clearest example of architecture of phenomenological derivation, where the Deconstructivist theory is backed up by great talent and applied with unerring taste. Peter Eisenman, one of the Princeton group "The Five", which had strongly influenced American architecture in the post-war period, was the creator of the winning design and the architect of the Wexner Center. Eisenman finally found the great occasion to realize a long-cherished dream. In the previous thirty years of his activity, no ambivalence appears in the direction of his thinking. His works are a continuous sequence, an indefatigable reproposal of the same theme, with infinite variations and nuances. He waited until the traditional phase of the Seventies had subsided before continuing unperturbed in his work.

While criticisms of the Wexner Center by the local public ranged from the purely dismissive to the vehemently polemic, debate in the profession and the schools was at high pitch. Finally there was the chance to analyze a phenomenological work of great significance. The discussions of Eisenman's architectural message reflect each critic's intellectual background; the readings of the work are very different but too biased to be impartial. John Dixon, the director, and Thomas Fisher, critic, of "*Progressive Architecture*", which published an exhaustive study on the Wexner Center, perceived primarily the Modernist matrix, which is certainly present in the grids of the construction scheme and in the past of its architect. Dixon writes: "This project is the most successful attempt so far to advance a plan of innovation and discovery of Modernism". Vincent Scully, in the same magazine, deals with the theme of Deconstructivism, quoting an article by Jacques Derrida on Eisenman's philosophy. In evaluating the center, Scully writes: "Eisenman's fundamental theory is anti-classical and post-humanist". Mark Taylor, professor of religion and director of the Center of Humanities and Science of Williams College, says of the Center: "At first sight the use of 'fortress' details (part of the construction is made up of brick towers) seems a classic Post-Modern gesture. But there are differences and these differences constitute an important critique both of Modernism and Post-Modernism". Taylor's final comment leaves no doubt as to how a traditional humanist sees this kind of architecture: "Wandering through the labyrinthine construction of Eisenman, we (re)discover that which we already know but struggle to repress: there is no way out of the labyrinth in which we are destined to wander".

It appears clear to all observers that in the Center the pseudo-rationalistic language of the grids blends with the image of the brick towers, whose theme is clearly traditionalist, thus creating a marked dissonance, typical of Surrealist aesthetics. The image of the grids which are reflected one in the other, suggests the reverberations of a symphony that has been playing for years in the mind of its architect.

Considering the social significance of this work and Eisenman's philosophy, it is impossible not to think of the very high cost involved in producing this type of building. Its intricate, complex geometry is, in fact, considered by many totally out of proportion with its function as a university structure. Accordingly, this philosophy appears inappropriate to a large section of the public, particularly when all cities and university campuses, hard-pressed by financial difficulties, are struggling to defend their existence. Moreover, in a moment of social and political awareness, faced with millions of homeless and the need for funds to solve the problems of the ghettos, a moral tendency to curtail excessive expenditure re-emerges on the architectural scene. Deconstructivism is seen by those who believe in the ethical and political component of architecture as a typical example of counter-culture. For its exclusivism and experimentation with costly projects this trend is accused, often unjustifiably, of moving towards a dangerous élitist personalism in search of new sensations, increasingly far removed from the problems of society.

11 - Contemporary Architecture is on Trial

In the Nineties the public, having experienced too many stylistic changes and conflicting ideas, appears to have lost faith in the architectural process, blaming it for much of the dysfunction in the contemporary urban fabric. The role of the architect was called into question by the failure of Modernism and by the accusations of superficiality and fatuousness brought against the Post-Modern and neo-Surrealism. Decisive action in defense of the environment has frequently been taken by communities opposed to new constructions in their towns. Architects have been perceived as promoting ideas of development unacceptable to the majority of people, and there has been a fundamental loss of faith in their creative capacity, no longer capable of capturing the public's imagination as in the past. Why, it was asked, is it not possible to reach a consensus on a few internationally famous architects, as was possible only a quarter of a century earlier? F.L.Wright, Le Corbusier, Mies Van der Rohe, Alvar Aalto, Gropius, Nervi and a few others were universally acclaimed and respected as masters. Had great talent, then, disappeared from architecture? And what had happened to the artistic leadership of our time? Certainly, excellence had not disappeared from the human psyche, judging by the many valuable contributions to various fields of knowledge and the arts, but the recent past has not helped to clarify ideas or to achieve a consensus of opinion on artists and their creations.

Certain episodes are symptomatic of the current mistrust in the architectural process, revealing the level of tension that has built up between professional architects and other members of the community. Concerned about this situation, the board of directors of the Connecticut Society of Architects, a member of the American Institute of Architects, decided in October 1989 to launch a public relations campaign "to improve the image of architects in the American community". The president of the Society wrote to all members saying: "During the last few years, we have become increasingly worried by the fact that the role of architects and their work has been largely misunderstood, or worse, that they are viewed negatively by a wide public, both in Connecticut and in the nation."

In Europe as well there has been a traditionalist reaction against modern architecture and town planning. The Prince of Wales is the acknowledged leader of this movement, supported by an ample public and a number of critics, in both Europe and the United States. But only a small percentage of architects, many of them American, have followed the dictates of Prince Charles. (7). The debate which has arisen within the profession and in schools on both sides of the Atlantic is rife, leading to further polarization of extreme positions. The tones of the debate between the Modernists and the Prince of Wales have been decidedly acrimonious as a result of his attempt to rescind contracts for projects for a number of buildings in the center of London awarded to well-known Modernist architects. For the first time in the post-war period the opposition between traditionalism and Modernism in architecture has become an open confrontation.

Given the opposition faced by the architectural profession, it is legitimate to ask why its image and effective power have fallen so low in the eyes of public opinion.

The truth is that in the prevailing consumeristic economy of our time the architect has lost control, in most cases, of artistic synthesis. In these years of non-consensus the tendency has been to convert the structure of the profession into a business mainly interested in profit rather than in designing a work of art which will repay its creator with professional satisfaction. Young architects coming out of school with the intention of producing original projects must immediately adjust to the management of a profession which is on the whole much closer to engineering than to an artistic activity, due to the increase in paperwork as well as the technical complexity of every project. From the viewpoint of society, the most important aspect of the profession is the guarantee of results from a functional and legal aspect, to provide a product that will be acceptable to the majority. The marketing of any successful architectural practice is thus based mainly on majority opinion. Even in schools of architecture of international fame the entrance requirements of today have become intelligence, culture and dedication, rather than artistic talent. In many western nations, including the United States, the tests to obtain the architectural licence do not require that the candidate demonstrate a clear artistic ability. In these exams no emphasis is placed on traditional architectural qualities such as balance, sincerity, authenticity of expression and sense of proportion in space and form, but rather on objective tests and technical data. The triumph of systematics, technology and economy over traditional humanistic values is quite clear.

4) The School of Administration (see photos on page 32) was built on the campus of the University of Ghana, Legon, Ghana, in 1963 with the assistance of the local government and the Ford Foundation. This was the first of the author's projects to be built in Africa; others were to follow in the next few years, in both East and West Africa. The moment of great hope seemed to have arrived and many African states, having gained their independence, began to control not only their economic resources but above all their intellectual ones. Ghana in particular, unlike other African states, showed itself capable of progress and self-government despite its limited economic resources. While the architecture of this building has a modern matrix, it uses traditional concepts. To obtain the continuous ventilation necessary in a tropical climate, the author designed a building capable of generating air currents deriving from the difference in temperature of the outside surfaces, even without wind. Both walls and roof are double, with a ventilated interspace providing greater protection against the heat of the sun.

5) The first high-rise apartment building to be built in the United States with an industrialized system (see photos on page 33) was constructed by the author in Yonkers, New York, in 1971, using a French system, the "Tracoba", modified to meet the needs of the American market. The system was made up of panels and three-dimensional elements made of reinforced concrete, produced in a factory located on the Harlem River in New York. This factory could produce a thousand apartments a year with a double work shift. Most of the workers, almost all of whom had no experience and had been previously unemployed, were Americans of African or Puerto Rican descent. With the training program offered by the project, they became skilled workers within six months. The Yonkers building was intended as a prototype, to be repeated in different form and size in programs for slum reconstruction.

The tower is still in perfect condition in the 1990s and has become a luxury high-rise condominium. The New York construction worker unions, who opposed the use of prefabrication because it would reduce the working hours of their members, won their battle against the newcomers, imposing limits on factory-assembled components, insisting that they be completed on site. The American government, for its part, considering the vastness of the problem, preferred to give up its search for a solution to the problem of slum reconstruction that had been launched with "Operation Breakthrough". Moreover, the building industry was not particularly interested in construction systems, since its profits derived from other factors, such as the prestige of the site location. Thus the problems of the American slums and of providing employment for Afro-American workers, frequently either untrained or unmotivated, remained unresolved, worsening continuously from year to year.

The training method based on the repetitiveness of construction systems still remains valid in the 1990s, particularly when each individual, non-skilled worker is allowed to learn and progress to the maximum of his or her capabilities.

6) (see photographs on page 42) The School of Agriculture at Spilimbergo in the Friuli region of Italy was certainly a new experience, in which I drew on childhood memories, in the desire to recreate that type of architectural space in which I grew up, as in a film by Fellini. In these contradictory feelings, irony had no part. Perhaps it was only a misunderstood appreciation of classicism which, for a European who grew up in Florence and lived for many years in America, becomes the dangerous game of a mime who sees himself skillful but indecisive in the liquid mirror of memories. The game, if it may be so called, as the commitment to produce a serious and balanced project, had become that of reinterpreting the message of De Chirico, since in searching for the guiding thread, the story had to emerge from a dream. But at the same time there was the continuous fear, as in the rapid movement of a dance, of falling into the arms of Walt Disney, of entering that lost land somewhere between playful childhood and oppressive commercialism. I had also to ask myself whether an important factor in the action was not the European complex, typical of American architects, that one succumbs to at times of psychological uncertainty, much like an illness. Once the work was finished, the joy of having avoided falling into the Disneyland trap of superficiality was undeniable. At the same time there remained this ambiguous feeling of having produced a "classical" work, of quality, but extraneous to its proper time, place and function, which is an oppressive contradiction in terms. Moreover, the idea of having created a coherent and serious three-dimensional setting, achieved almost cynically, that was visibly appreciated by the students and teachers of the School, was a constant source of doubt. Were they, then, also living the dream of an uncertain historical moment?

For an architect of Modernist formation the opportunity to experiment in the sphere of traditionalism was like an exciting pilgrimage, full of unknowns. It was like making a journey into the past and rediscovering sensations already felt before, living an experience of architecture without being an architect, being able to observe from the outside. At the same time, a progressive inner coldness resulted from the continuous pressures and dilemmas posed by the intellect, incapable of rejecting its formation, and thus generating severe psychological detachment. One begins to wonder, then, whether we do not show the best in ourselves at those crucial moments when we are willing to look inside ourselves with determination.

Some things can only be appreciated when one has a complete knowledge of them. Knowledge of classical architecture teaches us that the proportions of the past are supremely important in creating dignity and respectability, both of which have been lost in contemporary modern reductionism. In a special way, this knowledge teaches us that modern architecture, made up of so many small spaces, repeated in the hive-like creation of dwellings and offices, is perceived by the public as music consisting of one note repeated ad infinitum, distinguished by a few marginal variations.

Will we then be capable of reconciling the needs of mass society with the sensibilities of a limited group of individuals, interested in the defense of a traditional way of thought and environment?

The first project (see drawing) for the School of Agriculture was designed for contemporary agrarian technology, as a means and an end of teaching - it seemed to grow out of the fields and vineyards. Its roof was in part a glazed surface to be used as nurseries for plants and was conceived to provide a natural link with the sky and the earth and a scientific means for investigation and research. This solution was rejected by both the community and School as well as by the director of the A.I.D. project, sponsored by the US government. The teaching of agriculture and particularly viticulture, it was emphatically pointed out, is and always been an art in Friuli, not a science as the architecture of the project seemed to suggest. Consequently, the building that was to house the School had to have characteristics of a traditional nature rather than a technological one. Furthermore, following the enormous damage to their land by the earthquake of 1976, the people of Friuli looked to their past, rather than to the future, feeling themselves threatened by the development of technology.

It was in this state of mind that, during the reconstruction following the earthquake, the people of Friuli almost always rejected projects of contemporary design, opting instead for traditional solutions, particularly in the construction of new houses in villages hundreds of years old. This was true in the case of the Home for the Elderly at Buia, the cost of which was paid by the US government as part of its aid program for reconstruction. A modern proposal by a well-known local architect was rejected by the town administration and by the directors of the American program (A.I.D.) The project was turned over to the author with the recommendation to keep to the standards of local tradition.

Here again the author found himself in the same psychological situation of ambivalence experienced during the planning of the School at Spilimbergo, which was built at the same time. The Home for the Elderly at Buia was acclaimed as a success both locally and in the United States.

7) At a reception for the 150th anniversary of the Royal Institute of British Architects on May 30, 1984, Prince Charles succeeded in astounding its members by his speech accusing them of having "continually ignored the feelings and

wishes of the majority of the population". Following this, the Prince of Wales continued his campaign to stop building of modern derivation in England with public speeches and a book, published in 1989 and entitled "*A Vision for Great Britain, a Personal Vision of Architecture*". This treatise set out the Prince's philosophy in 10 points, defined by the press as "the ten commandments" of traditionalism. In short, the Prince set out guidelines for new buildings, ranging from criteria for respecting proportion and the existing environment to detailed proposals with suggestions for the decoration of façades. Precise examples were given by the Prince in favour of certain existing buildings, while he made a vigourous effort to block other projects of modern design.

Although many British architects opposed Prince Charles' action, the majority of the public, as polls showed, supported him point by point. In his inaugural address in July, 1989, the new president of RIBA, Maxwell Hutchison, expressed the official position of British architects, most of whom had adopted the credo of the Modern Movement, when he said: "The result of the Prince of Wales' intervention has been to make honourable that which would have been considered contemptible only half a century ago: the rejection of the new in favour of the old".

The main theme of the debate was obviously centered on the planning of new urban areas in England, but had widespread repercussions elsewhere. The disillusion with post-war New Towns and urban development projects that were interested in solving technical rather than human problems, had influenced the reaction of the British public. Prince Charles willingly became the spokesman for this discontent, given his social and philosophical roots of perfect traditionalist origin.

PART THREE

THE INFLUENCE OF MENTAL PROCESSES ON ARCHITECTURE

1 - The Significance of Tradition and Innovation in History

We may legitimately ask why in our present-day society there is a large scale confrontation between traditional forces and technological development, resulting not only in loss of valuable energy but also in the loss of faith in a better future. The negative repercussions of this situation on human activities as a whole must be acknowledged, at a moment when all possible intellectual and economic power should instead be focused on solving the global problems facing humanity.

The two opposing forces in the society of the Nineties represent two clearly defined positions growing out of the unification of cultural ideologies deriving from the same matrixes and the consequent process of polarization, which has greatly accelerated over the last twenty years. Scholars and the more culturally aware sectors of the public had already reached some kind of consensus, initiating debate on a global scale, on this phenomenon of polarization, which has surfaced in every continent and is typical of XX century society. The main themes of the debate were at last clear, although the precise causes of this social malaise were not, while the alternative solutions to the problem depended more and more on the personal evaluations of each individual. It was thus clear that in such a vast context the power of the two conflicting forces in society derived from the intensity and variability of their influence on the mental state of each individual.

The most conspicuous of these influences, traditionalist thought, is so called because it always makes reference to established ideas and concepts, which are hardly ever discussed or analyzed by their believers, being part of a system of acquired knowledge. The opposing force is the spirit of innovation, the raison d'être of which is the analysis of every element, whether physical or mental, the search for the meaning and significance of things, with the aim of modifying them in a beneficial way that will open up new frontiers.

In projecting the future image of society, these two forces have played very different roles: traditionalism has always tried to transpose the past into the future, thus denying the possibility of change. The innovative spirit, on the other hand, has tried to obtain the new directly, invoking the fascination of the untested and hitherto unseen.

The dynamic thought from which the innovative spirit derives is certainly stronger in some individuals than in others. This spirit has been present in all civilizations which have left their mark on history but has never appeared in primitive societies. The motivating force of innovation lies in the macroscopic desire to explore the universe to its limits and in the microscopic research into its cellular structure. It is an optimistic force, growing out of the search for an ever more radiant future and a solution to the drama of human survival in a universe studded with dangers and possible catastrophes, but seen as exciting and challenging.

Until the Sixties, many historians and anthropologists were willing to recognize the existence of a variety of different traditions, each with particular characteristics, but accepted traditionalism only as an abstract concept. During the Seventies however, all common elements such as forms, values and principles of the various traditions were analyzed and began to be assimilated by a spontaneous process into a single concept in opposition to the growing pressure of the technological world. The existence of a "tradition", or a traditional spirit, capable of representing a mode of thought common to all the different cultures, had finally taken shape, giving rise to a recognizable ethology and a new kind of unified front and philosophy unthinkable only half a century earlier. The members of the major religious communities started to communicate with each other, attempting to present a united front against the spread of atheism promoted by technology. Religious organizations and traditionalist groups buried most of their age-old differences, tending to formulate a common set of beliefs and a fundamental inheritance to be defended, although their doctrinal differences were still apparent. This new position was deemed necessary to keep alive the venerable values of the past under the onslaught of the new and transient constantly being created by the process of innovation.

The two modes of thought even use different systems of measurement for physical objects. Traditionalists think in terms of natural units: feet, inches and gallons, taken from their perception of the physical world, whereas XX century innovative thought uses meters, liters and kilograms, or the metric-decimal system, which facilitates calculation because the units are all related.

Even for an objective operation such as the measurement of time two different techniques are still used, one traditional, the other innovative, each having a different significance for its users. Innovation uses oscillations produced by a quartz crystal and electronic instruments to measure time with a precision hitherto impossible. With this technology a chronometer can measure time to a hundredth of a second, offering many other functions as well to satisfy a wide spectrum of users at a much lower cost than the traditional spring balance system. But at the same time tradition holds its own in this field where the art of watch-making is still celebrated. The mechanical watches of the past are still made today with great precision and style and are held in great esteem by connoisseurs who willingly pay much more for them, although their performance cannot equal that of quartz technology.

Another typical example of the clash between the two cultures can be seen in the 1988 victory in the "America's Cup" regatta of the American yacht over the New Zealand one. The American yacht sported a new design concept: a catamaran with a variable-profile sail designed much like an airplane wing. This boat was much faster than the New Zealand one, totally out-classing it from a technical point of view. The international controversy which flared up as a result centered around the question of accepted custom, which demanded the use of a traditional hull and sail. Although the Cup regulations apparently were not explicit, many sailing enthusiasts considered it unethical on the part of the Americans to have entered a new, technologically advanced boat, so different from those traditionally used.

The clearest example of the dichotomy under discussion, however, can be seen in the historical role of women in society. The traditionalist sees the role of woman essentially as that of mother, subordinate to man. In all religions, with some recent exceptions, the role of priest or minister has always been held by men. Technological society however tends to place women on a par with men, but only when they can demonstrate their ability to perform the same job, on both the intellectual and the physical level. The concept of performance, inspired by science and utilitarian philosophy, thus challenges the dogmas of traditional orthodoxy. Technology and medical science support the new female status by giving women freedom of choice in child-bearing, through contraceptives and safe abortion.

In traditional thought all objects have a specific origin, often belonging to one of the two sexes. They have recognizable characteristics and can be classified as coming from a determined geographical area. The symbols displayed by the form of each object, if authentic, bear witness to the period in which they were created, making them easily datable. In a techno-oriented sense the difference between the sexes is ascribed purely to difference of function, beyond any ethical or aesthetic consideration. For the same reason, in traditionalism sexual relationships are part of a much more complex emotional and ethical relationship, whereas in technological culture their basis is functional and hedonistic. A complex, emotional love story is typically traditional, while sexual mechanics and pornography, which became widespread after World War II, are derived from the concept of performance and are a result of polarization between the sex act and the sentiment of love.

In socio-political history there has always been a struggle between conservatism and new ideologies. Conservatism has retained basically the same characteristics throughout history. Innovation, instead, has often been identified with the process of continuous evolution of the ideological left. The left is constantly on the search for a new ideology to replace the previous one which rapidly looses its relevance, in much the same way as products of technology are modified to keep pace with social development.

In Japan the clash between tradition and innovation was especially sharp because the original Japanese culture, protected by the isolation of its islands, had remained virtually intact through the centuries up to the present day. The Western nations instead accepted large-scale multiracial immigration and the consequent cultural influences; they accepted pluralism whereas Japan rejected it.

The Japanese dilemma is clearly illustrated in the work of Yukio Mishima, who describes the drama of classical culture confronted with the new industrial era, promoting hedonistic capitalist ideals. In 1970 Mishima committed suicide in sign of protest against the loss of pre-war Japan. In the late Eighties, on the contrary, Shintaro Ishihara in his book "Japan Can Say No" theorized that advanced high technology would be the determining factor in future world leadership. The clash between the opposing theories of Mishima and Ishihara is noticeable in the contrasting inspirations of Japanese architecture.

2 - The Two Creative Modes of Thought

In their different directions, the defense of acquired values and the shaping of the new have preserved a continuity of inspiration, showing how each of the two represents an active mental process with a propensity for creation. This propensity is applied to all those physical aspects and the world of ideas which distinguish every epoch. The two basic philosophies, in fact, reappear clearly in every historical period, although in different guise, in all fields of knowledge. We will call **ANALOGICAL THOUGHT** the mental process which, on a social level, produces traditionalism, while the process which generates the new through science and technology will be defined as **ANALYTICAL THOUGHT**. These two mental processes, which aim to create artistic synthesis, are the only processes of the human mind capable of generating this synthesis and have always operated with in variable proportions. Their salient characteristics may be deduced from an analysis of their philosophies and from observing their production over the course of history. As will be seen, all known historical events have been produced by these processes, in balance or in opposition. These two modes of thought can be defined point by point in terms of their contrasting positions and their salient features. To every characteristic or aspect of one corresponds the philosophical alternative of the other.

INFLUENCE OF MENTAL PROCESSES

A) THE ANALOGICAL PROCESS : TRADITION

The analogical mental process is founded on the preservation of the meaning of each concept which describes every element making up the human consciousness, whether material or intangible. Each element is indivisible and unchanging, preserving its initial features intact.

1 — In architecture we find the concept of **immutability**. Construction materials are thus natural: stone, wood; and are used as far as possible integrally, without altering their intrinsic qualities. Respect for the material is fundamental. The details of construction are based on the same principles of design as were used, for example, in constructing Greek columns 25 centuries ago. In art, this approach demands a faithful, truthful representation of every natural element.

2 — Orthodoxy, one of the most important features of this process, is based on **accepted principles and rules**, inspiring confidence and credibility. Orthodoxy is founded on absolute belief in the defense of a pre-established order, where all elements are conditioned to retain their own place or role, whether this be social class or the appropriate moulding on a certain style of door. Those who adopt orthodoxy commit themselves to maintaining a hierarchy of **authoritarian** values. The holders of these values and those who will pass them on to the next generation are the **elders. Seniority** and **maturity**

B) THE ANALYTICAL PROCESS: INNOVATION AND SCIENCE

Analysis is a mental process founded on the ability to abstract the parts from the whole. Each part thus becomes a unit to be ordered and assimilated into a system of physical properties and concepts. In the development of its speculative activity this system produces more complex entities. The purpose of analysis is to isolate basic elements in preparation for the composition of the parts, assembled according to various systems. During this continuous state of change, new syntheses will be created and increasingly refined theories of aggregation will be devised.

1 — The materials used in architecture are the product of **transformation and synthesis**: steel, metal alloys, plastics, multi-layered glass, refined reinforced concrete and finally composite materials. The materials rarely display their natural characteristics, while the structural elements are always new, following the development of new techniques. The architecture of the Modern Movement derives from this philosophical stance, having experimented with new forms and techniques in the attempt to define artistic and scientific progress.

2 — Total liberty of thought is the cardinal rule which enables society to progress, allowing verification of every new concept. The analytic process presupposes a type of mentality in which no individual adheres to a pre-established system of ideas. It is this type of perception that has produced the theory of evolution, faith in free enterprise and the doctrines of rationalism and positivism. In a culture of analytic derivation there are no pre-set rules seen as immutable. Rules, even if based on principles of logic, change with the progress of research and are structured to cope with each situation or environmental

| ANALOGICAL | ANALYTICAL |

are virtues, in that a fundamental understanding of things needs time. Time produces a gradual, balanced maturing, resulting in **continuity** and credibility. Thus, an older scholar is described as a mature person, an expert, commanding the respect of the young. Education is, accordingly, initiation into the acceptance of a set of values which make up a culture.

Authenticity of expression is the most important aspect deriving from orthodoxy and the basis on which man's past and world history is founded. The principles according to which authenticity is judged determine rules of ethical origin and are therefore irrefutable and immutable. Architectural orthodoxy is based on well-tested laws and aspires to classicism; it defends styles, continuously re-proposing them as unchangeable. The classical features of the Western Tradition are the symbols of that society, as it has been preserved since the time of the ancient Greeks. For over two thousand years the structure of Western houses has had the same general features, based on the same principles.

Resistance to time is one of the important requisites for true works of art. When the authentic quality of such works is preserved for centuries they acquire the status of **antiques**. In this context, the authenticity of a work of art or architecture is the critical feature which guarantees its true origin and real value.

3 — Physical and historical **permanence** is necessary to achieve stability and immortality. The repetitive use, in architecture, of the same principles and structural features reinforces stability and continuity.

condition. The result is a socio-economic reality which is always new and in continuous evolution; from this derives freedom of thought. In this culture **youth** is a psychological security with its desire for change, its faith in development leading to a better future and in scientific progress. The new, where it represents an overall socio-economic reality, is, in fact, the most important objective of **innovation**.

The **values produced by freedom of thought** come from the ideas of relative esteem, utility and importance. They are thus of materialistic and essentially amoral origin. In architecture every new building is a **new affirmation of a principle** which can indicate a new direction. Every artistic expression is a new experience since there are no pre-established elements to generate it. The artistic avant-garde derives from the necessity to produce the new as both an end and a means.

3 — The working together of all parts: **performance** is the ability to repeatedly fulfill a given task and is itself a product of the scientific method. The aim of analytical thought at the end of the XX century is to restructure the human brain as an electronic apparatus.

The quality of performance is determined by three major factors: **efficiency, flexibility** and **speed**. Efficiency is the critical component which guarantees that nothing is lost, due to physical or

ANALOGICAL

ANALYTICAL

psychological friction or in terms of space and energy. Economic efficiency is one of the most important elements and is determined by three types of cost involved in the life cycle of a building. Flexibility is the capacity for responding to ever changing circumstances, with the speed required to make changes rapidly.

The **product** is a typical expression of the innovative process in search of something repeatable that can be used globally by an ever increasing number of people.

The Bau-Haus and the International Style of the Modern Movement aimed to create solutions of global value in step with the scientific spirit. The message of this Movement was clear and resolute: "Form follows function". In the same way, the words of one of its prophets, Mies Van de Rohe: "Less is more", are a good description of the essential nature of his architecture.

While Modernist aesthetics tended towards minimalism, scientific progress demanded complexity in solving the increasingly difficult problems posed by the search for a refined functionalism deriving also from humanistic matrixes. This irreconcilable difference occasionally resulted in contradiction, revealing the lack of a coherent artistic synthesis. On the level of pure image, Modernist aesthetics mimed essentiality of form without attempting to solve the problem of language, either as means of expression or as communication.

4 — Ethical thought introduces a moral dimension as a fundamental part of this process. A relationship between ethics and aesthetics can be achieved in pure art as well as architecture, in a complex communion which includes both moral principles and feelings. A multiform type of thought is preferred insofar as it is closer to human nature. In this context the most highly esteemed qualities of mind are the capacities for intuition and analogy, vital to the assimilation of new experiences. These are the guiding forces in man's search for a place in the universe. As a corollary, architecture is influenced by analogical thought insofar as, when conceived of as art, it possesses all of the attributes of sculpture. From a sense of balance, and of honesty, a relationship

4 — Specialization comes from the need to produce elements providing a constant level of performance in a specific field. It has a limited functional or intellectual relationship to the rest of the scientific process.

Mechanization is necessary to reproduce objects an infinite number of times. The Modern Movement was the first to propose the idea of the machine in architecture with Le Corbusier's "Machine à habiter", a dwelling designed to be entirely functional. This first step was followed by others all over the world, culminating in the Japanese pre-fabricated houses, mass-produced by robots. In this case the house itself is not a machine but a product of one. The emphasis on the concept of quantity derives from the notion of production.

ANALOGICAL	ANALYTICAL

ANALOGICAL

between ethics and aesthetics will arise naturally. The sense of proportion in buildings and in individual architectural elements derives from the validity of this relationship. The narrowest form of traditional art is **folklorism**; as its artistic contribution is restricted to a precise area, its influence on any other culture is limited.

5 — The expression of **individual personality** respects singularity and freedom of choice within the limits set by the principles. In the domain of aesthetics and morality, individual personality must be emphasized to nurture the uniqueness to which a work of art aspires. **Originality** derives from the union between authenticity and unique expression in a difficult and rarely achieved process.

All traditional buildings, including housing, are designed to offer their inhabitants various possibilities for personalization.

6 — **Metaphor** and ambiguity come from the intangible, the emotions and the supernatural. In this case language is an end in itself, and the need to use metaphor in all communications is vital. Metaphor, defined as a figurative image to express a concept by analogy, obviously gives rise to ambiguity. The understanding of a metaphor and the nature of its ambiguity is restricted to a specific area, a limited number of individuals or a closed circle.

ANALYTICAL

5 — The **impersonal** inspires **mass-production**, emphasizing the tangible and the commercial product that can be distributed in great quantity with a quality level acceptable to all. Production for a mass society was the aim of the Modern Movement from the start of the XX century. The **egalitarian spirit** of this period can be perceived in buildings which offered the same type of dwelling for all, to eliminate the economic discrimination deriving from differentiation in their quality. These projects proposed simple volumes, raised above the ground, with a roof terrace accessible to all. As the creation of units of different design and value was excluded, there were no private gardens or attics. Le Corbusier's "Unité d'Habitation", built in Marseilles, is a typical example of this philosophy, which had many followers in the Fifties and Sixties.

6 — **Precision**. A scientific system cannot operate without precise instructions. There must be no room for doubt arising from ambiguity or metaphor. The emphasis is on precise objectives and mechanical procedures capable of translating into reality any complex idea. The technological process thus uses a simplified system of communication where functions are described by symbols which make up a specific, universally comprehensible language. For this reason the terminology adopted by the Modern Movement was the same all over the world, using scientific references to express its architectural concepts.

INFLUENCE OF MENTAL PROCESSES

ANALOGICAL

7 — Uniqueness is the striving for a distinctive work of art, deriving from originality, individuality, metaphor and authenticity.

ANALYTICAL

7 — Uniformity is the tendency to adopt a product offering a consistent level of quality achieved through specialization, mechanization and precision.

3 - Two Concepts of History

The two modes of thought have influenced events, particularly in the last fifty years, in very different ways, dominating in alternating periods in the various geographical areas and generating two opposing notions of history.

Although history is a single progression of events, each individual's different comprehension of it creates noticeably different interpretations, particularly when critical parameters are so divergent, as in the case of a traditionalist or a modernist perception. Historical interpretation is of crucial significance since it gives rise to a conclusive judgement on every phenomenon capable of influencing or inspiring future action on the part of individuals, and thus of communities. Our future actions are indeed determined by a projection of ideas based on our personal image of the future.

The traditionalist view of history, essentially as defined by Giambattista Vico, is based on a **cyclical concept** and represented by a complex spiral progression of events recurring with varying degrees of frequency. The phenomenon of repetition is due to the recurrence over the course of time of similar events when like circumstances prevail. The dynamic principle of this process is of great significance, since as soon as the context for recurrence of certain events is identified the consequent historical developments become predictable.

Thus it is that, in accordance with the cyclical view of history, the original symbols of western architecture, such as classical Greek columns, have always been positively reaffirmed by analogical thought whenever historical circumstances demand a restatement of the link with the past. Such a return to classicism may, however, be negative, as during the XIX and XX centuries in Europe and the United States, when classical symbols were used in a pompous and grandiloquent manner in a stilted, unnatural reaffirmation of the past. In this case the true humanistic values of classicism were absent. The grandiose proportions and ostentatious decoration of XIX century buildings were dictated by a false inspiration to copy architectural styles from the past. This clearly revealed the insecurity of the traditionalists of the times, who reacted in an excessively defensive manner to the crushing pressure of technological advance.

The cyclical recurrence of an analogical theme in the history of western architecture is exemplified by the development of the large-scale house. For the western traditionalist the ideal home has always been the Roman villa, developed in various, but always coherent, forms throughout the Renaissance and the following centuries. It was Palladio's influence first on English architecture, then on American in the XVIII century which expressed the continuity of traditional principles within the Western Tradition. In more recent times the Post-

Modernists have revived the Palladian influence in the design of suburban homes in America. In these houses, the concept of setting as well as the general development of form and decoration was basically the same as in the I century A.D. This was the result of a philosophical continuity producing an architecture that became immutable through the centuries, just as the western élitist tradition retained those same guiding principles.

The analytical view of the historical process is, instead, the history of science. It can be represented by a **linear progression** created by an irreversible sequence of new discoveries and changes brought about by society. This type of progression, which works towards greater efficiency, speed and flexibility, continually changing in search of the next step ahead, produces a form of architecture in constant evolution.

Thus two philosophical poles give rise to two easily discernible scenarios based on two contrasting images of the future. The analytical process is consonant with a theory of architecture in evolution, driven by a society in constant expansion, an environment yielding to the demands of a developing population. Such an architecture is imbued with democratic and populist themes and is at the service of an ever wider community. At the other extreme, traditionalist philosophy tends to idealize a numerically stable and balanced society, since only in this way can equilibrium be maintained without change.

While harmony of proportions and a certain poetic inspiration can be seen as valid in a society with a strong cultural tradition, concepts of mechanization and technological performance are more easily comprehensible in evolving societies where development is initially quantitative rather than qualitative. A society in expansion needs a means of immediate communication and a sense of self-assertion, while traditional society requires above all reassurance and reaffirmation of its principles. From these two conflicting aspirations derive two divergent ideas of history, giving rise to two opposite concepts of architecture.

4 - The Linear Concept of History in Modern Art and Architecture

The ideas formulated during the 1930s began to reappear after World War II, with the timidity of a long-cherished hope finally about to become reality. While post-war reconstruction was progressing at great speed, the desire to create a new world had already manifested itself, backed by the power of science, inspiring and exciting with its ever more amazing discoveries. The pace of life suddenly accelerated. Things hitherto inconceivable were now becoming part of logical thought, and thus obtainable. The new, the incredible, the unimaginable discoveries fascinated artists and architects who rapidly tried to catch up with the times and to vie with scientists. Never before had the words "old" or "obsolete" taken on such negative implications. In the early Fifties the meaning of the word "antique" was defined and glorified and made applicable to a period ending at least two centuries before, thus avoiding any contamination by the undesirable concept of "old". In the Seventies however the qualification of "antique" was extended to encompass works produced in the XIX century and even the early years of the twentieth, for the obvious reasons of an expanding market and enormously fast-paced change which placed even the recent past in a new historical perspective.

In the early Fifties Modernist art and architecture, mostly untouched by the vestiges of an opaque traditionalism, already rejected by the intelligentsia, wholeheartedly but unconsciously identified with the linear history of science. A period of great angst began, in which artists and architects sought at all costs to mark the line of history with their own personal discoveries. Each artist attempted to contribute something startling, shocking, totally new. The possible incomprehension of their work was justified by its total newness. The object of artistic research was to define the most advanced concept, deriving from an idea never before expressed or explored, analogous to a revolutionary scientific discovery. The avant-garde thus became a necessary factor in the exploration of a new, as yet uncharted, territory of art, while at the same time the artists' frustration increased as their search for the absolutely new became ever more difficult.

The classical artistic synthesis which produced works of art with a clear message expressed through a conventional medium gave way to research that resulted in unusual works adopting revolutionary materials and techniques. The evolving modern artist developed and changed rapidly from one year to the next. In the desperate search for the new and untried, canvases were first covered with layers of color applied by new techniques, sprays or jets for instance, and were then torn and slashed. Canvases and frames were taken apart to symbolize the breaking up of the traditional classical schemes, becoming strips of colored material and objects of strange shape.

Many paintings created with new, untried techniques rapidly deteriorated, revealing their physical fragility, often equalled only by the frailty of the ideas behind them, where the search for an astonishing effect stifled any intelligible artistic message. The same phenomenon could be seen in sculpture when figurative interpretation was abandoned; three-dimensional works of art were reduced to total dematerialization or abstraction. Marino Marini's horses began to show signs of restlessness, shortly afterwards rearing suddenly, only to fall to the ground in pieces.

Modern artists, despite the impossible task of competing with science on its own ground in trying to produce new discoveries, often succeeded in creating works which will hopefully be appreciated by posterity. Such artists were undoubtedly able to draw on the humanistic quality of the analogical process in their works. Henry Moore was one who, using essentially modern forms, was able to convey a message in which the balance of an authentic inspiration of classical origin reaffirmed the highest values of Greek and Roman sculpture. The well-deserved acclaim of a number of acknowledged masters was offset by the accusations of incapacity and insincerity brought against artists of the new generation whose lack of talent and inspiration the public judged to be easily camouflaged by the incomprehensible language they used. The talent of many painters and sculptors thus took time to emerge from the confusion and uncertainty enveloping both their own ideas and society as a whole.

The total predominance of the analytical mode leaves little space for the true creative potential of the modern artist who devotes all his or her energy to inventing new concepts while forgetting how to draw, paint or sculpt and thus loses the ability to communicate with the vast majority of the public. Modern art, when it becomes identified with the analytical process and with linear history, loses all the characteristics and humanistic qualities of the analogical mode of thought. In classical artistic synthesis these characteristics played a highly significant role in imparting depth and communicative capacity to works of art. The analytical synthesis tends only to delineate the general concept and ensure the performance of the work, while all the values associated with the search for proportion, colour and tone are inexorably lost. Moreover, in linear history technology ages rapidly, making obsolete the production of every period, including the artistic one that has chosen this course. Linear history thus seems to tragically deny its past, in contrast with traditional history which celebrates and glorifies it. Similarly, modern art in refusing to transcend time, totally rejecting traditional values and placing its relevance only on the time of its creation becomes inevitably dated and rapidly subject to obsolescence.

The public now wants an answer to the crucial question: what is the difference between the celebrated realistic art of the past and contemporary art? The difference between a Renaissance masterpiece and a contemporary one is quite visible. Most contemporary art lacks any description of the complexity of the society it is supposed to reflect. The tendency to abstraction and minimalism results in an inability to provide a historical representation of contemporary society, which far from having lost the depth and variety handed down from the Renaissance, has, in fact, acquired new intellectual value deriving from scientific and artistic research as well as a deeper psychological introspection. A Renaissance portrait gives us a total vision of the society of the time, a precise image of the persons portrayed, from the overall concept of the composition to the minute details of the fabric used in the dress. The physical and social portrayal of these characters is of great historical value from all perspectives. The same is true of the architecture of that time which can still today communicate to us not only factual messages but also vivid sensations.

What will modern works be able to tell about today's reality five centuries hence? Apart from wondering how many of today's buildings and works of art will survive physically, we expect that their image will appear blurred and insufficiently detailed to give an accurate representation of the modern era, unless the art of our time is to be perceived only as a total panoramic view of a multiform image made up of many diverse and contradictory episodes.

Part Four

THE BALANCE BETWEEN THE TWO MENTAL PROCESSES IN HISTORY: REALISM AND META-REALISM

1 - From the Balance Between the Two Processes: the Birth of Realism in Art

In a comparative analysis of historically significant events and works of visual art and architecture, a certain number of phenomena can be seen to appear recurrently. Whenever signs in works of art reveal that both analytic and analogical processes are present in the collective mind of a given society at a given time and are equally balanced, we always find a distinct period of progress in all domains which leaves its indelible mark on history. In such societies, founded on both humanistic and scientific values, judged by them to be of supreme importance, great esteem is shown for a life based on realism, as commonly understood and accepted. This occurs when realism is not interpreted as a reductive phenomenon tending towards pessimism, seen as the opposite of idealism, but when it is instead based on a positive, optimistic attitude leading towards understanding and control of reality. This context generates the realistic mind, capable of a balanced vision of human life in its complexity; a mind that can produce lasting solutions, projections of reality encompassing both logic and instinct, creativity and continuity of judgement. This is the mind that contemporary psychologists, also in search of a new equilibrium, have described as balanced and positive, and thus capable of resolving complex problems and ensuring lasting stability and contentment.

In those societies distinguished by a balance between the two mental processes a clear, inspired realism can always be observed, both in the visual arts and in architecture. In this realism, authenticity is accompanied by the expression of genuine human feelings and emotions which in turn give rise to inspiration; a realism that is the exact opposite of a mere copy. Thus, the equation:

BALANCE BETWEEN ANALOGICAL AND ANALYTICAL = CONSENSUS = PROGRESS = INSPIRED REALISM BOTH MENTAL AND ARTISTIC

represents the sequence of events that has produced the **great and celebrated art** of the past.

This formula has certainly remained valid from pre-history up to the present time. All visual art, painting and sculpture as well as architecture that has been universally recognized as great art by public, critic and consensus among artists, has always and invariably been **realistic**.

Our thesis has been developed by analyzing the historical events which have determined visual art and architecture in order to find the recurring phenomena that have produced inspired realism. First of all, the significance of realism should be defined at this moment in time when its definition is somewhat problematical. The definitions found in the texts of the Sixties through the Eighties vary considerably, due to the influence of phenomenology, which has interpreted the external world in many different ways.

Our description of realism is the classic one, as found in Webster's dictionary and used in texts on the history of art up until the Fifties. According to these texts, realism in art enhances the similarity with the reality of things, whether inanimate objects or animate beings, reflecting the proportions and details of the physical form.

Realistic art is thus the direct projection of the realistic mind. Moreover, one of the characteristics of realistic art of the highest level is the ability to communicate the emotions of the subject. This is why sculpture of the human figure is the quintessential measure of realism of the society that produces it. Realism in sculpture is unequivocally and immediately recognizable, being the form of artistic expression closest to human understanding, while the painted portrait comes next.

Realistic representations are comprehensible to all, requiring no particular initiation or cultural education. They have the power of immediate communication that can last for millennia. For this reason classic visual art, celebrated as one of the most perfect manifestations of humanity, has always been an inspired realistic art, as represented in sculpture by Phidias and Michelangelo, or in painting by Piero della Francesca and Rembrandt.

The resemblance of a portrait to its subject is a testimony of the artist's ability to reproduce the physical, psychological and emotional characteristics of a person. The Egyptian queen Nefertiti can be easily recognized in a number of sculptures. Her attractive features and fascinating personality can be perceived in whatever medium is used, either basalt stone or painted wood. The crowds who flock to the museums where the sculptural portrait of Nefertiti is exhibited are made up of people from all social and cultural backgrounds. Realism undoubtedly unites sentiment and intellect to create an ample consensus, a clear sign of a pluralistic form of communication.

The fact that great architecture was designed and built by the same artists who produced celebrated paintings and sculptures suggests a direct relationship between realism in buildings and realism in other works of art, both deriving from a mind able to produce a balanced synthesis resulting from equilibrium of the two mental processes. But while realistic sculpture can be recognized at first glance, realism in architecture can be perceived only through lengthy observation. A building is a much more complex manifestation, coming from the communion of ideas from various spheres and sources and made up of many elements, both technical and functional. More time is needed to decipher all the signs and levels of thought, ranging from pure spatial concept to social significance. Architecture is the result of a multilateral synthesis of interests from many directions, all with the same aim. The architect, the builder, the owner and the local community directly influence the final result, uniting in one process historical and future projections.

Realism draws from the analogical process all humanistic elements such as proportion, tone, capacity to communicate emotions and sensations. The analytical process generates innovation in techniques and methods. But a common realistic aspect of the mind is also shared by society and must be present in the majority of the members of that community in which realism appears. In examining the work of major artists from the past, we discover that it is characterized by the typical signs of the time and the level of realism, considering the type of symbology used, is identical to that of the period. Although Picasso embraced cubistic experimentation, his achievements as a realistic painter and draftsman are universally admired. He accepted the challenge of his time while his true genius was basically of a realistic nature.

The alternating predominance of one or the other of the two mental processes has led to different types of civilization and thus different kinds of architecture. For this reason Graeco-Roman science was threatened by the rise of Christianity, which destroyed all the classical texts in an attempt to cancel the heritage of the Western Tradition. Subsequently the analytical process died out in the minds of the inhabitants of Central Italy with the triumph of Christianity, which reigned supreme for almost ten centuries after the fall of the Roman Empire. The analogical process prevailed during early Christian and Medieval times, in tune with the need for ideological permanence of Christian doctrine.

The predominance of the analogical process in a given society almost always results from a religion becoming a totalitarian political power, where moral tension is paramount and economic production and the search for progress are neglected. When traditionalism has become oppressively established in a society, completely suffocating any innovative process and culminating in the triumph of fundamentalism, it inevitably results in depression, both socio-economic and intellectual. No society has shown itself able to protect its achievements and further its progress without including an element of innovation in its social structures and its architecture. As had been the case in many prior civilizations, the great realistic Christian art and architecture appeared only after the XIII century when the two mental processes finally found an equilibrium that softened the rigidity of orthodox Christian ideology by combining it with the secularity and rationality of the Western Tradition.

Conversely, the predominance of the analytical process tends to emphasize economic values, resulting in an overpowering materialism and hedonism which prevail over moral and traditional values, leading to a dangerous estrangement from realism. In this case too, visual art and architecture languish and are unable to find a stable, accomplished form of expression worthy of being recognized as among the greatest achievements of mankind. This is what has happened in the Western world in the latter half of the XX century.

2 - Meta-realism in Art and Architecture

A state of perfect equilibrium between the two mental processes produces both the mental capacity for judging realistically and a realistic artistic synthesis. Their coexistence represents a state of grace which has been achieved only a few times in history. We find it in those societies where an initial positive tension, heralding progress, produces a driving force, active for many decades and capable of uniting all of the physical and moral energies, talents and abilities of its people, harnessing them in the move towards a goal which is both material and spiritual. We may define this extraordinary achievement as the state of Meta-realism, expressive of the total success of the capacities of a community, united by a common drive to create a new reference point in the scale of human values. At this stage both the traditional humanistic values and innovation, typical expression of invention at all times, must combine in one artistic synthesis. The contribution of innovation is absolutely necessary in this case because it represents the image of the future of each society.

In the history of some societies Meta-realism has been achieved on different occasions for a certain period of time. Other societies have attained a type of realism that, while similar, does not exactly and completely fulfill all the requirements for Meta-realism. In any society, the period of Meta-realism has always lasted for only a limited time. It is obviously difficult to maintain such a positive tension, which invariably gives way to growing mental inertia, followed by social and economic slackness leading eventually to decadence. Once again, changes in sculpture provide a precise description of this phenomenon, as has been noted by other authors in discussing the transformation of realism in the course of history. At the high point of Meta-realism, when society reaches its long-sought objectives, strength, beauty and simplicity are always manifest in the representation of the body and gestures of the human figure.

3 - The Levels of Expression of Realism

In painting, sculpture and architecture, four levels of realism may be distinguished; they refer

Modern Art develops along the linear notion of history: The sculpture of Marino Marini from the Forties to the Sixties

Is the last stage of Marini's work an early form of Deconstructivism?

Could the negation of a balanced form in sculpture and architecture be the ultimate denial of unity and continuity in western society?

Marini's horse begins to show signs of restlessness at the end of the Fifties, shortly thereafter rearing suddenly to fall to the ground in pieces.

Below left - "Piccolo Cavaliere", 1946. Plaster in color.

Below upper left - "Piccolo Cavaliere", 1948. Bronze.
Below upper right - "Miracolo", 1953. Bronze.

Below lower right - "Il Grido", 1962. Bronze.

The ability to produce realistic art is innate in the human mind

Below left - Paleolithic rock paintings of Lascaux, France.

Below right upper and lower - Rock paintings in the Sahara region, 4,000 B.C.

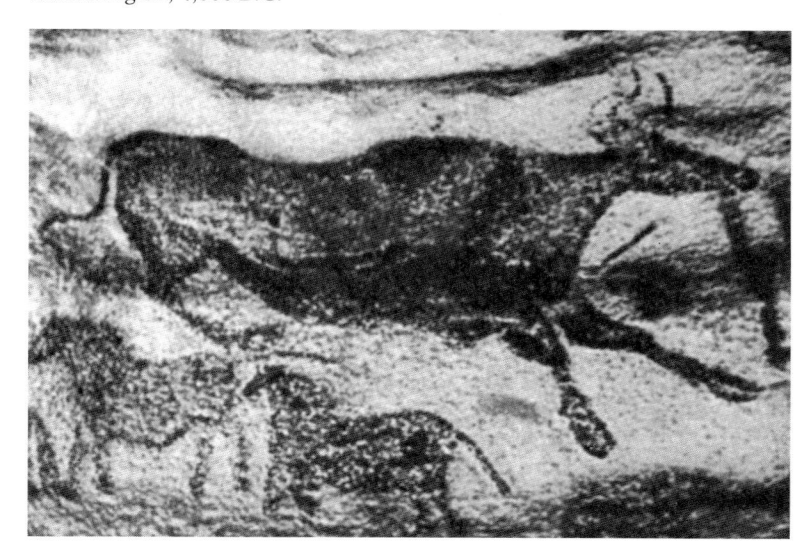

directly to the social setting of the historical period in which they appear.

Meta-realism. An inspired realism communicates emotions and sentiments and through its idealism and immediate comprehensibility transcends on a global level any kind of division or barrier. There is perfect mental equilibrium between the analytical and the analogical processes. All the qualities expressed by the two processes appear to be in total harmony, uniting innovation and tradition in a synthesis of permanent artistic value.

The concept of formal composition is the most important characteristic of a work of art, reflecting in its solidity and completeness the general situation of the community in which it is created.

In this society we find:
– on an ethical level: respect for the principles of intellectual freedom;
– on a social level: equilibrium in pluralism;
– on an economic level: growth in large-scale activity; profit is deemed a necessary but not sufficient condition.

To define the state of perfection, Meta-realistic architecture should be described in detail.

GENERAL COMPOSITION - a specific structure is expressed through fundamental geometric rules, without the use of ambiguous or contorted forms. All elements, of whatever origin, are in harmony and form part of a system consistently adapted in the whole building. Form derives from a physical and metaphysical conception, representing the most advanced invention of the time, generating the sense of stability that true equilibrium demands. The sequence determining form comes from the interrelation of spaces and is simultaneously new, functional and emotional. The aggregation of all parts must produce a continuous sequence of emotions. A minimal difference of proportion in the representation of the human body, for example, produces a noticeable difference in the final formal result.

AESTHETIC SPIRIT - The formal language must be familiar to contemporaries but also timeless. The sincerity of the form reflects the clarity of the content. Decoration is reduced to a minimum and is in any case an integral part of the composition, using complex formal or sculpturally derived elements.

SOCIAL AND ECONOMIC SIGNIFICANCE - The social purpose of each building is clearly apparent, totally accepted and respected. The space is of necessity a reflection of the complexity of the community, providing an answer to problems of both functionality and social expression. The economic feasibility must be accepted by those who promote the new architecture as well as by the society which inspires it. A building conceived in this way has always been considered a moral entity capable of lasting for centuries.

TECHNOLOGY AND FUNCTIONALITY - The technical and functional levels must be the most appropriate as well as the most advanced possible, suited to the size and function of the building.

Realism tending toward Aestheticism. Here realism becomes more refined and, while retaining a high level of communication, tends towards the decorative and toward preciosity of style. The analogical process is slightly predominant, and is uncertain about its principles as a result of a growing state of psychological insecurity. The objective of artistic composition moves away from pure form towards a search for beauty as an end in itself, tending towards traditional symbolism. Formalism prevails over the force of emotion and reason, leading towards mannerist solutions. In society we find:
– on an ethical level: a tendency to hedonism;
– on a social level: predominance of elitism;
– on an economic level: positive financial results deriving from a marked propensity to seek profit on the part of the majority of individuals.

Descriptive Realism. A more rigid realism begins to lose its comunicative capacity, showing a visibile tendency to the detriment of clarity.

Imbalance between the two mental processes appears, resulting from the distorted logic in which materialistic gains predominate.

With the stylistic imposition of an oppressive mannerism, artistic composition of analogical derivation, its systematic application is analytical; thus image and form prevail over content.

In society we find:
- on an ethical level: a tendency to hedonism;
- on a social level: predominance of elitism;
- on an economic level: positive financial results deriving from a marked propensity to seek profit on the part of the majority of individuals.

Hyper-realism. A realism overloaded with complex, highly visible details is now at the extreme limit of its ability to communicate. The quest for opulence is a further barrier to understanding of the artistic message, which becomes ever more vague. A state of decadence can be observed in this society. The equilibrium of the artistic form gives way to the flaunting of technical detail and proportion is lost as the content of the work is overpowered by a distorted, even violent image. A tendency towards giantism twists the message of the work of art, producing a surrealist formalism. An obsessive symbolism of analogical derivation is applied through a feeble analytical method.

In society we find:
- on an ethical level: overpowering materialism becoming widespread moral decadence;
- on a social level: marked differences between groups and widespread non-consensus;
- on an economic level: protectionism and lack of confidence.

4 - The History of Realism

The following research is an attempt to distinguish the manifestations of realism in the visual arts and architecture, from the beginning of history, in every part of the world. Although this would seem at first sight a difficult task, given the great diversity of artistic expression, it soon becomes apparent that the identification of realism is almost immediate as far as painting and sculpture are concerned, for meta-realistic works always have the same basic characteristics. These reflect aspects common to all humanity, in general physical forms and in details as well as in the expression of emotion. Such similarities between realistic sculptures from different eras are particularly visible when much attention is given to detail and all the more so when Meta-realism is achieved, since in this case local elements added to the composition play a minor role. This is because Meta-realism prefers the essential representation of human subjects, as near life-size as possible. A common matrix can thus be observed in the general character of these sculptures, deriving from the mental state of their creators; accordingly, they have been essentially the same for five thousand years.

A demonstration of continuity of the human mental structure can be found in the cave paintings of Lascaux in the Dordogne region of France, dating from the Aurignac-Perigord period of the Paleolithic age, about 25,000 years ago. These paintings, along with other cave paintings of the same period, demonstrate the incredible ability of people of that time to represent animals realistically. This is proof that the ability to produce realistic art is not linked to a cultural level but rather to a mental state. In other words, realism is not necessarily a point of arrival but can be, instead, the point of departure of the human mind, particularly when the way of thinking of a group of individuals is not influenced by the imposition of religious or ideological beliefs. The mind of the cave-dweller, primitive but already possessing a certain level of knowledge obtained through observation, was able to produce realism, showing the capacity to see reality as it was, without the imposition of myth and ideology which blur and distort truth. This ability to reproduce basically the same reality is further proof that the philosophical parameters of human beings have never really changed. Humans have had at their disposal the same measures of realistic judgement and have seen with the same eyes, although this faculty has been lost during certain periods of mental imbalance.

Defining realistic architecture over the centuries is a more complex matter. Realistic buildings cannot be recognized at first glance, as they tend to be characterized by technical elements of local derivation, since traditional construction techniques have always been pervaded by a strong sense of symbolism, even of religious influence, translated into conventional signs. In realistic sculpture, on the other hand, the physical matrix of the body and the facial expression were common to works produced in different periods and places. In the case of architecture, while the visible elements may differ greatly from the aesthetical point of view, they always have in common the geometric and physical characteristics that regularly reappear in different periods, expressed in a variety of languages but with the same meanings.

Realistic thought in architecture may be evaluated by analyzing the dominant philosophy of each period with its specific characteristics and degree of technology, utilizing data from all traceable examples as well as the knowledge available to historians in all fields. An interdisciplinary approach is important here, since the available data must be coordinated to draw as detailed a picture as possible of every period. This thesis, in relating all evidence from every society, can be implemented in a research method applicable over a long period of time. When this method is put into practice, discrepancies in earlier evaluations often become clear, particularly in areas where people of different origins and at different stages of cultural development lived contemporaneously. An example is provided by Mesopotamia in the period 2000 to 1000 B.C. In this area with its rich and varied past, many attributions appear today unsatisfactory and contradictory. Examination within the system of cross-referencing offered by the more investigative methodology inspired by Meta-realism could perhaps provide a more precise historical collocation.

In this regard, from the Fifties onward a number of qualified critics, having accepted the validity of non-realistic languages in modern art and the concept of linear history, have indirectly influenced the qualitative judgement of the art of the past. Frequently no distinction was made, and complex, refined works of manifest artistic talent were considered on the same level as others of primitive derivation and uncertain inspiration. Other critics, at the same time influenced by the analogical process and inspired by a driving spirit of revival, judged as very valuable art copies redundant with traditional symbolism, such as the works of the XIX and early XX centuries. The result is the patent confusion in the visual arts criticism of the late Eighties. This was true mainly of the United States, where poor reproductions of XIX century European architecture abound. The criteria of judgement in this case are compromised, since there is no possible reference to a recognizable state of authenticity.

With regard to the art produced in times of imbalance between the two mental processes, certain formal similarities may be noted between the art of the early Middle Ages, the work of the cubists and the fauves and the less celebrated art of African folklore. In the Eighties some critics, returning to a theme already discussed in the Fifties, discovered that cubist art was in fact inspired by traditional primitive African art. But obviously these modern critics could not see that the final stage of decadence of a civilization, where imbalance between the two mental processes is apparent, has always produced in painting and in sculpture a flight from realism with forms of typical primitive matrix. A perfect example of this can be seen in cubism. The physical signs of this phenomenon in art are the same: necks are elongated, eyes are enlarged while the sockets become deeper and the human body is distorted and out of proportion (8).

8) In Livorno, Italy, in 1984, a hoax that had international repercussions was perpetrated on a group of well-known Italian modern art critics. Some Livornese jokers faked the discovery of two sculpted heads presenting the general physical characteristics of the works of Modigliani, an artist of great fame and undeniable stature. The roughly modelled heads were recognized and authenticated by noted critics as original works by Modigliani before the truth was discovered. In brief, the search of modern artists for uniqueness and immediate awareness of their stylistic diversity made the recognition of the artist more important than the overall message conveyed by the work itself.

When the analogical process is totally dominant, there is either no architectural creation whatsoever or it is reduced to very simple forms as in the early Christian period. When there is a marked predominance of one of the two processes, the resulting synthesis is disproportionate and incapable of responding to the expectations and demands of a balanced society, which needs instead more complex solutions derived from both logic and feelings.

Accordingly we will attempt to understand, in identifying the societies that have derived a form of architecture from realism, what relationship exists between the two mental processes when they produce the same phenomena. A purely aesthetic interest in the works becomes merely an instrument of investigation in this context, for it would be inappropriate and illogical to disregard all non-realistic art. The undeniable fascination of some of these non-realistic works depends on the very absence of rationality, which liberates psychic forces and deep sensations springing from the marked predominance of a particular feeling or mental state. There is in Medieval art, for example, a subtle but powerful poetry which communicates in subdued tones a contradictory message containing myths, fears and constraints. Abstract art, on the other hand, seems to free our instincts, putting us in a state of ambivalence between the need for immediate comprehension and acceptance of the challenge which compels us to explore a new dimension of life. The violent colors of abstract art incite an immediate response, as in the case of Rothko's paintings, communicating the stratified and sedimented angst that precedes suicide.

These different types of artistic expression with their uni-directional force, their unbalanced exploitation of a certain feeling or mood, their impact which we absorb as total experience, are important for the human spirit. Civilizations that are stable and lasting have always required more than the mere experiencing of moods and emotions. In delineating their future they have tried to influence the course of history, to protect human life by creating a permanent environment in defense of its equilibrium. A great civilization has never accepted unbalanced or partial solutions unable to guarantee the propagation of its achievements and progress. Meta-realism is the materialization of this principle, capable of projecting the power of its achievements into the future, because its ideals have remained clear and valid for centuries.

Mesopotamia - The Sumerian nation was the first community to develop to a very high level in Mesopotamia three thousand years before the birth of Christ. While many peoples of different origin contributed to the civilization of this region, only the Sumerians left precise documentation of their discoveries. They succeeded in building a complex social and economic structure and were capable of solving second-grade equations and making complicated calculations. They invented the letter of credit and organized detailed systems for recording contracts. But over and above these achievements of pragmatic origin, the Sumerians delighted in literature, handed down to us through their writings, and in music, as demonstrated by their refined instruments. They employed a precise logic in the building of houses, which were designed on two floors with an internal courtyard, where an underground tank collected rainwater from the roofs, using the same system as the compluvium later adopted by the Romans. Sumerian visual arts, however, were far from being developed to the same extent as other disciplines in this society. It was a schematic, almost primitive art, as far removed from realism as from creative fantasy. Only after the domination of the Semites from Accad did Sumerian art become more refined, at least enough to suggest an approach to a kind of realism which cannot be called fully descriptive since it is lacking in detail and precision. At this time, definite economic progress appeared in this society, defined by historians as severe and rigid in its respect for basically oppressive rules. It was a society where analytical thought dominated the analogical, and where religious sentiments were exploited for pragmatic purposes, using the temples destined to the cult of the gods for the discussion of business, the administration of justice and the safe-keeping of registered contracts. Art and architecture obviously suffered in this situation where the humanistic element springing from freedom of thought was totally absent. Perhaps this lack of artistic communication explains why the knowledge of such an important civilization was lost for so long. Averardo Chierici, a noted scholar of Sumerian civilization, writes: "Strangely the Sumerian civilization was forgotten; even its name was cancelled from human memory." Was it, then, the absence of a high level realistic form of art that made the message of one of the earliest civilizations incommunicable?

Mesopotamia is without doubt an example of an area where the human mind successfully projected its complex image through achievements in many fields. But the most fascinating aspect of the diversity of the Mesopotamian peoples is the simultaneous presence in their minds of myth and pure reason, clearly in continual conflict, bringing about significant changes in socio-political situations determined by the temporary predominance of one of the two forces.

While it can be said of the Sumerians that their civilization saw the triumph of pure logic over humanistic values, it was during the Assyrian Empire that myth and reason found common expression. In Assyrian sculpture a precise and refined inclination toward reality is expressed by an extraordinary ability to dream and to transform these dreams into fantastic mythical forms that are also skilfully detailed. Assyrian architecture, with its clever use of space and richness of decoration, is an example of elaborate elegance tending toward decadence. The splendour of the courts reveals an excessive search for refinement in the unusual non-religious art of this period and is a symptom of that precarious equilibrium between the search for the new and tradition. The Assyrians showed an equal respect for physical courage and intellectual fortitude. Assurnasirpal, their warrior king, was worshipped in the same way as was the god Nebo, patron of scribes and priests. For these reasons, all of the art and architecture of the Persian period was based on attractive decorative solutions but never reached the state of full realism. Later, in the same region, the Phoenicians who became the bearers of Mesopotamian civilization throughout the Mediterranean area did not manifest any distinct personality in their artistic production, since they absorbed different cultural influences from the surrounding countries. For this reason it is hard to judge their intrinsic level of realism.

It would be highly interesting to know more about the reign of Israel, which rose to great political and intellectual power around the year 1000 B.C. All its great architectural works have been lost or buried under new buildings as in the case of King Solomon's Temple, on the ruins of which the mosque of Omar was built. The loss of much of the heritage of this civilization represents a great misfortune, considering the knowledge it would have provided of the artistic and socio-economic development of the region.

Asia Minor and Mesopotamia are testimony to the rapid changes and vicissitudes marking the coexistence of dissimilar peoples, inspired by different ideals. But despite their substantial contribution to human culture, its seems that no lasting, stable mental equilibrium of meta-realistic inspiration was achieved by any of the societies in this geographical region. The tendency to make economic power the guiding influence in human actions explains the predilection of these peoples for ostentation and their excessively decorative taste of clear hedonistic origin. The only realism possible was at best based on aestheticism. Mesopotamian reason, despite its great contribution to humanity, did not succeed in achieving a stable balance between tradition and logic and thus failed to find the proper meta-realistic medium of artistic expression, capable of transmitting its culture to future generations.

Egypt - During the Neolithic period in the northern Sahara, human thought had already reached the first stage of equilibrium, as shown by evident signs. A people of shepherds and hunters painted scenes of daily life on rock walls with a descriptive realism impressive for the sense of proportion in the humans and animals depicted and for the precise detail and sense of movement of the composition. But it was during the pre-dynastic period and the Trinitan Kingdom that Egyptian art began to develop its classical themes, showing a disconcerting analogic predominance which obscured the realism that, although expressed in naive forms, had dominated the same geographical area in the preceding centuries. Again it is interesting to note a phenomenon often found when a human community passes from the primitive state, such as that of cave-dwellers, to a higher stage of development which ceases to be realistic insofar as it derives from a predominantly analogical mental state. In the course of Egyptian history the period of transition between the two states of realism, the neolithic and that of the Old Kingdom, is however relatively short. With the beginning of the Old Kingdom in 2778 B.C., one of the most magnificent phenomena of human history was set in motion. Egyptian culture, both artistic and scientific, achieved the status of one of the greatest and most balanced civilizations that had ever existed. But even as this was happening, Egyptian religious fervour revealed itself in acts of profound, secret and invisible homage to the gods, as can be seen in the tombs of the sacred bulls near present-day Cairo. In these tombs, made up of a series of tunnels tens of metres below ground, are sarcophagi made of enormous blocks of stone containing mummies of the sacred bulls. This enormous undertaking was obviously intended never to be seen by human eyes. Unfortunately the interiorizing of such deep religious fervour was to mark the limits of Egyptian culture, becoming more evident with the passage of time.

The great inspired sculpture of pure meta-realistic origin was first created during the Old Kingdom. Egyptian architecture was unquestionably on the same level as its sculpture. What remains of the monumental constructions of the time is clearly exemplified by the Saqqara Complex, designed and built by Imhotep, remaining forever a magnificent example of the strength of simplicity.

Egyptian art, which lost the power and balance achieved during the Old Kingdom, was nevertheless to reach the highest degree of refinement and opulence during the period of Tutankhamun. But the aesthetic realism that produced this kind of fabulous artistic treasure, arousing the amazement of the public in every age, is a sign of the end of a great civilization. This realism became descriptive and finally, during the reign of Ramses II, acquired tones of hyper-realism in the gigantic Temple of Abu-Simbel. For the same reason the temple of Amon at Karnak has oppressively heavy volumes and an exasperating sequence of obsessive detail and repetitive decoration. The decadence forecast by these

Mesopotamia: Different forms of civilization inspired by myth and by pure reason

The Sumerians

Left - Neo Sumerian art. Gudea, ruler of Lagash. XXII Century B.C.
A governor of Lagash. XXII Century B.C.

The Assyrians

Top left - Wounded lions. Niniveh Palace. VII Century B.C.

Bottom left - Winged bull. VIII Century B.C.

Statue of King Assurnasirpall II. IX Century B.C.

Egypt: From the Meta-realism of the Old Kingdom to the
aesthetic realism of the New Empire

Old Kingdom

Below - Detail of statue of Chefren. Basalt.

Right - The Scribe. XXV Century B.C. Painted stone.

New Empire

Right - Head of Nefertiti. Detail. XIV Century B.C. Quartz.

Coffin of Tutankhamen. Detail.

Realism of Mentemhet

Above - High official of Mentemhet. VII Century B.C.

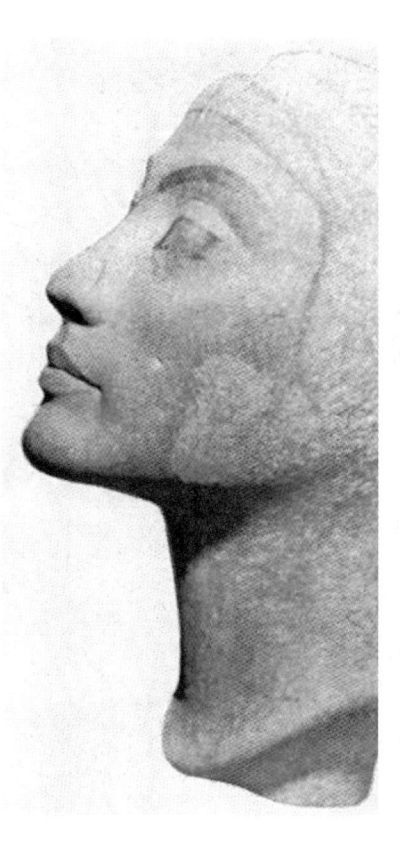

Greece: The foundation of Western Tradition takes shape in the Greek mind
Meta-realism at its highest level was then able to produce the greatest contributions of all times

Top right - Head of Hypnos. IV Century B.C. Bronze.

Center left - Statue of a young woman. Hellenistic period. Marble.

Center right - Statue of a divinity, detail of head. V Century B.C. Bronze.

Bottom left - Parthenon. V Century B.C.

Bottom right - Temple of Zeus in Athens. II Century B.C.

Rome: the Western Tradition creates the first model of a technological society that produces aqueducts and theaters for the masses while building palaces and villas for the elite

Top left - Aqueduct of Gard, Gaul. I Century a.C.

Top right - Hadrian's Villa in Tivoli. II Century a.C.

The scheme of the Roman villa becomes the model for the large houses of the Western Tradition in the span of twenty centuries.

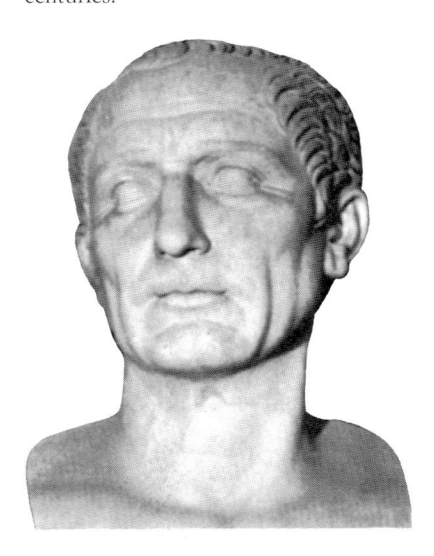

Center left - Head of Caesar. I Century A.C. Marble.

Center right - Statue of Augustus. I Century B.C. Marble.

In sculpture: Meta-realism of the Greeks versus descriptive realism of the Romans.

Bottom: - Colosseum. (Dwg. by L. Duc). The structure of the velarium is visible at the top. Made of silk and linen, it was installed on each occasion to protect the spectators from the sun.

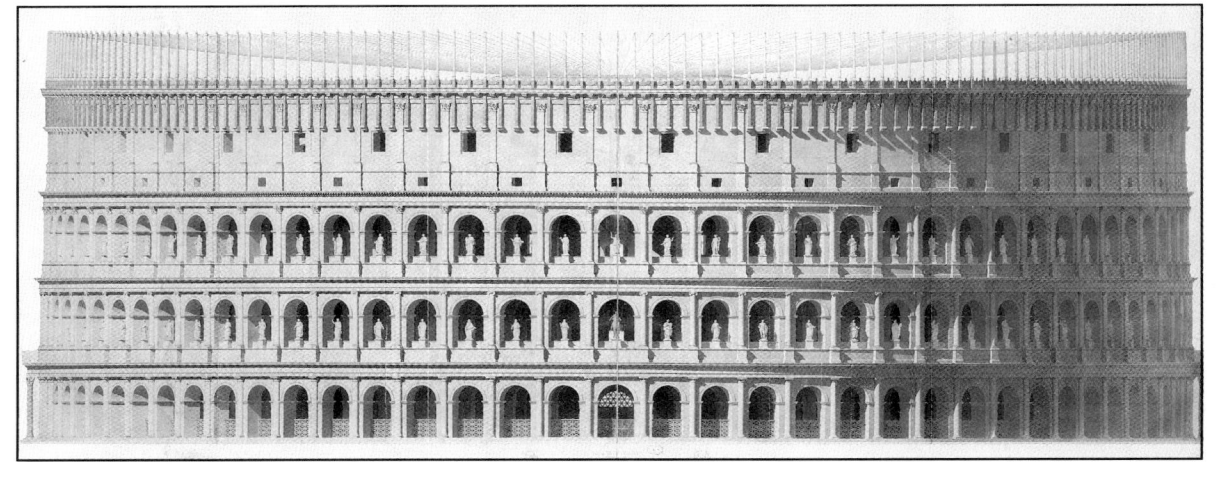

monuments was to take rapid hold of the Egyptian world, now dominated by foreigners. The artistic level of this period is poor, producing primitive, redundant works.

Under the Ethiopian kings Egypt appears to have regained at least part of its old spirit. During this period the so-called realism of Mentemhet is visible in sculpture. Following this short parenthesis, Egypt was once again laid prostrate by the invasions that destroyed its social fabric and national spirit. The Egyptian soul, overwhelmed by fear, vainly sought protection in mythical amulets to the god Bess, a little monster in the form of a monkey; it no longer felt able to determine its own destiny by facing reality.

Crete and Greece - The remains of the palaces at Knossos and Festos give us an idea of the breadth of the Mediterranean civilization, which began in Crete some two thousand years before the birth of Christ. The architecture of this island was resplendent with vivid colors, reflecting a joie de vivre never before experienced in the Middle East or Egypt.

The Greek cultural phenomenon embraced the spectrum of human knowledge reaching its highest point, after several centuries of incubation, in the V century B.C. at the time of Pericles, with one of the greatest social, political, economic and spiritual advancements ever known. This period was to give a new dimension to human thought, outlining the parameters of the philosophical debate which was to continue for the next twenty-five centuries on the same intellectual themes and with the same unchanging spirit. The basis of the Western Tradition, as it is still understood today, took shape in the minds of the ancient Greeks from whom it drew its ideals and inspiration.

V century Greece unconditionally represents the clearest and most genuine architectural expression of Meta-realism, springing from a collective ideal pursued with clarity and determination. But, as always happens in every civilization, at the moment of its triumph, the complexity that follows the satisfaction of basic needs opens the door to weakness and hedonism. The new socio-political situation was also reflected in art which, during the pre-Alexandrian period, took refuge in descriptive realism, moving ever further from classical realism. Aristotelian rationality asserted itself when Greece, under Alexander, was projected into the conquest of an Empire, and became increasingly attracted by materialism rather than philosophical speculation. The art of the late IV century reflects this determination before its transition into the refined, decadent realism of the III century B.C. Subsequently Hellenism triumphed with a form of art and architecture which was still realistic and elaborate, substituting sensuality for the pure beauty of the images, the poetry and the silent composure of classicism. Once again decadence was heralded by the elegance of the forms, seen by many in later centuries as an element making the works of art more immediately communicative, in contrast to the difficult message of classicism which bears the intellectual and moral weight of a society capable of dictating the meta-realistic terms of its contribution.

Greek architecture of the leader-cities is an indication of the works achieved by a society that gave absolute priority to communicating with its citizens. The Greek city is, in fact, the first example of an urban space, which was to become typical of the Western Tradition, conceived to facilitate human interaction, with its theatres, stadiums and agora; thus capable of accelerating all the activities deriving from the two mental processes.

Rome - Roman culture has been seen as a continuation of Greek culture but with a shift in the balance of the two mental processes towards the analytical. Its development was, in fact, directed toward consistent technological process, paralleled by a cataloguing and classifying of natural phenomena, its forces concentrated on organizing the services necessary to the community.

Roman architecture, on the whole, was close to Meta-realism, but succeeded in fully achieving it on only a few occasions, as for example in the Colosseum, the Pantheon and many buildings of the 1st or early II century A.D., such as the Villa Adriana at Tivoli. It is certain however that Roman sculpture and painting never equalled the best of classical Greek art, although they provide a good example of realism in descriptive details. The sculpture of the time of Flavius acquired its own personality, freeing itself of the local Italic and Hellenic influences but never really attaining Meta-realism. From the high point achieved at the time of Trajan, artistic expression first passed through a period of aesthetical realism, followed in the II century by a phase of descriptive realism, soon leading to formal distortion as the Empire neared the brink of crisis. The phase of hyper-realism, announcing the approaching loss of a sense of reality, was now imminent. The huge IV century head of Constantine is vulgar and unnecessarily out of scale, representing in artistic terms the dire political situation in which the Emperor has become absolute monarch while the citizens have lost faith in the state, already collapsing.

Roman civilization represents the first serious attempt by humanity to build an empire where the legislative and technological systems guaranteed a safe and sure environment for a community that was multiracial, although the social differences of caste and slavery typical of the time existed practically unopposed. This was the first civilization that besides being pluralist was open to the masses, since it directed its efforts to the community as a whole with such constructions as aqueducts and sewers, building stadiums designed to hold tens of thousands of spectators. From this time on, the efficiency of the community environment was to be judged by its physical performance, in terms of the urban fabric and the quality of the services offered. The organization of life in Ancient Rome thus became, after that of Athens, the second testing ground for the Western Tradition.

In parallel to the Western Tradition of the Mediterranean and the Middle East, other major civilizations were developing in the rest of the world.

China - Despite the very high level of Chinese art, we cannot find any example fully exemplifying Meta-realism, although many forms of realism can be distinguished, particularly in the Sung period. Any expression of Chinese art is filtered by an immediately visible but very rarefied traditional symbolism which permeates the entire spectrum of communication. Especially in architecture the ritual approach is so powerful that it is difficult to evaluate a building above and beyond the local cultural context.

Chinese visual art has never projected a sense of action or strength but has always offered a detached vision through an enchanted poetry of nature and social rites, in a tone that is generally serene, at times melancholy. In Chinese life the analogical process is only mildly tempered by the analytical one, in which the Chinese have historically excelled with their valuable contributions to mathematics and science. But here the two mental processes never seem to have found the necessary fusion capable of providing an objective vision of life globally acceptable beyond traditional rites and local customs.

India - Indian art has over thousands of years produced an enormous quantity of sculpture, painting and architecture without, however, truly approaching full realism. Indian art has great force and seductive power in its presentation of myths and legends. At the same time the contradictions, emotions and exuberant

Japan

Meta-realism was achieved several times in this country throughout its history, particularly when Zen philosophy triumphed during the Kamakura period.

Top right - Statue of Uesugi Shigefusa. XII Century A.C.

Top left - Statue of Furuna, one of the ten disciples of Buddha. VIII Century A.C.

Bottom right - Statue of Basu Sennin. XIII Century A.C.

Bottom left - The south portal of the Todai-Ji. XII Century A.C.

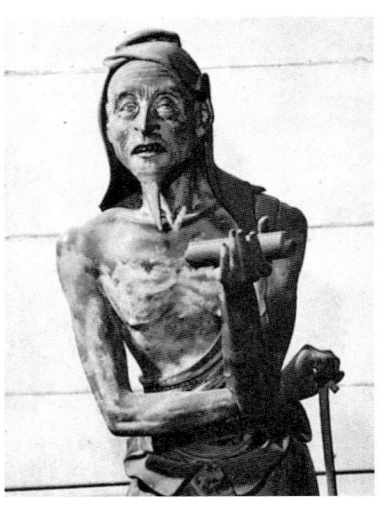

China

Refinement and poetry continuously permeated the traditional symbolism of its many artistic expressions. Architecture is highly integrated in this process and part of a very stable synthesis. Meta-realism was never fully achieved during the long history of this country.

Left - Main building of Toshodai-Ji in Nara, Japan.

Right - Figure of Buddha follower. Sung period.

India

Mysticism is always prevalent in the extremely rich and sophisticated panorama of its art and architecture. Therefore, Meta-realism was never achieved in this country.

Right - Sculpture of Yakshi, Goddess of Fertility. II Century A.C.

Left - Corridors of Rameswaram Temple. XVIII Cent. A.C.

aggressivity of the images communicating all the different variations of thought, feelings and human instincts present in Indian works of art, seem in continual conflict with each other, making realism impossible. Whereas in Chinese art the two mental processes barely meet, in Indian art they clash with force and sagacity, producing a sense of relentless tension and motion. Decorativism, omnipresent and obsessive in architecture, seems to arise from the artist's need to escape from the devouring energy produced by this tension through a gargantuan production.

Japan - Japanese visual art and architecture clearly reveal why in the XX century this country is striving to succeed in competing with the nations of the Western Tradition. Japan wishes to project its personality upon the rest of the world while maintaining its distinctive Asiatic culture. This tendency is a manifestation of inner force, equilibrium and self-control over thoughts and actions. For these reasons, as one would expect, in the history of Japanese art realism begins to appear as early as the VIII century A.C. during the Nara period, with the T'ang style.

During the Kamakura period, in the XII century, Japanese art influenced by Zen philosophy produced a direct and dramatic Meta-realism, represented by bare, essential forms. This is one of the best examples in history of perfect equilibrium between the two mental processes. At that time the sculpture of the school of Unkei produced vivid images of a circumstantial and detailed realism. The figures are described both physically and emotionally in great detail, resulting in an image which is not introverted, but projected towards the external world. It is a realism resembling that of Roman art of the I century for its fidelity to physical detail, but is much closer to the realism of the Old Kingdom of Egypt in terms of the emotional communication of the figures, who appear to seek direct human contact with the observer.

In the Kamakura period, a balance deriving from simplicity and clarity and from a logical structural form produced an architecture which is both bold and light, revealing a personality that transcends the Chinese models from which it derives. The accusation that Japanese art is derivative, emulating continental Asiatic influences, and is thus inauthentic, comes from a critical view that looks only at the symbolic matrix and not the real inspiration of the composition. In fact, Japanese art has shown over the centuries a strong personality of its own and a remarkable continuity, developing in accordance with unchanging principles through the centuries, aimed at the same goals. In this process, the Japanese spirit appears to try to influence nature according to a predetermined plan. A typical example of this is the technique of the Bonsai, where the plants are lovingly nurtured but allowed to grow only to a limited size and shape. The Japanese character, with a realism made up of logic, creative ambition and respect for accepted principles, strives to dominate the unpredictability and impermanence of natural things within a predetermined plan.

West Africa - An undisputable example of totally achieved realism is the art of Ifé, a religious community of the Yoruba population dating somewhere between the XI and XV century A.D. The Ifé heads cast in bronze on cire perdue demonstrate artistic qualities of balance and composure that somehow recall painted figures of the Italian Renaissance. The art of the Yoruba tells us clearly and unequivocally that a sophisticated society once existed in the area that is now Nigeria. The production of these profoundly realistic works is proof of the existence of artists whose minds where capable of perceiving reality in all its aspects.

Close analysis of the Ifé works of art indicates a local cultural inspiration and not, as some scholars have suggested, the influence of Islam.

West Africa

An unquestionable and seductive realism was achieved during the Yoruba period in the XIII Century A.C.

Heads of Ife'. Bronze.

Central and South America

Pre Colombian art was at times close to realism, especially during the Maya culture.

Top left - Funerary mask. Olmeca civilization, Mexico. Green stone.

Top right - Vase shaped like a head. Mochica culture.

Bottom left - Statuette of a warrior. Classic Mayan period.

Bottom right - The Palace of Palenque. Classic Mayan period.

The works, in fact, show no perceptible symbolic or decorative sign of Islamic derivation but are of a decidedly African matrix. Moreover, as we know, Islamic art has never reproduced human heads or bodies because this is against its religious principles. If more detailed research were carried out in the area of the Yoruba, the resulting finds would doubtless provide proof of a refined and multifaceted civilization. Well planned excavations would throw new light on the past of that area while providing more detailed knowledge of the history of Africa.

Central and South America - The Pre-Columbian art of the Indios has too often been defined by scholars as primitive. It thus seems appropriate to attempt to define the meaning of "primitive" in art, since this terms has been interpreted in very different ways. Leonard Adam, for instance, in his book "Primitive Art" published in 1954, includes in his definition Assyrian, ancient Egyptian and even all of Oriental art, provoking a negative reaction from those art historians capable of appreciating the high artistic complexity and social level of these civilizations.

Our historiographic vision of art tends to define "primitive" as the opposite of realistic. By this we mean that, from the socio-economical point of view, primitive art is produced by a society not fully developed, which expresses its thoughts through forms typical of communities that have not yet attained their final stage of civilization.

The definition of primitiveness offered by critics in the post-war period was almost always imprecise due to the fact that they placed the emphasis more on the notion of "primitivism" deriving from the influence of primitive arts on XX century art. These critics thought that art had progressed through the centuries, like science, finally to arrive at maturity of the art of our time. Such a theory has been developed as a justification for modern art, to explain its abstract conceptualism far removed from realism.

Another important element which influences judgement in delineating the concept of primitive is the level of architectural production of each society. In our opinion primitive societies are those that have never produced buildings of quality, constructed with lasting materials. Architecture, in fact, reveals the high level of organization of those societies that have produced habitable buildings used for complex functions and not merely sculptural monuments constructed for religious cults, such as the pyramids. For this reason, the level of art and architecture of the Indios of the Americas varies enormously from people to people, from the primitive state of the communities of hunters in North America who never constructed large-scale buildings, to the last Aztec societies who were capable of building elaborate cities such as Tenochtitlan, described in superlative terms by the Spanish conquistadors in 1525.

During the last period of Mayan civilization, around 1000 A.D., only a form of approximate realism appeared in the art of this culture. Mayan architecture instead reached a high level of creativity and a grandiose monumentality, producing palaces, temples and pyramids of balanced inspiration, very imaginative and powerful. But the overwhelming presence of myth, in abstract and obsessive forms, intensely felt in these splendid works of great skill, appears to have limited the development of thought in the Mayas, definitely dominated by the analogical process.

The development of an autochthonous Mexican culture was brought to a halt during the Aztec period by the Spanish conquistadors in their efforts to colonize and convert to Christianity the populations of Central America. The change in cultural and political atmosphere brought about by the Spaniards was total. Probably never before had a colonizing power coming from thousands of miles away succeeded in not only radically changing the destiny of the native peoples, but also in imposing their own culture and totally halting the development of the original civilization.

The last period of the pre-Columbian era had begun with the founding of the Inca Empire in 1430. The powerful, well defined architecture of these people indicates a predisposition for a sound socio-economic structure, although it was unable to achieve high levels of technical and formal complexity, as can be seen from the ruins of the city of Machu Pichu. The art of the Incas is less well developed and less appealing than the architecture, but since it has undergone little mythological influence we may observe a slight tendency to realism, visible in the polychromic decoration of vases.

The culture of the Incas was in many respects similar to that of the Sumerians, although never reaching their intellectual level. Its basic mental equilibrium showed a tendency to analytical thought directed towards productive systems and logical organization, but it was never capable of producing exceptional art.

At this point, we may return to the development of the Western Tradition.

Early Christian Art - After the fall of the Roman Empire the descriptive realism of Roman art rapidly becomes clumsy, approximative representation before dissolving slowly during the V century into a pale, repetitive and depressive decorativism, retaining however some realistic elements, as in the art of Ravenna. Byzantine art, on the other hand, takes on Oriental forms, initially seeming a heavy-handed and insecure exercise in decoration, while its dull and uncertain realism begins to disappear in the VI century. The level of Christian painting and sculpture has by this time sunk to the level of primitive art, while Christian philosophy directs all manifestations of Medieval life in Europe towards asceticism, rejecting the so-called pagan science. Greek and Roman texts are lost or destroyed by Christians who see in them a negative influence on the faithful because they promote freedom of intellectual thought. These texts, mostly written in Greek, the language of science, were saved by Islamic scholars who translated them into Arabic. During the Renaissance the texts were then translated again from Arabic into Latin.

In Europe the Christian art of the 5th to the 10th centuries, although it had lost touch with realism, produced some sublime works of architecture where the humanistic component predominates. Masterpieces were built in Tuscany, particularly during the late Romanesque period; the Cathedral, Baptistery and Tower complex at Pisa and the Baptistery in Florence stand out clearly from the general architectural situation of southern and northern Europe. These works already show signs of a new development, announcing the Renaissance with a gradual return to realism. In coincidence with the development of the Romanesque style the Italian mind had, in fact, begun over the course of several centuries to regain equilibrium. The simplicity and logic of Romanesque architecture indicates the evolution of a society capable of creating a balanced and well-designed urban environment. In these congenially conceived spaces the city-states grow and prosper just as the capacity of the individual to perceive realism blossoms out in all directions. From one generation to the next the Renaissance takes shape. Stone by stone emerge the hill towns of Tuscany which we still today climb with emotion. Tuscany thus becomes the center of a unique artistic and social phenomenon and the ground for affirmation of the Italian city-states in the 10th to the 13th centuries.

The break-up of the typical Medieval hierarchy, God-lord-populace, was started by those who began to free themselves from this form of slavery, finding the capacity to communicate their thoughts and take part in the government of

Early Christian and Medieval period. From III to XI Century

Soon after the collapse of the Roman Empire, Christian art shows all the signs of a deep involution. All the forms and principles of Greek and Roman classical origin are negated; gloom and unsophistication are the distinctive traits of a period that lasted in Europe for more than seven centuries.

During this time all the intellectual vestiges of the preceding Mediterranean civilization were destroyed or ignored by the Christians. Only during the XII century were the first signs of a new awakening visible in Europe.

Top left - History of S. Martin. Detail. Spanish Romanic period. XII Century.

Top right - The Triumph of Christ. Mosaic in the Basilica of Santa Prassede. Rome. XI Century.

Center - Church of St. Angel. Perugia, Italy. V Century.

Bottom - Cathedral and Leaning Tower. Pisa. 1063-1270.

Islam

At the beginning of the VII Century, this religious and cultural movement became the defender and continuance of the Mediterranean culture, opening new roads to civilization.

The new Islamic culture flourished in the Mediterranean and Asian geographical areas with an ideology common to many diverse people and was very close to achieving Meta-realism.

Top left - Omeiade Period. Mosaic floor of Caliph Malik Palace near Gerico. Mid VIII Century A.C.

Top right - The Mosque of Omar in Jerusalem. End of VIII Century.

Center - Patio de los Arrajones of the Alhambra of Granada. Nasride period.

Bottom - The "Blue Mosque", Istanbul. Ottoman period.

their towns and villages. The clarity and elegance of the Renaissance was beginning to make its appearance, stimulated by the civic conscience and community spirit that inspired its artists to attain their highest achievements.

Islam - The culture of Islam, spreading from Spain to the Gulf of Bengal, created a politico-religious phenomenon which united peoples of diverse origin in a common philosophy, achieving a civilization that could absorb and utilize each individual contribution.

Islamic science expressed the continuity of European and Middle-Eastern scientific tradition, becoming the link between Graeco-Roman and Renaissance science. Many discoveries of the human mind would have been lost had they not been conserved by Islam. No other religious doctrine, either before or after, held science in such high esteem. Islamic art, retaining a uniformity of concepts, particularly in the construction of religious buildings, left local artists complete freedom of expression within the pre-established schemes. This philosophical frame of mind generated a vast and admirable architectural production, showing similar characteristics but quite different personalities.

A very important aspect to be borne in mind in evaluating Islamic art is the ruling imposed on artists by religious orthodoxy prohibiting the depiction of human subjects, particularly in a realistic way. Obviously this poses limits to a clear recognition of realism in the Islamic visual arts. Undoubtedly, however, there is an equilibrium between the analogical and analytical processes in Islamic urban planning and architecture, as can be seen in different regions and under different dynasties. This equilibrium of the two mental processes, which could be termed indirect, combines all the elements of religious orthodoxy, but always with a genuine spatial intuition obtained by an exciting use of volumetric assembly, while evidence of logic and reason appears in the vertical and horizontal composition of the buildings.

Gothic - During the XIII century a new civilization began to emerge in Northern Europe. The Roman legacy via the spread of Christianity gave impetus to a new way of thought in which the analytical process developed rapidly. The peoples of northern Europe were inspired by a new vigour which led them for the first time in history toward uncharted horizons while they sought a new dimension in life through solid social and intellectual conquests. The Magna Carta of 1215 is a milestone in the foundation of the new civilization in need of a social contract that will sanction its rights and offer new perspectives for freedom. The signing of this historic document in England marked the beginning of a series of philosophical and legislative contributions that were to build over the following centuries the modern social structure of the Western Tradition. In parallel to these social conquests, northern Europe resumed the study of Greek science with the theories of Aristotle, while scientific thought began to take its first timid steps.

French architecture was the forerunner of significant new initiatives soon emulated by the English and the Germans. The Gothic style spread with great vitality, revealing the extent of change in northern European thought. Ideas seemed to have finally found the necessary force to be expressed in the elegant skeletal structures of flying buttresses built onto the naves of cathedrals. Gothic sculpture follows architecture step by step and is always an integral part of it, expressing a timid realism in its first self-assertive phase, still restrained by the Medieval nightmare. Although there is more control over detail in sculptural compositions, the result appears, in general, unsure and redundant. Only during the late Gothic period did realism make headway with a more balanced control over both architectural and sculptural composition, although some of the inspired purity of two centuries earlier was lost.

In the late XIV century a positive ferment of ideas and sentiment indicated the now permanent presence of the analytical process as an integral part of the European artistic synthesis.

The Renaissance and the XVI Century - This period marks the point of contact between Roman cultural heritage, Christianity and the new analytical European mind. Christianity, in fact, triumphed for the second time in its history, but in a much more realistic way, as an active part of the Western Tradition, with the new political direction of the Roman Church of the Renaissance spurred by the victories of Pope Julius II.

It took nearly two hundred years from the beginnings of realism in the XIII century to reach the glorious Meta-realism of the Quattrocento Toscano. This process of development is a constant factor in the history of positive growth of any period. The same slow progress towards realism has been seen in the civilizations of Mesopotamia, Egypt, Greece, Rome and Japan where changes took place slowly, step by step, since ideas take time to become established and receive consensus. For this reason, the period of transition between the late Middle Ages and the XV century still displayed a humanistic, or analogical, predominance, which was then slowly modified by the analytical European attitude to create, at last, a new meta-realistic equilibrium.

Here we may remark that the real and most interesting story of mankind would seem to be the history of changes in human thought in the light of historical events, in that they can disclose the real significance of human action, and not merely the chronology of recorded events. In this context, the Renaissance must be seen first and foremost as a mental attitude which favoured a new opening up of ideas, brought about by re-evaluation of the Greek-Roman period, thus adding another link to the Western Tradition.

The Renaissance, however, had neither the philosophical strength of ancient Greece nor the capacity for achievement shown by Roman civilization. The Renaissance "universal man" appears to be an ideal character of Greek-Roman concept who, having escaped from the Inquisition, sets out again on the difficult road in search of absolute human perfection. In contrast to the Roman ideal character who struggles for a balanced but aggressive society with a broad popular base, the "universal man" is generated by an élite, divided between idealism and pragmatism, welcoming only those individuals endowed with superior qualities and a vast culture who seek to achieve the best. It was this ethical approach that was to prove to be the intellectual limitation of the Renaissance on a wider social level. As a result of this situation the clarity and beauty found in the works of Piero della Francesca or Brunelleschi could surface for only a limited time; within a few decades it had become more and more difficult for other artists to achieve such outstanding quality. This particular Renaissance phenomenon exemplifies the difficulty of maintaining such a high level of pure creativity within the rapid succession of socio-political events of the 15th and 16th centuries. Such changes tended to subvert the initial meta-realistic harmony of the compositions, and emphasized the inevitably limited duration of a state of perfection, possible only in a very restricted area such as the Florence of the early Quattrocento.

The Italian Renaissance and northern European Mannerism, deriving directly from the Renaissance, are responsible for the greatest cultural heritage ever produced by a civilization, with priceless works of art created by many different artistic personalities. Within two centuries they established precise standards of excellence for works of art, producing new dimensions of depth and clarity. Renaissance architecture, however, despite its elegance and balance, apart from a few constructions such as

Gothic

The northern European mind evolves and begins to generate a new dimension of intellect. Gothic architecture is the most accurate representation of this progress.

Top left - Cathedral of Bourges, France. XIII Century.

Top right - Elisabethkirche of Marburg, Germany. XIII Century.

Center - Tympanum of Princess Portal in the Cathedral of Bamberg. Detail. XIII Century. A secular and popular realistic art surfaces after centuries of oppressive religious fervor.

Bottom left - Castle of Marburg, Germany. XIII Century.

Bottom right - Abbey of Westminster, London. XIII Century.

Renaissance

The Italian spirit rejoins the Western Tradition which is now moving northward and thus is also sustained by the emerging European mind.

A new peak of Meta-realism is reached in Italy during the XV Century, introducing a major historical era.

Top - Medici Villa in Poggio a Caiano, Florence. Giuliano da Sangallo, Architect. XV Century.

Center - Reliquary bust of San Rossore. Donatello. Early XV Century. Gilded bronze.

Bottom left - "Venus" painted by Giorgione and finished by Titian. Late XV Century.

Bottom right - "Flagellation of Christ". Piero della Francesca. Mid XV Century.

The flagellation is portrayed in the background of the painting while the classical architecture framing the depicted event and the main figures are given predominance in the foreground.

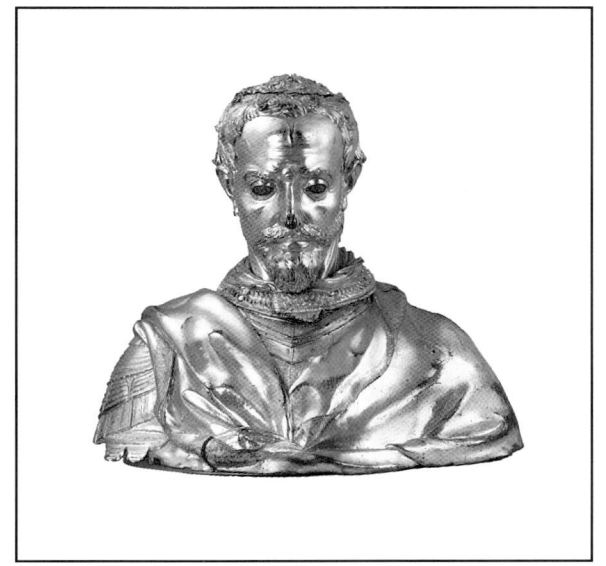

Brunelleschi's Dome, does not provide new spatial concepts or new functions, for it does not address itself to large-scale social problems as did Greek and Roman architecture but limits itself to producing harmonious spaces for human interaction.

With the affirmation of international Mannerism, French, English and Dutch architecture also achieved solid realism. Despite some mutations, XVI century realism reigned supreme over the whole of Europe, producing a remarkable sequence of masterpieces of various derivation, and successfully maintaining a constant balance, sustained by a wellspring of inspiration. Against this background the many leader cities of Europe took on the role of catalyst in the new society then being formed, preparing for the period of expansion that the Western Tradition was to undertake with the conquest of America.

The XVII century in Europe - The Baroque, particularly in the works of Bernini and Borromini, may be said to be the last architecture of truly classical origin. Roman Baroque was the swan song of classicism in its attempt to imitate the complexity and tortuousness of time in a composition that was dynamic, complex, coherent and always controlled, but on the point of formal explosion. To ask more of stone would have been impossible.

With the Baroque, an era that had placed before humanity a new order of problems and decisions came to an end. In the whole of Europe the art and architecture of the XVII century produced many and various works inspired by classicism, naturalism and romanticism, but always with a fundamentally realistic balance, enlivened by great intensity and bravura.

Europe of the XVIII century: "The Age of Reason" - The relationship between the intellectual positions of individual leaders and the relative importance of social classes has had a determinant influence on the architecture of every period. The unique composition of an Egyptian pyramid derived from the undisputed uniqueness of the absolute monarch, the pharaoh. Conversely the Greek temple, the first large-scale totally rationalized architectural system, cames out of a society where there was a clear dialectical structure in relationships between individuals and society. Republican Rome produced an urban fabric, inherited from the Greece of Pericles, for a society that revolved around the axis of the "senatus populusque romanus", while Imperial Rome returned to a great extent to the worship of a supreme leader, with an architecture dedicated to his power. Christianity and Islam brought individuals into contact with their divinity, the architecture of churches and mosques providing the only true direct link. The Renaissance, while paying homage to the absolute ruler in conceiving the idea of the universal man, also suggested the possible multiplicity of leaders in an élitist society. This concept obviously led to the architecture of palaces for the rich and educated bourgeoisie, destined to become the connective tissue of Western society. The structure of European cities stems in fact from this social condition, as the absolute monarchs one by one became constitutional ones. But it was only in the XVIII century that the Enlightenment opened the doors to democracy, bringing about the first break in the age-old social balance with the French Revolution and the American Civil War, and setting in motion the growth of the modern city which gradually took on a new shape, structured to meet the demands of industrial development.

The Age of Reason, so called by those who accepted the predominance of science, saw an increase and acceleration in all human activity in the name of progress and gave rise to one of the most resounding disputes of all time in art and architecture. It is in this century, in fact, that we find the most disparate images, the decorative complexity of the XVII Century contrasting with

The XVII Century in Europe

The Baroque marks the last century of classical architecture created within a unitary artistic conception. Hyper-realism becomes the major trait of architecture and the arts of this period.

Top left - Church of San Andrea of Quirinale, Rome. G. L. Bernini, architect.

Top right - The Cloister of San Carlo alle Quattro Fontane, Rome. F. Borromini, architect.

Center - Bust of Costanza Bonarelli. G. L. Bernini, sculptor.

Bottom left - The western facade of the Palace of Versailles. L. Le Vau, architect.

Bottom right - Gallery of Mirrors, Versailles.

The XVIII Century: The Age of Reason

This period sees the disappearance in the arts of the unified aesthetical equilibrium as seen in the preceding centuries. Many diverse intellectual contributions propose a new innovative trend developing along scientific speculation.

Top left - Shelter for the rural guards. C. N. Ledoux, architect.

Top right - The Cathedral of Carignano, Italy. B. Alfieri, architect. The Baroque influence is still alive.

Center left - Library Hal.. E. L. Boullee, architect.

Center right - Mirrored room. Amalienburg Mansion in Numphenburg, Germany.

Decorations by J. B. Zimmermann. An outstanding example of Rococo style.

Upper bottom left - Metropolitan Church. E. L. Boullee, architect.

Lower bottom left - Circular Hospital. B. Poyet, architect.

Bottom right - The House of the Guard, Berlin. K. F. Von Schinkel, architect. Typical neo-classical architecture.

The XIX Century in the Western World

Beginning with this century, architecture is either forcefully traditional or decidedly innovative. A new dimension of socio-economic reality produces this fracture while a totally new concept of space is born with the steel structure.

Top left - The Reading Room of the National Library in Paris. H. Labrouste, architect.

Top right - Restoration of the Chateau de Pierrefonds, France. E. Viollet-Le-Duc, architect.

Center left - Cumberland Terrace. Regent Park, London. John Nash, architect.

Center right - Interior of the Crystal Palace, London.

Bottom left - Fine Arts Building, 1893 World's Fair. Chicago. Charles Atwood, architect.

Bottom right - Wainwright Building, St. Louis. Louis Sullivan, architect.

the bare essentiality of the first rational projects for French public and monumental buildings. European architecture was influenced by Rococo in Germany and Austria and at the same time by neo-Classicism and neo-Palladianism in England, Italy, Russia and Austria. Remnants of the Baroque influence remained everywhere, while in France functionalist doctrines, already clearly showing modern characteristics, were becoming accepted. Moreover, in France, Boullée, Ledoux and Poyet put forward a new concept of architecture containing surrealist elements, indicative of a psychological revolution in the European mind and a situation of instability and change. In the early XIX century these contrasting tendencies were defined by the opposition between the Ecole des Beaux Arts and the Ecole Polytechnique.

With the growing power of science in intellectual terms, and of technology in terms of production, the equilibrium necessary for realism was clearly in crisis. While in painting and sculpture of so-called Romantic derivation the lines of the figures became blurred, in neo-classical art the delineation of the figures tended to take on a photographic and idealized precision derived from late Greek art. Despite these dichotomies, the average level of European artistic production was still very high, albeit presaging an imminent crisis of great proportions.

XIX Century Europe - The architecture of the XIX century presents the first example, without historical precedent, of a drastic split between very different conceptions. At one extreme of the spectrum, the neo-classical became very imposing, loaded with decoration, while on the other the new steel structures, in search of a permanent place in the architectural panorama, produced bare buildings, both stimulating and balanced. Between the two tendencies we find the organic aesthetics of so-called "art nouveau" which explored new modes of expression, often with considerable success among intellectuals but more limited acceptance by the public. At the same time the French Impressionist movement won international consensus that was destined to last throughout the XX Century. In this panorama of idyllic realism the anguished expression of Van Gogh stands out with a vitality and modernity that was to be particularly appreciated after World War II. His comprehensible synthesis, derived from the juxtaposition anguish/vivid color, attracted a wide public.

The late XIX century is marked in northern European and American architecture by a clear, if brief, period of realism, appearing at a difficult time when the growth of technology was becoming more threatening. Within a few decades this state of equilibrium was destined to disintegrate, making way on the one hand for art and architecture increasingly tending toward abstraction and Modernism and on the other for a dull carbon copy of classicism.

The United States - The late XIX Century was a period of great inspiration for the United States, now finally ready to take its place among the great nations of the world, having successfully combined intensive industrial development with a new model of individual and social freedom. By the early 1900s the Middle West had become the industrial and moral center of America, where puritanism and positivism combined to produce a new society both idealist and realist, led by a president of great energy and culture, Theodore Roosevelt.

Between 1883 and 1893 Chicago had been the leader-city. The art and architecture of the Chicago School are an example of inspired American realism, deriving from amalgamation of the modern spirit and influences from the past. It is in Chicago that Louis Sullivan, Le Baron Jenney, Daniel Burnham and many other architects have left an example of clarity and strength in their projects. At the same time Frank Lloyd Wright brought a freshness of approach, first to the conception of the American home and then, in a variety of building types, to all future architecture. The genius and vast productive capacity of Wright has been a guiding light for generations of architects in conquering for America a well-deserved place in the Olympus of timeless artistic contributions. Wright achieved a new formal expression, combining the accepted logic and balance of the past with an authentic contemporary inspiration. Later, changing social influences in America led to deprecation of the realistic architecture of the Chicago School in favor of the so-called "mercantile classicism", coming from New York and derived from Beaux Arts ideals. While the realism of the Chicago School marks the happiest period in the development of this great country, "mercantile classicism" is a prelude to the hedonism of the Twenties and the subsequent Great Depression.

The realism of the late XIX century architecture of the American Midwest is very close to Meta-realism, although it does not fully achieve it. Apparent also in the painting and sculpture of the period, this realism in art sanctions the new leader nation of the Western Trend. This architectural phenomenon has a parallel in the Roman Empire, where the creative emphasis was likewise on building rather than painting and sculpture. The two societies, that of America and that of the Roman Empire, developed along similar lines, in quest of an ever higher standard of living for a growing society. The Western Tradition thus finds in American society continuity and new affirmation.

The Western World prior to World War II - The 1930s witnessed a rapid change in world equilibrium. There was growing tension among the western nations, emerging from the ideological awakening of the working classes who, having contributed with considerable sacrifice to the industrial revolution, were now demanding a better socio-economic status. The essentially populist theories of modern art began to evolve, particularly in Europe, where a great spirit of renewal spread through the lower classes, feeding ideologies on the national as well as the international level. Throughout the world, the tension that would lead to the outbreak of World War II was on the rise.

The Modernist movement, which started in the 1920s, became increasingly influential in Europe during the next decade but was contrasted, particularly in architecture, by a reactionary movement promoting a return to classicism. This reaction was advocated by three different ideologies: National Socialism, Fascism and Communism, which shared the European political scene, each acquiring ever more absolute power in its own area of influence. The emerging political situations in Germany, Italy and Russia, inspired by these popular ideologies, found models of a new social order in Hitler, Mussolini and Stalin. These three leaders had in common their modest origins, limited culture and the military rank of corporal. They favoured traditionalism in architecture because it conveyed the coveted sense of grandeur and pomposity that seemed to give authority to the regime and personal security to their limited intellectual roots. The same type of architecture adopted by the three regimes is indicative of the common matrix shared by these ideologies. The rest of Europe, including England and France, appeared with the exception of a few outstanding artistic figures to be in intellectual limbo, showing little signs of rapid revival. Meanwhile, Modernism continued to survive in the intellectual background of European art, assuming different forms in the attempt to withstand the traditionalist pressures.

In Germany, after many successful initiatives, Modernism was violently stamped out by Nazism. Gropius, Mies, Breuer and other architects and artists emigrated to America to inaugurate a new season of rationalism and the International Style.

Meta-realism in the United States

The true innovative spirit of the twentieth century architecture first appeared in Chicago. A wider social dimension with its own distinctive aesthetics produces the first meta-realistic phenomenon of the new world.

The Chicago School:
Top left and top right - Carson, Pirie, Scott Department Store. Chicago 1899. Louis Sullivan, architect.
Center - Leiter Building. Chicago, 1889. William Le Baron Jenney, architect.

Bottom left - First department store served by a passenger elevator. Built with a cast iron facade. New York, New York, 1857.

Bottom right - Willitts House. Highland Park, Illinois. 1902. Frank Lloyd Wright, architect.

The Modern Movement of the 1920's

The principles of this philosophy in architecture were already clearly stated both in Europe and in the United States from the middle of the preceding century. The "Modern Movement" subsequently produced an intellectual minimalism derived from rationalism as a form of idolatry of science; the essential without intricacy is, in fact, fundamental in the scientific procedure.

For the Europeans, the sameness and impersonality of modern architecture became instrumental to escape the oppressive stratification of social classes that had totally structured their life. The upper classes had in fact built their urban environment using their power and the symbols of their wealth.
The failure of the modern city is also due to the social upheaval that produced an architectural philosophy which opposed the classical urban patterns and, instead, adopted impersonality as an expression of democracy while rejecting the traditional elitist values of artistic synthesis.

Top left - Convention Palace, E.U.R., Rome. 1942. Adalberto Libera, architect.

Top right - Settlement Houses, Pessac, near Bordeaux. 1926. Le Corbusier and P. Janneret, architects.

Center - Project for a Glass Tower. 1921. Mies Van Der Rohe, architect.

Bottom - The Bauhaus of Weimar. 1926. Walter Gropius, architect.

In the USSR as well, Modernism was totally suffocated. The Constructivist movement which had contributed much to Modernism in terms of search for new forms and means of expression was completely obliterated by Communism.

In Italy, on the other hand, a new atmosphere was created by the division of power between the socio-political forces linked to Fascism, to the monarchy and to the Vatican. These three forces produced the only equilibrium that was still possible on the social as well as the artistic level. Fascist architecture, reflecting this situation, is viewed by many as fairly positive, perhaps because it represents once again the typical Italian situation of compromise. This was true at least until Fascism became the predominant social force and the country was obliged to accept the onerous, but at that point irrefutable, terms of Nazi friendship.

Italian architecture of the thirties gives the impression of a fine balance drawn between permanent contradiction and quick intuition, looking both backward and forward, reflecting a society that turns towards the future but resists change. A significant example is the Palazzo dei Congressi at Eur in Rome, designed by Adalberto Libera and completed in 1942. Here we can distinguish a latent realism in the integration of traditional influences and a rationalist vision hinging on a highly controlled minimalist logic. This influence was to carry over into the architecture of the post-war period, but only for a short time before consumerism began to dominate over certain positive aspects of the intellectualized vision of the best Italian architects such as Libera and Terragni.

The America of the Depression seemed a country that had lost faith in itself, as the architecture of this period clearly shows. Houses, schools, churches and other public and private buildings copied English styles or attempted pompous solutions while genuine creative invention languished. The Modern, very little in evidence, was opposed as both style and philosophy. Traditional pragmatism became definitively established in the American architectural panorama, building a stronghold that stands out clearly in the twilight of history.

Following victory in the mid-forties, America rediscovered the lost direction, but only a few decades later had to face a difficult period in terms of social and economic balance, thus achieving only partial realization of her highest ideals.

* * *

For almost five thousand years, the leading societies of every period have marked the course of history with a culture that offers its contribution to the whole of mankind. In the XVIII century, the "Age of Reason", based on science, began to construct a new world dimension. Industrialization created a grand illusion of being able to solve all human problems in a brief space of time. As a result, however, by the mid XX century the social and ecological situation of the world had changed profoundly, leading to the drama of contemporary society which has now become aware of the obstacles to finding a new and acceptable equilibrium.

Part Five

META-REALISM IN THE FUTURE OF ARCHITECTURE AND URBAN PLANNING

1 - Utopia and Meta-realism

At the close of the XX century, in the aftermath of a long period of development, the socio-economic and ethical situation of Western nations has changed once more. Considering the positive elements as well as the many tensions present in our society, it is legitimate to ask what events will determine the near future.

We are living in a historical moment which has witnessed the demise of the last century's great ideologies based on technological development. Communism is everywhere in self-acknowledged crisis while capitalism is exploring its limitations and possible remedies. On a purely speculative level we begin to see a change of direction in western thought. In the wake of the experience of the modern and the moderate reaction of the past decades, it is tending towards reconciliation and realism, although certain extremist tendencies cannot be ignored. Our time has been termed post-modern, post-industrial and post-ideological, thus defining the past without trying to determine the present, and even less the future. At the same time it must not be forgotten that opposition between traditionalism and the advance of technology is wide-spread all over the world; and this could lead to destabilization of global equilibrium with open conflict between the two cultures that have now become the ideologies of our time. Nonetheless, the growing power of balanced critical judgement in many industrialized countries indicates that consensus on the most crucial problems to be debated may be hoped for.

Moreover, a growing tendency to logic is emerging in all aspects of human aspiration, where the economic dimension of every activity serves to curtail the inefficiency and contradictions of the world by giving a basically realistic form to every solution. But it is just in this new situation that western society, clearly in search of a new mental equilibrium, needs to regain a thorough meta-realistic perspective.

A meta-realistic basis is also essential for the schools, plagued by the split between scientific and humanistic disciplines and unable today to envisage the future clearly or to establish a precise philosophical relationship between competing demands. This is particularly true of architecture and art schools, where much talent is wasted. A new perspective would be highly useful to the architectural profession in helping it regain public confidence after the rejection of Modernism and the modern city.

Those who aspire to a new Meta-realism must logically uphold the thesis of a creative process in continuous transformation. Progress must be achieved, since the human spirit is always in search of a new frontier opening up vast horizons of consciousness and freedom, within the framework of a stable mental equilibrium.

Here the question of realism versus utopia arises. Utopia is clearly the opposite of Meta-realism in that it advocates evasion from reality through unattainable dreams. This situation was apparent in the Sixties when techno-utopias proclaimed the rapid resolution of all human problems, while equally visionary philosophies of humanistic derivation contested the modern world and sought to build a new society. It is conceivable that Meta-realism might seem at first glance utopian in tendency, because of the undeniable difficulty in attaining it, given the coincidence of circumstances necessary at any particular historical moment. Meta-realism has always been characterized by the highest powers of the human mind, unrestricted to race or creed or to any specific geographical area. While the particular circumstances determining its occurrence are only rarely present, they are always predictable, since the factors announcing its appearance are precise, quantifiable and immediately recognizable. Utopia, when it remains on an intellectual level, is an intangible, perfumed powder blown away with the first evening breeze of one historical period, to return again with a different illusory aroma at the dawning of a new day. When codified in an affirmed ideology however, utopia may become an organized, dictatorial process, as recent history demonstrates, accompanied by a dangerous mechanism of constriction.

The meta-realistic tendency is essential to environment planning in a democratic society, since it affords a detailed awareness of the ideas, principles and values pervading every action that aspires to consensus. Utopia, on the other hand, lives on rapid partial solutions, recreating the past or superficially hypothesizing the future, where civilized society demands instead precise answers, based on proven fact and logical analysis.

The setting in motion of a complex and circumstantial process is never easy, particularly when elements of diverse nature coming from very different spheres are involved. Whenever subtle differences between phenomena enter into play, theories and formulas are reduced to barely visible signs while each individual's instinctive capacity for judgement becomes crucially important. This ability has always been a rare quality, extremely difficult to convey or to teach. For this reason the most easily transmitted theories are schematic, quantifiable in a clear and mechanical process. They are easily applicable and demand only a limited capacity for personal judgement and are therefore capable of attracting mass consensus.

Such theories have prevailed in a period of growing specialization, marked by a widening gap between complex disciplines and the ability to manage them, as individuals have been bombarded by a mass of information coming from every sector while their capacity for coordinating and controlling this information was still limited.

But the most crucial question concerns the ethical dimension of Meta-realism in architecture. The difficult point of this topic rests on the sense of responsibility of the planner and architect, on whether they should assume personal obligations and actively participate in crucial decisions on the socio-economic level or should merely implement decisions taken elsewhere on a higher level. In future it will be increasingly arduous to find a clear line of demarcation between the total or partial involvement of the architect due to the complexity of decision-making when dealing with social reality and environmental issues.

2 - The Three Variables Determining Architecture in a Meta-realistic Perspective

In a situation where the best conditions for the creation of a meta-realistic societal context pertain, the three variables determining its architecture would reach their highest state by faithfully reflecting the existing intellectual environment. Consensus, the first variable, would pave the way for a balanced relationship between tradition and innovation, the second variable, since society would be able to control their development, preventing any excess on either side. Language, the third variable, would take on the forms freely conferred by the architects. This can come about when the relationship between language and content remains in the sphere of authenticity and formal balance, expressing the real significance of a work without adopting camouflages derived from superimposed aesthetics.

a - THE FIRST VARIABLE: CONSENSUS IN URBAN PLANNING

The consensus of the community is the necessary moral, social and economic basis for the development of the leader-city, since it is within this fabric that human relations establish the social contract. This consensus reflects on and greatly influences the architectural process.

Past experience shows that the attainment of a stable consensus within the democratic process becomes increasingly difficult when a society moves towards marked pluralism, becoming multiracial and naturally multicultural, as has often happened in various periods of western civilization. In this context a social contract must be stipulated between various groups of different ethnic or religious origin, based on common principles acceptable to all which respect the different origins and political or religious beliefs of each individual. Yet to achieve an active consensus, it is essential to create proposals that can be analyzed, examined and tested from all aspects. Such hypotheses must exist within a mode of planning in which the logic necessary for the functionality of the city of today and that of the future is combined with all of the elements of humanistic derivation.

b - THE SECOND VARIABLE: THE RELATIONSHIP BETWEEN TRADITIONAL INFLUENCE AND INNOVATION

History has demonstrated that Meta-realism derives from the equilibrium obtainable between tradition and innovation. This equilibrium is indeed very unstable due to the changing weight of technology and its rapid accelerations. Thus meta-realistic art production will change in accordance with the prevailing characteristic of the balance.

The role of technology in the future of western nations will be ever more crucial, considering the situation of uneasiness it has already brought about in the world. The influence of traditionalism remains stable or expands only within known parameters, since it can produce no new principles. Technology instead can run out of control and is capable within a few years of generating a totally unexpected situation. Such events produce sudden change in human life and limit the capacity of all individuals to evaluate the phenomena around them.

Technological development must be controlled, not by curbing scientific research but by developing only its positive aspects, to be implemented by society within a pre-established plan. The age-old debate over the total and unregulated freedom of science becomes senseless when the survival of humanity is at stake.

It is very difficult to make a summary decision as to which technological developments to accept, since evaluation, in addition to the defense of ecological equilibria, implies correct prediction of future needs.

It is increasingly obvious that, while every production sector is striving to reduce energy consumption and curtail pollution, a determined effort to adapt to the new ecological demands must be made in urban planning and in architecture. The annual energy consumption of buildings in the United States, which in 1990 was about 11% of total national consumption, continues to increase in absolute terms due to the greater use of air-conditioning and of telecommunications and electronics in general. On the urban level the consumption of energy constantly increases, with a soaring rise in pollution. The problem of limiting energy consumption thus becomes a fundamental challenge. The adoption of techniques that utilize renewable energy sources: the sun, wind and temperature of the earth, take on major importance in architectural projects, representing a viable alternative to the use of conventional energy. In reality too little has been done to make the use of natural energy feasible in architecture, by adopting design systems and applied mechanical engineering, apart from the limited number of serious experiments on single-family houses when the energy crisis first struck. These experiments were successful only in the case of passive absorption of solar energy, while active systems proved to be too expensive as well as inefficient (9).

Most of the research on solar energy has been in terms of small systems. Very little attention has been paid to large-scale structures such as apartment or office buildings. In calculating energy costs, the expense of controlling pollution must be added. As a consequence, many solutions currently deemed unaffordable become economically viable and capable of achieving results in a global environmental context.

What is needed in this case is a type of ecological architecture, conceived of as an organic structure, like a tree, that can exchange energy with the surrounding atmosphere without producing pollution or burning energy brought in from elsewhere. These questions must be confronted on both a limited scale, in finding solutions to individual problems, and on an urban scale, by establishing new criteria to meet ecological standards for every community, in setting stricter limits on pollution per capita.

c - THE THIRD VARIABLE: THE LANGUAGE

Our study now moves from analysis to synthesis, confronting the problem of the communication of content through architectural form.

Realistic communication requires the involvement of sentiment, a sense of logic and all the other qualities of the human spirit, made up of sensitivity and rationality. All these components of the two mental processes nourish the artistic synthesis and can be communicated without using accepted pre-established symbols, through an architectural form that is not already known and taken for granted. This type of expression is very different from the one using accepted forms such as columns, gables and trabeations or from structurally or mechanically derived concepts. In other words, it is possible to communicate through architecture using a means other than languages pre-established by tradition or technology. The message of architecture that uses symbols of the past is invariably time-worn, while an excessively innovative solution is initially incomprehensible and quickly outdated. It is even worse when the two languages are merged in an artificial manner, producing dissonance and formal imbalance, giving out contradictory messages, as in the case of neo-Surrealistic compositions. The preconceived languages communicate through clichés of traditional or technological intimidation, often becoming psychologically overpowering in their demand for admiration and respect. The forceful, dogmatic expression of traditional symbols in particular has always represented a governing power more interested in affirming its authority than in persuading by reason. The inauthentic, overstated use of classical colonnades in pompous façades was, as has been seen, a typical feature of Fascist, Communist and Imperialistic buildings. Industrial powers have also employed this type of ostentation. On the other hand, technological expressions, which start by communicating the new and up-to-date, soon age, becoming outdated. An architecture based on stable, comprehensible human values must therefore avoid all kinds of symbolism.

When a language is used with excessive force and precision it can become overly dominant in the architectural composition. The language itself, as can be seen in XVI century Mannerism where very complex forms were used, may become more conspicuous and important than the fundamental meaning of the whole composition.

It is however possible, on the ideational level, to produce architectural solutions that comprise both humanistic and technological inspiration, that is to say realistic. The highest quality message is the one limited to its essential nature: conciseness, therefore, and not reductionism or minimalist schematization. Achieving it requires a long period of clarification and distillation, avoiding both the obvious and the sensational, the overly complex and the simplistic, the intricate, the naive and the superficial. Simplicity must be reached via the most difficult path: by continually examining, evaluating, clarifying to retain all that is essential to the composition without losing the immediacy of intuition. Pomposity and overstated formality must be avoided because they negate sincerity of expression. Formalism can be compared to reciting a well-learned lesson, it becomes easy with repetition. On the other hand, a totally informal communication, when made up of preconceived ideas, indicates uncertainty and confusion.

An overly constructed image, when cosmetic art is used in architecture, must be seen as a distorted or falsified vision of reality. A superficial treatment, if not an outright lie, is certainly the glorification of a less than brilliant situation. Meta-realism has never required more than the essential.

There is no truth in the assumption of a number of critics that a particular education is a requisite for understanding high-quality art and architecture. Great works of art that emanate persuasive force and communicate a clear message have always been understood by everyone. Only highly refined but decadent works, on the other hand, transmit a message that is limited to a section of the informed public able to under stand it and interpret its code.

The creation of an image designed to attract immediate public attention has been a well-known characteristic of the artistic process in western countries. In these societies, imitated by all of the other communities which follow capitalistic leadership, an oppressive predominance of the image syndrome became the rule in architecture as well as other fields. For this reason the achievement of Meta-realism implies a change in a number of values on the part of society, which lately has accepted image as proclaimed truth and impermanence as a way of life.

In the final years of the XX century it has become clear that to attain a basic clarity it is imperative in the visual arts to avoid all of the "isms" that have created recipes for erudite artistic production and ideologies with an unreal vision of the world. Deleting from our minds all the preconceptions of an unbalanced time would certainly involve extensive analysis and philosophical clarification on the personal level. We live in a world that has become overly competitive and economically demanding, while people's expectations are rising. In this global perception, architectural solutions limited by provincialism or by inferior functional performance are unacceptable.

9 - The house designed and built by the author in Greenwich, Connecticut, in 1979, as his family residence, (see photos on page. 113) was conceived of as an interior three-dimensional space, lit by windows and skylights situated at various levels of the roof surface, which is angled at 45⁻ and faces South. The feeling of the interior changes according to variations in the brightness and quality of the light, of both the sun and the moon. The interesting aspect of this project is the presence of solar technology in a house of quality, built in an exclusive, expensive area generally deemed more suitable for traditional projects.

3 - The Meta-realistic City

Throughout the vicissitudes of history, the only comforting message of hope to humanity has been that of Meta-realism. It has been shown how this message, clear, unequivocal and coherent, has come down to us bearing the same characteristics, from all continents, different countries and civilizations and from all historical periods. Undoubtedly, what is most positive about the Western Tradition is meta-realistic. In history it is also apparent that the tendency to recreate such a state of grace exists in the minds of those people who have achieved it in the past, because the spiritual objective has remained alive and rooted in their intellectual tradition. In this context, defense of the meta-realistic values of the Western Tradition appears supremely important.

The Western Tradition is under attack from outside by all those who accuse it, often justly, of being oppressive and even racist, while seeking an alternative to its philosophy and its established authority. We may assume that this accusation will be made more emphatically as the presence in western nations of non-western ethnic groups continues to expand. But the Western Tradition is also being challenged from within by those who object to its rationality and systematic nature, deemed excessive and restrictive of total freedom of expression. This attitude became manifest when the surrealist and the anti-rational, always part of western thought as the antithesis and the spirit of opposition implicit in every culture, made a dramatic reappearance during the last thirty years. All the manifestations of anti-rationalism and surrealism that have surfaced in architecture have proposed solutions that are clearly seen by the traditionalist as destabilizing and subversive. These architectural solutions are explicitly critical of the institutions of our society, and undoubtedly lead to profound modifications designed to alter western historical continuity and balance.

More widespread phenomena of potential destabilization, now visible in all sectors, have developed along two contrasting lines. One is the extreme globalism deriving from the analytical thought of the Sixties-Nineties period, which introduced an excessively competitive economic system all over the world, encouraging soaring hedonistic expectations among vast social strata. The opposing phenomenon takes the form of localism, defensive provincialism and religious fanaticism. The consequence of this event is the balkanization of many geographical areas which seem to have adopted a new kind of medievalism. The forces of globalism and localism are, unfortunately, already in fierce conflict, bringing new tensions and instability everywhere. The balance between these two phenomena is crucial to the future of the whole world and more specifically to urban planning and architecture, which for their development require peace and stability.

In the case of globalism, which thrives on free enterprise, the city is fertile ground for rapid speculative change and impermanence. Although racism is not accepted in this system, the unbridled speed of change puts a heavy strain on the weaker groups of the community, creating social divisions and segregation of the poor. The urban space becomes an uncontrollable metropolis broken up into many separate areas, some blatantly wealthy, others desperately poor.

In the case of localism instead, the city tends to become introverted and impervious to outside influences, erecting psychological or even physical barriers to keep out the foreign, the different and the new.

The true medieval city is a clearly defined entity, in many ways fascinating because it has a measured and balanced architectural form with a livable internal space on a human scale. However, because this physical and intellectual space is limited to a single, self-contained, local cultural tradition, it could never grow or change. All medieval type cultures, after a period of intellectual and economic prosperity, die of asphyxia, while their cities become beautiful empty shells stranded on the shores of history. These shells were recovered in many ways but only to be used for something quite different from the function for which they were created.

The future directions of architecture in every area depend on the philosophical definition of urban planning derived from socio-political decisions. Therefore the evaluations and intellectual contributions of the architects and planners are very important in influencing this definition. In this context it is necessary to defend the concept of the city, as conceived by the Western Tradition, based on stability, continuity and controlled growth as well as openness to new ideas and new people. The extremes of globalism and localism can and must be avoided.

a - The multi-racial and monocultural city

Without being aware of it, modern society has brought to the brink of catastrophe a world that humanity slowly and painstakingly built up over thousands of years. While placing its rational, scientific logic at the service of this new global society, it has allowed its population to reproduce on a grand scale as one of the most prolific of the animal species. As a result, the analytical predominance in the minds of those who had global decisional power is now accused of having caused imbalance in the world, producing distress and insecurity at the base of the human pyramid that has almost tripled in half a century. As a consequence, the world community of developed countries has had to employ its resources in ephemeral production and in the creation of new fictitious needs to artificially support its own growth, instead of investing the fruits of its labour in lasting, permanent structures. Unbridled consumerism has thus become the last stage in a rampant process that has turned cities into hostile, undesirable areas, while all too often the countryside has become a place of solitude plagued by psychological and economic depression.

The society of western nations is becoming progressively multi-racial and it is clear that steps must be taken to integrate the non-western cultures within the established western one. The formulation of a society that is multicultural becomes more and more difficult for practical reasons of governability, since the immediate assimilation into an established society of principles and standards deriving from totally different cultures poses major problems.

A single unified culture derived from the transformation of the Western Tradition, although modified by contributions, evaluated and tested, from other cultures, still remains the most logical option and appears to elicit growing consensus. The Western Tradition is in fact already changing internally, as a result of the input of the new generations, influenced by philosophies and cultures of non-western origin and by an increasingly more open vision of the world.

It should be emphasized that the United States is the only country in the world which has opened its doors to people from every continent through legislation permitting wide-scale immigration, accepting the obvious problems arising from this situation, many of which are still unresolved. It is not mere chance that this legislation has been enacted in the country that has been for many years the standard bearer of the Western Tradition, thus creating a multiracial society and partially absorbing its different cultures. The race-culture dualism perceivable in the United States clearly indicates that the problem to be resolved is not always mainly racial but mostly economic and cultural. People of different race and credo can live and work in harmony when they achieve a similar economic level and basically believe in the same laws, the same science and the same multifaceted art, actively participating in these disciplines. The Western Tradition can, therefore, help to establish peaceful coexistence, directed towards a possible unified culture, offering a supportive organizational structure that is more than two thousand years old.

b - Permanence in the urban environment

In art, architecture and all other human activities, the rapid changes and uncertainties of recent times have been represented by the avant-garde of Disneyism, Surrealism and finally Deconstructivism. Seen in this light, these phenomena appear to be the symptom of a latent challenge to western stability. The determining factors of this situation are now clear.

To fall back on traditionalism alone is impossible, although, as the most natural defensive measure, this would seem to many to be the easiest answer. Logic gives no respite to those who try to stop time. There are no examples in history of societies that have succeeded in maintaining the acquired status quo by freezing it for the future. On the other hand, the exasperated experimentalism in search of novelty which seeks a short cut to the future has produced unbalanced, fragmentary answers. This situation cannot be easily evaluated, understood or accepted by a wide public. The divertissement, irony or surrealism of avant-garde projects produce only astonishing stunts, holding public attention only for their brief duration. Consumerism demands in fact an instantly visible and marketable product, but it is not interested in long-term investments and social benefits.

The hope for a permanent meta-realistic city must now be placed in the new generation of architects, who may be able to unravel all the contemporary contradictions. This could be done by interpreting the desire of a society that is trying to re-establish an equilibrium and find the right direction, after the errors made in the recent past.

The major objective is that of outlining a clear image of the future in order to delineate a consensus that can also restore to the artist a responsible independence, in tune with the needs of society. The role of the artist is fundamental in giving the work character and historical dimension. But the world of the future needs more than the great contributions of exemplary artistic personalities. It needs above all a moment of psychological peace, where the comprehension and sharing of a common reality can become the enduring heritage of all.

A new urban structure is now being sought, not only to resolve the urgent problems of the contemporary world community, but also to recreate that golden dream that the city has always represented. A new sense of social responsibility demands from architects a new commitment in that direction. Apart from works of new conception, a great deal of reconstruction work will be necessary to restore to the meta-realistic splendor of their past many western urban areas. There is an urgent need to create and experiment an urban fabric conceived and designed as a lasting entity.

Wise and precise decisions are called for. They will have wide-reaching implications, producing healthy crises that are needed to deal with the problems of the future. Meta-realism should be considered, in this perspective, as a method for resolution in perpetual evolution. Its speculative contribution will thus become a philosophical vehicle of great moral power.

An ecological house: a passive solar system

Severino residence in Greenwich, Connecticut, U.S.A.
Renato Severino, architect.

The house was designed to demonstrate that a "solar" building can also have an exciting interior space. The natural passive system of solar heating provides about 30% of the energy requirements of the house.

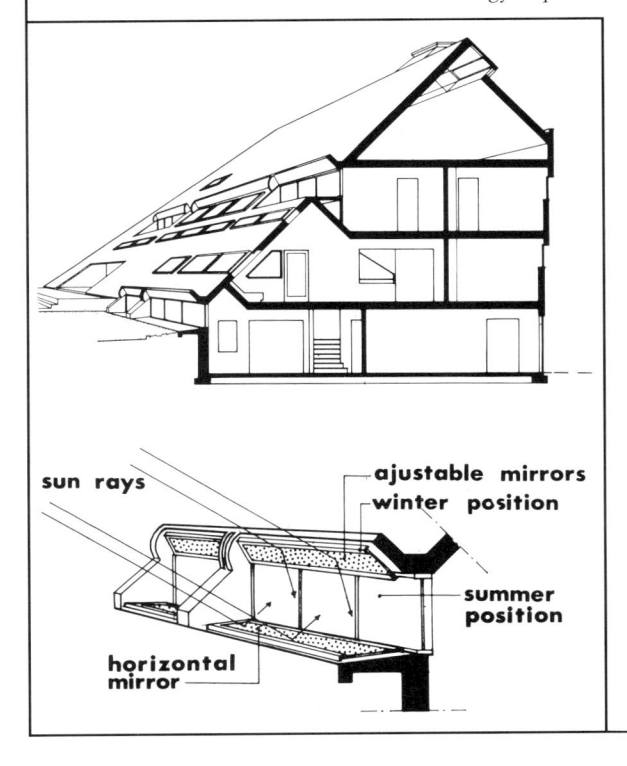

APPENDIX

1 - Preface

I have decided to keep the introduction to my latest work separate from the main text that deals with my speculation in historical perspective. I did not want to give the false impression that these new designs that I am now showing with this text should be considered self-certified examples of Meta-realism. A much larger, more profound consensus will be necessary as well as a long process of intellectual dialogue with critics and the public before such an occurrence can come about. The new work that I have produced intends merely to offer ideas for a new testing ground, after so many years of confused and contradictory architectural production world-wide.

My decision to pursue this new design research has derived from the need for clarification in my own mind, after more than thirty years of intense activity in the profession. During this long period, I have always looked to other disciplines for a clearer understanding of the development of societal influences and trends. The "style" of my production has changed accordingly from Modern to Post-Modern and, finally, to a series of solutions probably not yet stylistically definable. As a result, my work may be perceived as discontinuous, as regards both style and professional marketing. In the visual arts, changes in the aesthetic production of artists or architects are subject to disapproval by critics, art dealers and the public. These three groups prefer, especially nowadays, to deal with a continuity of production, both physical and intellectual, with an already classifiable entity that can be immediately and unmistakeably recognized.

In today's climate of challenges, contradictions and opposition, it is hoped that this research will offer useful material for clarifying in the architectural field some of the issues of the next ten years. In my opinion, most of the best work in architecture and urban planning done worldwide during the last two decades will go down in history mostly as outdated and will be seen as depicting an unbalanced and insane historical period. This is why I strongly felt that a pause for reflection was also necessary in my own case, to define for myself a clearer image of the future.

This intellectual self-evaluation has taken quite a long time. But it has also been exhilirating to look deep into the labyrinths of my mind in the attempt to extract its best, especially that which never had the chance to surface, being overlain by a deep stratum of cliches produced by professional routine. I now sought to stay away from preconceived languages and to avoid uncommunicative personal jargon.

I felt that I had to be completely alone while thinking through my ideas and then attempting to express them. I did not want to discuss alternatives with anyone, so as to avoid being influenced in any way. It became the perfect ego trip away from team work, computers and friendly advice. I was working against the current of our time but in very happy solitude, at last.

A positive spirit of collaboration emerged again when the design stage was over and I began working with Florentine artisans to construct the models of my projects. These excellent craftsmen possess both perceptive critical sense and reassuring intellectual honesty, unusual in today's industrial world controlled by economic power rather than traditional sensitivity and respect for artistic values. But certainly the pace of work in Florence is quite different from that of New York. After a period of "rinsing out my garments in the Arno River", I found myself again torn by two conflicting forces, even more in need of restoring that link between reality, dream and pure thought.

2 - Restoring the Broken Link: Reality - Dream - Pure Thought

At the end of the Eighties, western architecture saw the conclusion of a period marked by

APPENDIX

tireless and often frenetic activity that had begun after World War II. With the ensuing global recession a new period has begun and reappraisal of the situation has been initiated to define future action. The crucial social problems driving this research towards a new intellectual frontier in architecture may be summarized as follows:

a - The failure of urban planning in the last forty years and especially of the modern city in all its functional, aesthetic and social aspects.

b - The general public's total rejection of the anonymous, overbearing buildings typical of the Modern Movement. Our contemporary cities look like a heap of boxes carelessly piled one on top of another, overcrowded by day, a wasteland by night.

c - The need to manage the urban fabric with a new respect for ecological requirements. The necessity for reducing pollution by using renewable energy and adopting a more sensible attitude towards nature.

d - The abandonment of certain urban and suburban areas which became untenable for the manufacturing and service industries in the Eighties. Many old and new buildings, now ghostly, are standing in cities today, testifying to a floundering western economy hard struck by global competition.

In this difficult and multifaceted context, research is too often perceived, in both didactic and professional fields, as utopian, in sharp contrast with active practical experience. This dualism conceals a dangerous lack of confidence in new ideas, since research is seen as a flight from reality. But it is precisely within this psychological context that we must distrust research conceived as an end in itself, as has been the case in modern art and in many educational establishments, because it has produced a serious rift between active intellect and social processes. This is why intellectuals who isolate themselves in ivory towers end up by producing ephemeral avant-garde works that negate the reality of the process of artistic, technical and, lastly, professional development. It is then that the profession, especially that part of it which is short on ideas and interested only in economic-administrative and technical-political strategy, can isolate itself and proceed undisturbed to construct all of those inferior buildings to be seen in our contemporary cities.

The real hope is that research in the next few years will be able to restore the broken link in the chain of reality-dream-pure thought, thus offering new prospects to young people capable of making an intelligent, optimistic contribution.

The incommunicability of modern and contemporary art stems from the desire to propose ever more novel discoveries, which then turn out to be incomprehensible to the general public. Today, especially in our consumer society, because of the belief in progress in art, all works begin to show their age very quickly, soon becoming hopelessly dated, in contrast to what occurred in the meta-realistic periods of the past. There is even talk of revivalism, in which the merits of works only twenty or thirty years old are reconsidered. This happens because most of the techno-innovative components of such works tend to destroy their own history and to believe only in the completely new. On the contrary, the traditional element in any composition defends its historicity, thus tending to extend its life into the future. This is yet another demonstration of the fact that equilibrium between the analogical and the analytical components in an artistic synthesis is absolutely necessary for the construction of enduring work.

It is thus imperative that architectural research succeed in reconnecting the traditional elements of sensitivity and artistic instinct for proportion with the current innovations of any time. The more perfect is the balance between these two elements, the more likely it is that our hope of enjoying a future of meta-realistic quality will become reality.

Bernard Tschumi, Dean of the School of

Architecture at Columbia University, writes in 1992: "Today, one can distinguish two main approaches to architecture as educational establishments. In the first, one learns from certainties, from the lessons of history, whether distant or recent. It boasts a curriculum and a rational course of action. It borrows its inspiration from architecture itself. The second one learns from uncertainty, doubt, experimentation. Instead of a curriculum, it exhibits a frantic quest for fresh sources. It often borrows its inspiration from everything except architecture: from the arts, from literature, or from remote areas of molecular physics. The two approaches are not mutually exclusive". It is certainly to be hoped that an approach that derives its inspiration from all areas of thought will not be exclusively concerned with the production of painting and sculpture, showing only limited interest in architecture to be built.

On the other hand, the accusation of lack of realism in this quest may actually come from those who, in refusing to change, remain bound to a reductive, pessimistic reality. In this regard, it must be acknowledged that research in Deconstruction thinking has already yielded practical results in buildings now in the stage of experimentation and evaluation.

A brighter future for architecture must be invented by experimenting with new ideas, within the limits of Meta-realism, that is solving all aspects of program and construction at once. But these ideas should be evaluated using models built to a very large scale, as was done during the Renaissance, or through contemporary techniques based on virtual reality. Before construction begins, buildings should be thoroughly studied and visualized, much more than has been done in the recent past. Littering the urban fabric with buildings that are unsuccessful experiments must come to an end.

A sophisticated research laboratory should be organized in each school to produce positive, realistic proposals. These should then be analyzed and presentations made to interface with the largest possible audience. Schools of architecture as well as the profession should leave behind them the syndrome of the old-fashioned art school. Now they must enter the arena of ideas immediately communicable to the public, interested in seeing and knowing its future environment before it is built.

It is time for a new concept in architecture to declare obsolete those bulky buildings constructed during this century that have become a visual and spiritual barrier in our cities. The theatrical facades of the past are now anachronistic. A contemporary notion of spatial perception has evolved from the way we move about today on the land and in the sky, the way we penetrate and use buildings, absorb and reverberate the stimuli of life.

Relations between man, space and time have changed drastically in the last twenty years, becoming rapidly more dynamic. Modern man's evaluation of space is definitely altering the principles of architectural design. We are now aware that the parallelepiped building conceived as a multi-functional container is a static and paralyzing form that negates the continuity of space between its interior and exterior. Drastic separation between these two spaces is created by the vertical walls. The visual contact provided only by doors and vertical windows totally impedes perception of the outside. In this situation, the interior becomes a sequence of boxes for users who are obliged to move about only on vertically superimposed floors.

Now at last it is possible to enjoy from the interior of buildings an extended, uninterrupted perception of the changing quality of light and the surrounding landscape. The technical means of obtaining this spatial perception are at our disposal.

In our proposal, dynamic continuity between these two spaces can be obtained by:

a - raising the structure above the ground to

let the exterior space continue throughout; contact between sky, ground and the interior of the building now becomes total;

b - setting the building into the ground and moulding its top surface so that it becomes visually and physically penetrable. A building of this kind will not be an insurmountable visual and physical barrier, particularly on a hilly site;

c - by slanting the structure, the exterior space will reach skywards and underneath, on the other side, space will penetrate the building. The entire top of the structure is now in visual contact with the sky while the underside is in contact with the ground and the lateral spaces.

Ecological concerns are clearly expressed in this approach, which shapes buildings in such a way that natural energy can be easily exploited. Especially in an urban context, the contemporary way of moving in a built environment must be provided for with spatial continuity obtained by stratified pedestrian routes, all connected through walkable, graded surfaces. This architecture employs neither old schemes nor preconceived modes of linguistic expression, of either traditional or technological derivation, since these can describe only the past.

Our ambition is to proceed toward an architecture resulting from a state of equilibrium between the traditional inspirations present in every human mind and innovation, derived from technological advance and ongoing research. These solutions will be generated by the minimum effort required, as in organic proliferation, not constrained by any aesthetic formula. Our buildings should not be recognizable by any distinctive style, as expressed by repeated paradigms, but by their lack of it, while still projecting a coherent personality of their own. We should find the right architectural forms to be inserted into each and territory and adapt them to a whole range of local necessities, much as happens with plants that can live in their proper natural setting.

The program for such an architecture will develop within the three dimensions constituting the social fabric:

– The ethical dimension: both community and architects must be jointly committed to an architecture that is acceptable to the public and is functionally sound, ecologically conceived and well constructed, thus ensuring its enduring life.

– The social dimension: public buildings must be accessible to a considerably enlarged society. Enrichment of the community and particularly the teaching of history should be a major goal in uniting cultural interest to practical knowledge. In this process the new didactic museums should not be conceived as intimidating institutions but as mega-centers for entertainment appealing to the largest possible segment of the population.

– The economic dimension: public architecture should be economically self-sustaining, being appropriate to its function, offering to each community the necessary space and the sense of belonging to a built environment of its choice. Multi-functional buildings, operating day and night, represent the best social investment from every point of view.

CARTESIA

3 - The concept of a traditional city seen in the present

While the world-wide rejection of the modern city by its inhabitants, by sociologists and by the western public is a current topic of discussion, the construction of new urban areas goes on, repeating the same errors made by planners over the last fifty years. Despite our disillusionment, we all realize full well the difficulties inherent to resolving the problems of contemporary cities, given their complexity and the number of conflicting forces. But it is exactly here, where the problem appears most difficult, that the solutions proposed by the various parties involved become simplistic in their attempt to capture public and political attention. This is exactly what has occurred in the newly developed areas of recent years, which have been subjected to the errors and horrors of buildings going up too quickly with no thought given to possible alternatives.

On the other hand, a misconstrued respect for old, historical cities has conditioned the development of new parts of them. The construction of these new areas has often been dull and limited in scope, banning any exciting contemporary idea that might visibly compete with the pre-existing antique urban fabric. This is still another example of short-sighted traditionalism, stemming from the reaction against Modernism and denoting great insecurity and fear of the future. The most serious consequence of this situation is undoubtedly the fact that, by acting in this way, contemporary society forfeits the chance to hand down to future generations the fruits of its best efforts.

A new urban culture, to which all inhabitants would contribute both personally and as members of the community, would be the ideal. Accordingly, we may hypothesize a contemporary township aggregation and evaluate its guiding principles.

We have called our city Cartesia, since ideally it aspires to Cartesian clarity; but our choice has also been influenced by the dualistic nature of this philosophy which distinguishes between thought itself and the extension of thought to reality. However, we must add that the relationship between the architectural proposal (thought) and social consensus (extension to reality) has not yet been established, since for the moment this proposal for a new kind of city is purely unilateral, designed merely for the purpose of opening the debate. Moreover, we must recognize an intrinsic dualism in the planning of Cartesia, and thus for the moment its aspirations to Meta-realism, as exemplified in terms of perfect and univocal synthesis, are necessarily limited.

In this plan dualism is represented by buildings which derive from a traditional relationship with nature, and are thus opposed to solutions proposing a connection with the sky and earth using new volumetric design concepts. In the planning of Cartesia, buildings that are to be used for dwellings, schools and other daily activities which have evolved over the centuries tend to be more traditional. On the contrary, office buildings, museums and all constructions for the service sector, entertainment and leisure take on new forms.

We have developed the basic concepts of this idea by hypothesizing an urban fabric that has the ambition and potentiality to become a leader-city. This proposal has five fundamental precepts which aim to establish a coherent logic and common principles. What is presented here is a section of the city, providing a schematic representation of the relationship between its different components, inasmuch as the methodology acknowledge many solutions within the given formula. The freedom of the architects who plan the individual parts of these urban structures will be expressed within the limits of the regulations produced by consensus of the community. Such regulations will certainly be more elaborate and complex, describing buildings no longer conceived as modern containers. This new proposal for town planning will offer a three-dimensional solution, with a form resulting from artistic synthesis capable of producing a unified entity and not a sequence of buildings coordinated only by a two-dimensional plan based haphazard addition rather than an initial global concept.

POINT 1: THE BASIC CONCEPT OF PLANNING AND SPATIAL SEQUENCE

The first step in the planning of the new city is the creation of a base structure, called multi-traffic Platform, which will contain heavy traffic, stations for all types of vehicles and car parks, since solving the traffic problem is the most crucial factor in present-day urban design. The Platform contains the road network and all of the utilities: sewers, gas, water mains and electric power distribution. The basic concept of the Platform is that of total programming and regulation of traffic in a positive, not a restrictive sense, as adopted by cities all over the world during the latter half of the XX century. It is logical however that cars and other vehicles should be visible as little as possible in the city, as the oppressive presence of shiny metal and their rapid movement destroy the spatial equilibrium of architecture.

The Platform must always be the first phase of development of any part of the city, since the local administration will coordinate its design and assume the initial cost, subsequently to be shared by all the developers. This structure represents the active medium of control in the hands of the community and the guarantee of logical, orderly growth. The buildings, as described in the zoning ordinances, will then be constructed by the developers on the Platform according to the established rules and the requirements for interface with the road network beneath it.

The building types must comply with the concepts set out in the plan, adhering strictly to the main principles, but not to any pre-established forms on the level of minor architectural interventions. This planning proposal is purely indicative, although it refers to a three-dimensional plan in which the architectural volumes are important and an integral part of the conception of the urban fabric. On this subject it should be recalled that modern planning has been basically conceived as a road system layout with areas on which schematic volumes were superimposed, with no attempt made to foresee the final balanced form of the urban structure.

The Cartesia proposal recreates a traditional concept of space within the urban plan, counterbalanced by newer and more contemporary three-dimensional areas also conceived as part of the composition. The traditional space, with its familiar proportions and qualities, offers its inhabitants protection and reassurance, and is thus suitable for personal relationships and all forms of leisure, commercial and religious activities, typical of the "old world". The more contemporary area, instead, provides visions of suspension, flight, horizontal and vertical spatial openings, giving an extensive sense of movement and deep perspective. This concept is suited to the "new world" activities which imply a large concentration of public, offering an exciting sense of psychological freedom of action and the conquest of new intellectual territory.

Spatial continuity between the parts of the city must be guaranteed by the accessibility of every area, with the added possibility of walking on the external surfaces of inclined buildings. Only in a few cases, in fact, are the buildings free-standing, being for the most part totally integrated into the urban fabric. They are conceived as structures to be entered on different levels since the space is not designed as a compact volume in contact with the outside only via vertical walls, as is the usual case. While a hierarchy between the volumes of the buildings and the spaces of the streets and squares is necessary, it is essential to establish a physical continuity that can be covered on foot. This does not mean that the walkable spaces must be of limited area and volume. The large cities of the past were in fact made of vast spaces, but all in communication so that they could always be reached on foot.

POINT 2: THE SOCIO-ECONOMIC PLAN

The average density of the city will be high, although it will vary from zone to zone. High density, when it is well-structured, facilitates communication and interaction among people. The urban spaces must always be alive and occupied for most of the day by all kinds of activities. Thus every area of the urban fabric must possess the right proportion of various functions in order to be continually in use. Many support facilities, such as parking lots, can be placed so that they serve various activities at different times of day. Public areas can be used for a longer time throughout the day, thus guaranteeing their efficiency and economic viability. Used in this way, these areas will be more attractive and more easily protected from crime.

Community Consensus will be represented by the Commissioning body for architectural projects with the financial support of all citizens, in order to guarantee correct development of the city. This public body will have to monitor the functional and aesthetical permanence of the buildings, roads and bridges. It will also be necessary to reject new building developments promoted by financial groups interested only in immediate profit rather than the long-term welfare of the city.

When a planning program obtained by Consensus has been drawn up and studied in detail, a developer who can guarantee both the economic viability and the quality demanded by the people will be designated. To assure the functional and visual permanence of the project, it must be kept in mind that the technological elements of a building change more rapidly than the traditional ones. Quality built internal space is much more easily reusable, as can often be seen in historic buildings, even if their financial value varies over time, while technological systems and internal partitions can be changed as needed.

Planned economical use of all parts of the city results in greater administrative control of all construction and maintenance costs. The Cospace (Community Space Program) will plan the coexistence of community functions, on all levels, and the necessary structures (theatres, schools, sports facilities, etc.) to house them. The use of structures must be programmed to meet logical standards with adequate financing, the time-sharing and relevant costs having already been agreed upon by the organizations involved. This program must take into account the life cycle of every building so as to prevent malfunctioning and obsolescence, which are part of the pathology of the city. At the same time, competition between various areas and functions must be kept alive, because without this the city will not progress.

Cartesia advocates a new economic dimension for buildings, which must be constructed to last and be appreciated for their ability to serve the functions for which they were designed and for their aesthetic appearance. Some of these Mega-functional buildings will be able to serve both the local community and a larger public coming from other areas, producing continuous interest in the city as well as income. Designed for multi-medial communication, they will cater to tens of thousands of visitors a day, efficiently carrying out complex functions. Moreover, the buildings designed to serve the local community (multi-functional) will provide for various activities (scholastic, sports, entertainment and meeting halls for groups of all sizes) for at least eighteen hours a day.

The energy efficiency obtained with the structures of the new city must be evaluated not only in terms of direct economic saving but also of ecology. Solar heating systems will be used in winter and systems will be developed to convert concentrated heat into the high temperatures needed for air-conditioning in summer. Photosensitive cells to produce electricity will be easier to install on horizontal and sloping buildings. Moreover, it will be necessary to protect the façades and their skylights from the sun during the summer to reduce the cost of air-conditioning. The flues of heating and ventilation systems will not emit polluted air directly into the atmosphere. This air will be extracted, filtered and used to generate hot water by a system located in the Platform.

POINT 3: THE MULTI-DIMENSIONAL ORGANIZATION OF TRAFFIC

Heavy traffic and transporting goods by road certainly cannot be avoided in a city of the future because the automobile is indispensable for movement over a vast area. Traffic however, to be manageable, needs only to be programmed, regulated and directed in all aspects and details.

The Platform includes three levels of traffic. Level One is for heavy local and through traffic. A part of this level is used for parking beneath low-rise buildings and for unloading and storage areas. Taxis and emergency services also move on Level One, going up to Level Two only at certain pre-established places. Pedestrians move down from Level Two to the bus stops on Level One, either walking or using elevators and escalators. Below Level One is the Sub-Level containing a Subway System and an Intercity railway. Openings of various sizes on the streets of Level One provide orientation and ventilation for drivers, in zones that are lit naturally. There are other openings in the inner courtyards of the buildings. From Level One there is road access to the multi-storey parking garages located in high-rise buildings or high density zones.

Level Two carries low-speed foot traffic and Ulsy vehicles (ultra-light, slow and silent) designed to cover short distances. Culsy (commuter Ulsy vehicles) light buses can also circulate on this level, carrying a maximum of 20 passengers over short distances. Buildings on Level Two may cannot exceed the height of height four storeys.

Level Three, approximately 45 metres above Level Two, will be used by young people (particularly between school and home) and by the elderly, as well as for recreation activities, walks and sport, tourism and short-distance traffic between high-density zones. This level, which offers panoramic views, particularly in the High Park area, is for pedestrians, bicycles and Ulsy and Culsy vehicles. Level Three is partly covered but always very light and airy with one side often protected by glass to prevent wind cross-currents. Levels Two and Three are linked by open-air ramps, covered escalators and elevators and moving floors on open-air rack railways. Light first aid vehicles are permitted on level Three, while heavy emergency services operate from Level One. There will be a certain number of commercial activities on Level Three (restaurants, bars, essential shops) near the panoramic terraces, the Culsy public transport stops and the vertical transport points. Traffic on Level Three can be easily monitored for security since it is controlled at a limited number of intersections with the other levels.

The cost of the Platform will be economical in the long run because it is logical, efficient and practical, making everyday life and movement easier. The Platform drastically limits pollution and represents a considerable saving of energy by reducing the speed and travelling time of vehicles. Exhaust fumes of cars will be filtered before being expelled into the air above the buildings. Noise and vibration are controlled by means of absorbent panels and flooring that is detached from the vertical structures.

ULSY: ULTRA-LIGHT AND SILENT TRAFFIC. In the city, only very light, slow vehicles will mingle with pedestrians. These vehicles, with very low total mass and specific weight and limited speed (maximum 13 MPH), are silent and non-polluting, involving no danger to their users or to pedestrians. The engines of the Ulsy may be electric, aided by solar cells, or may operate with combustion systems of very small size but with high specific power using non-polluting fuel. Private cars, carrying two to four 4 passengers, will be protected by inflatable bumpers. Public transportation vehicles, the Culsy, have the same features and can carry up to 20 people. Two-wheeled light vehicles will also be slow and silent. Internal city traffic must be ultra-light to avoid congestion and the psychological pressure on pedestrians invariably produced by speed and noise . The average difference in travelling time for distances under six miles between traditional vehicles and ultra-light ones is minimal, since the rapid acceleration of traditional vehicles as normally regulated by traffic lights causes congestion that slows down the flow of traffic. The number of accidents caused by collisions will also be drastically reduced. Accordingly, the atmosphere in the city will be much more relaxed and conducive to all levels of human interaction.

Point 4: Architectural form of buildings and their design

The architectural forms shown here derive from tested concepts based on accepted functional and constructional logic, but not from the existing examples or from preconceived clichés. There is no symbolism of traditional or technological derivation in the compositional synthesis. Inspiration is derived from natural forms, used with immediacy but after a long period of reflection, attempting to eliminate the futile and superfluous by concentrating on the logic of the function. The sense of movement combined with the balance of natural growth in this architecture results in fluidity and continuity of lines, in sharp contrast to functionalist geometry linked to purely economic concepts. Each building is conceived as an active sculpture, solidly constructed with simple and precise details designed to last well with minimum maintenance requirements. The possible future substitution of buildings that are part of the urban composition should be avoided, since this would alter the balance of the whole conception and encourage the use of products that have a limited life and are soon obsolete. Continuity and permanence of the urban concept are the indispensable conditions for maintaining the spirit of the community. Internal changes may be made in the buildings, but only minor corrections in the overall arrangement.

The architectural definition of each building will depend on the development program and the solution that the architect in charge wishes to implement. In the proposal, ample space is left for the creative imagination of each individual designer. The basic concept of the various buildings calls for projects featuring creativity and problem-solving ability, where decoration is unnecessary. The architecture of building types is based on a sculptural three dimensionality which presents a greater challenge, that of being able to take advantage of all of its exciting possibilities.

Point 5: Growth and Change

Every area of the city must attain a balanced compositional aspect with its own particular features and a pre-established level of functionality. These areas will germinate and grow in accordance with a precise vision inspired by an image of the future of all western society. The concepts of urban planning proposed here are the means of achieving this vision, which, moreover, must be integrated with the insertion of buildings symbolizing particular events or situations that cannot at first form part of the plan but will develop within the future detailed program.

The continuity and permanence of the city must be guaranteed both from the strictly physical aspect, by maintaining the buildings in good condition, and as image, which must always be stimulating for its inhabitants to keep inspiration alive, striving toward still higher goals. To achieve this, uncontrolled consumerism must be restrained, as it tends to replace existing buildings with newer, larger ones that benefit only speculation and commercial property transactions. Inflation of property values and other related negative phenomena eventually cause serious socio-economic damage. For this reason even the replacement of some buildings, seen as a corrective measure, must be done slowly and with great caution.

APPENDIX

A DESCRIPTION OF CONSTRUCTION TYPES

Construction Type 1 - Housing

High density dwellings of various types are provided by multi-storey buildings, either vertical or sloping, with panoramic terraces. Multi-storey parking facilities and entrance for service vehicles are on Level One. The communal pedestrian areas and a covered plaza with shops and a café are on Level Two. Access to Level Three is near the schools and sports zones. Pedestrian traffic across the inclined surfaces and direct access from the walkways to the terraces of the apartments favours interaction among inhabitants.

Average public presence per day: 18/24 hours.

Construction Type 2 - Upper Park

High Park, superelevated and equipped for leisure activities and a children's playground, with a panoramic view over the city. Moving stairways and elevators provide connection to Levels One and Two.

Construction Type 3 - Shopping Malls and Housing - "Old World"

This is a traditional type of architecture with plazas, streets, alleyways and arcades and a maximum elevation of four storeys. On the first floor at Level One is the commercial zone with restaurants, hotels, meeting places and other structures such as book shops and places for religious worship. The offices are on the second floor while on the upper floors will be housing, which must occupy at least 50% of the available space to create density and life.

Pedestrian traffic and Ulsy transport will be on Level Two, while heavy traffic and service vehicles move on Level One, reached by the public via the courtyards of their buildings. Here the type of buildings to be constructed will be decided by private enterprise, the only set requirement being that of interface with traffic on Level One.

Average public presence per day: 18/24 hours, becoming 24/24 in certain restricted areas.

Construction Type 4 - Highways

The highways are mostly concealed ones built beneath Level One. They surface only in certain areas to give drivers a sense of direction.

Construction Type 5 - Public Buildings

Designed for city administration offices, this type of building consists of several floors with a sloping roof, providing a pleasant panorama of the city. Under the building is a garage for private cars with access from Level One. Bus stops and subway stations are also located in this area. The zone has pedestrian connections with Levels Two and Three, has access to the museums and the park and is also a tourist and panoramic area. Consequently, it should be a landmark building of lasting quality with distinctive characteristics.

Average public presence per day: 18/24 hours becoming 24/24 hours in limited areas.

Construction Type 6 - Lower Park

Wooded area equipped for recreation.

Construction Type 7 - Commercial, Entertainment Buildings, "The Young World"

This zone contains an exhibition area, department stores, theatres, cinemas and all recreational and social facilities as well as restaurants, bars, night clubs and the necessary services. There are courtyards and gardens within the continuous structure which is entirely covered in glass and totally air-conditioned. Parking for private cars is below this area, which with its inclined plane provides the third dimension, facilitating access to the upper floors easy by means of moving stairs and ramps. This structure, situated near the train and bus stations and the big car parks, is the commercial and recreational port of the city. Ulsy vehicles are allowed to circulate in this area. An ecological roofing system uses solar energy at all seasons, curtailing pollution and allowing significant energy-saving. This area represents the contemporary equivalent of building type 3.

Average public presence per day: 18/24 hours with 24/24 hours in places.

Construction Type 8 - Transportation Center

All the train, bus and truck terminals are situated in this multi-level facility which also has a heliport and ample parking space for private cars. All roads on all levels of the platform lead to this Center, making it the most important traffic junction in the city. An electronic system gives visitors directions and information about buildings and parking availability.

Average public presence per day: 24/24 hours.

Construction Type 9 - Office Buildings

This zone contains buildings 10 to 20 storeys high, for businesses that need space in which to use electronic systems economically for the production of data or for the creation and distribution of products. Office space will be organized around courtyards with waterfalls and evergreen plants growing on metal trellises. If large-scale headquarters conceived as landmark skyscrapers visible from a distance are to be built in the future, they will be located in another area of the city.

Ulsy transport vehicles will have access on Levels Two and Three, while other traffic will be on Level One.

Per day presence of tenants and the public in all areas with adequate services: 24/24 hours; in other areas: 12/24 hours.

Construction Type 10 - Museum - Mega Communication Center

This type of building is dedicated to museums and exhibitions. Built horizontally on a pedestal structure, it is totally open to sunlight, with a park beneath the entire structure. The park can be seen from all upper portions of the museum. Service roads to the building run underground and reach the structure via the pedestal buildings which house offices and storerooms. Parking space for private cars is provided beneath the inclined planes of Construction Type 1 and has access to the museum.

Public presence per day: 12/24 hours.

Construction Type 11 - Central Park

A large green area with high trees conceived for relaxation and for concerts and political events.

Construction Type 12 - Schools - Polyhedric Community Center

The various types of schools have direct pedestrian access to the parks and sports areas via ramps on the inclined planes in contact with the ground. Access to the schools is from Levels Two and Three. Parking facilities and access for service vehicles is on Level One.

Average public presence per day: 18/24 hours, including evening community use.

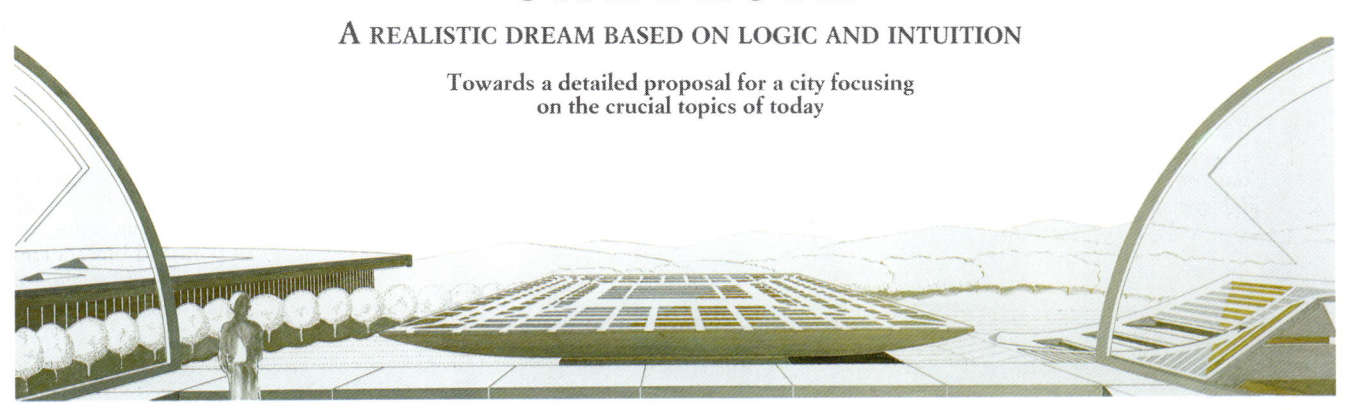

CARTESIA
A REALISTIC DREAM BASED ON LOGIC AND INTUITION

Towards a detailed proposal for a city focusing
on the crucial topics of today

General plan of Cartesia:
1. Housing
2. Upper Park
3. Shopping malls. "Old World"
4. Highways
5. Public buildings
6. Lower Park
7. Entertainment buildings, "The Young World"
8. Transportation center
9. Office buildings
10. Museum - Mega-communication center
11. Central Park
12. Schools - Polyhedric Community Center

General plan shows only a portion of the ideal city and typical aggregations of buildings to describe spatial and volumetric relationships.

Above: Perspective view from Upper Park of Aerospace, part of the Mega-Communication Centers, the multi-functional complex designed as one of the poles of attraction of Cartesia.

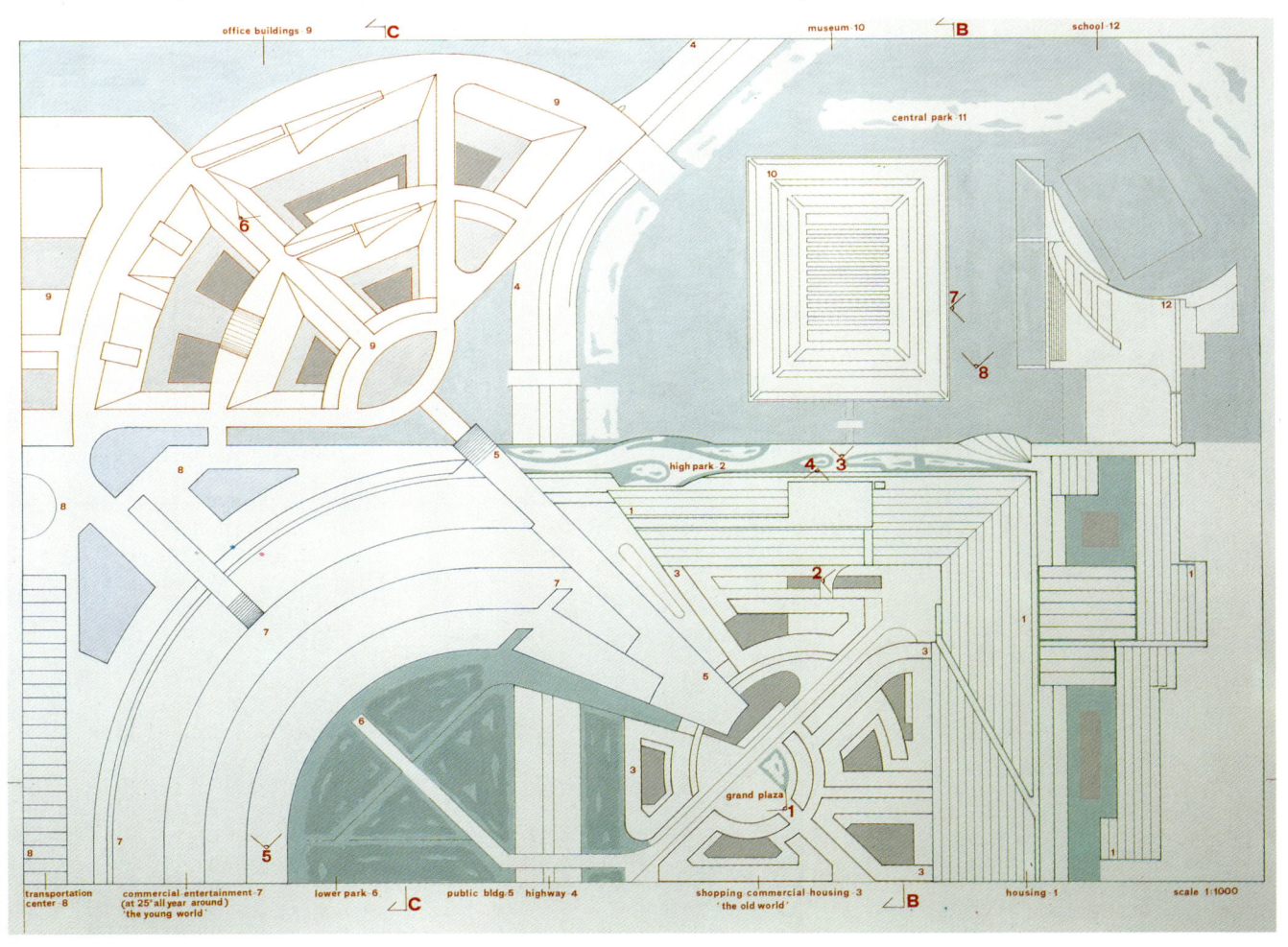

This is a study to create a blueprint for a conceptual urban pattern that retains the fascination of the classic tridimensional leader city, while offering all the logical solutions necessary to the contemporary world. It is an ambitious concept of city inspired by aesthetic, ecological and functional principles that seeks to propose a new method of confronting the urban design process.
This planning system adopts three-dimensional zoning rules to define the relationships between buildings and the total urban space.

The material shown in the following pages proposes only schematic and conceptual views of the planning guidelines. These guidelines will eventually be interpreted by the architects selected to design each building when the urban concept of Cartesia is implemented.

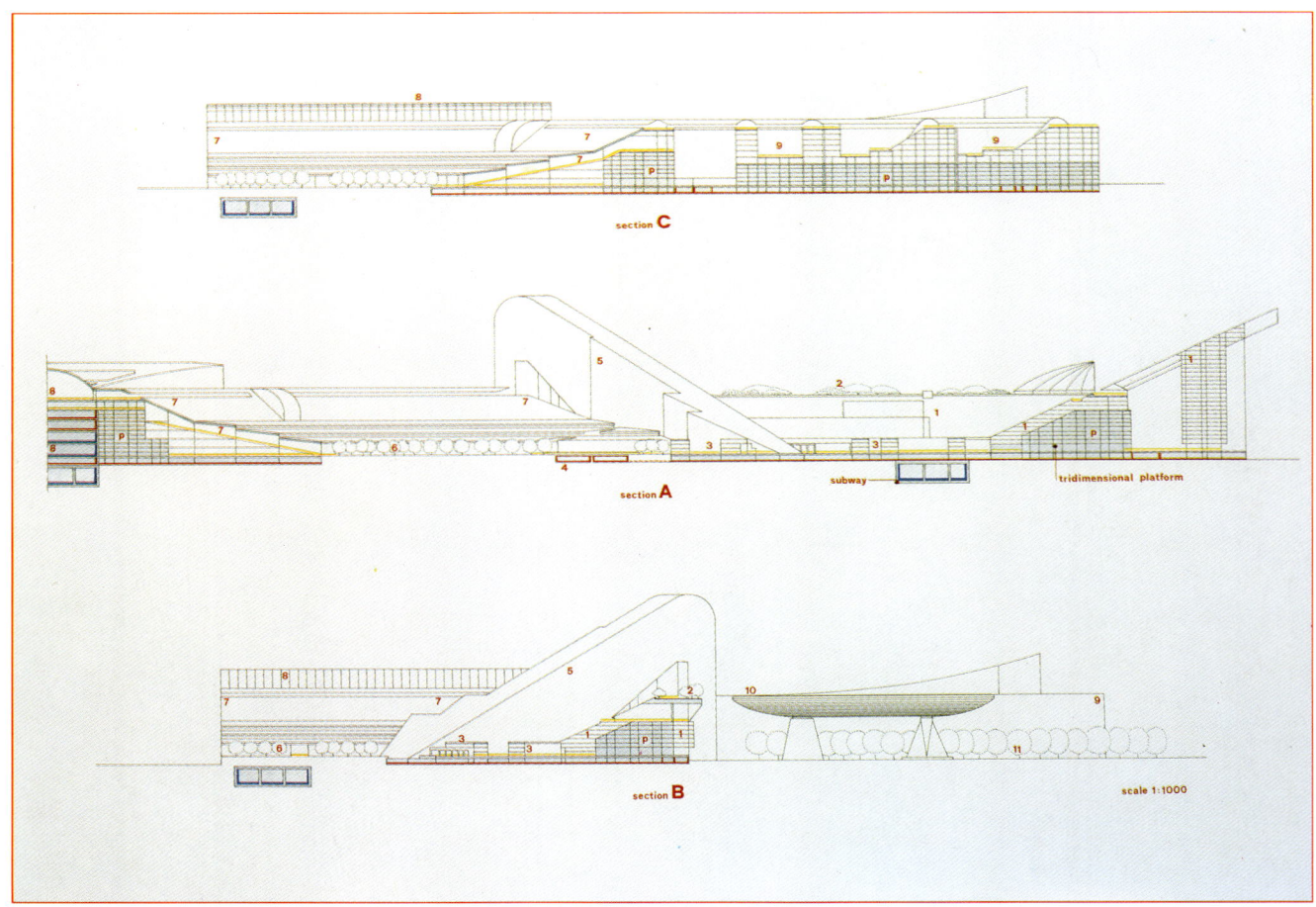

This page above: Perspective view of the Grand Plaza, facing the Town Hall.

This page below: Various levels of urban traffic: pedestrian and ultra-light, slow and silent Ulsy vehicles in yellow; private cars, busses, trucks, etc. in red; trains and underground transport in blue.

Next page above: View of housing from the "Old World".
Next page below: Cross sections of Cartesia.

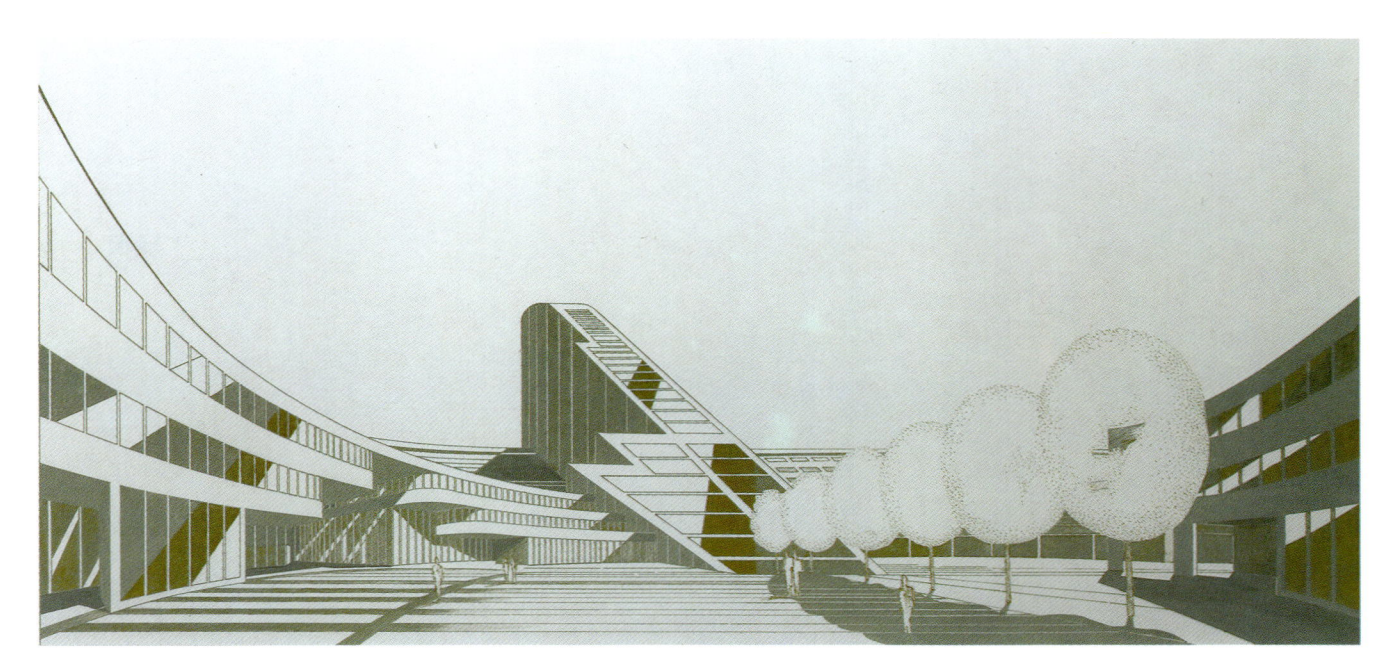

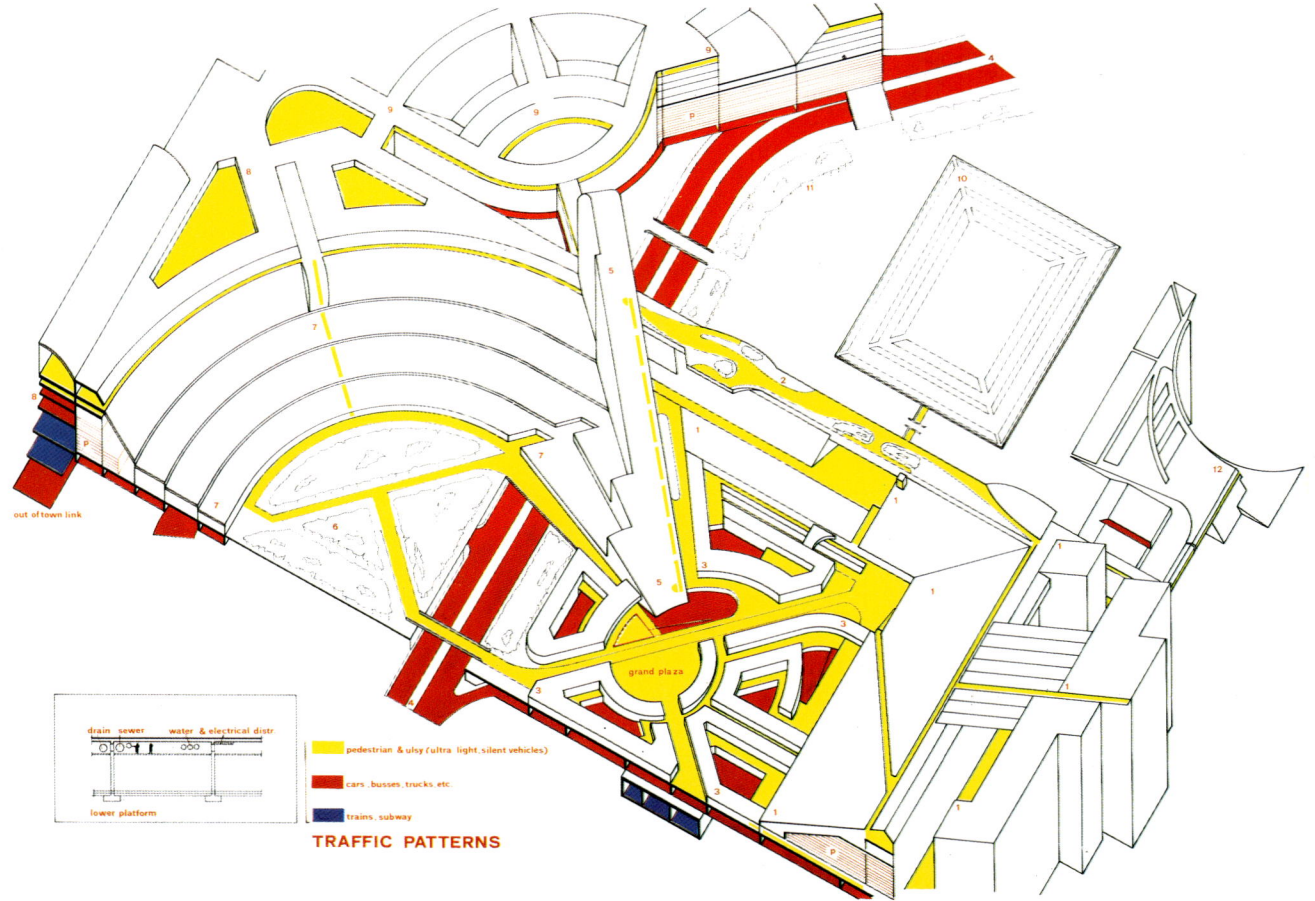

TRAFFIC PATTERNS

Top: Interior view of the "Young World".

Middle: Perspective view of a typical courtyard surrounded by office buildings.

Bottom: Perspective view of the "Old World" from High Park, at Level Three, 45 meters above ground level.

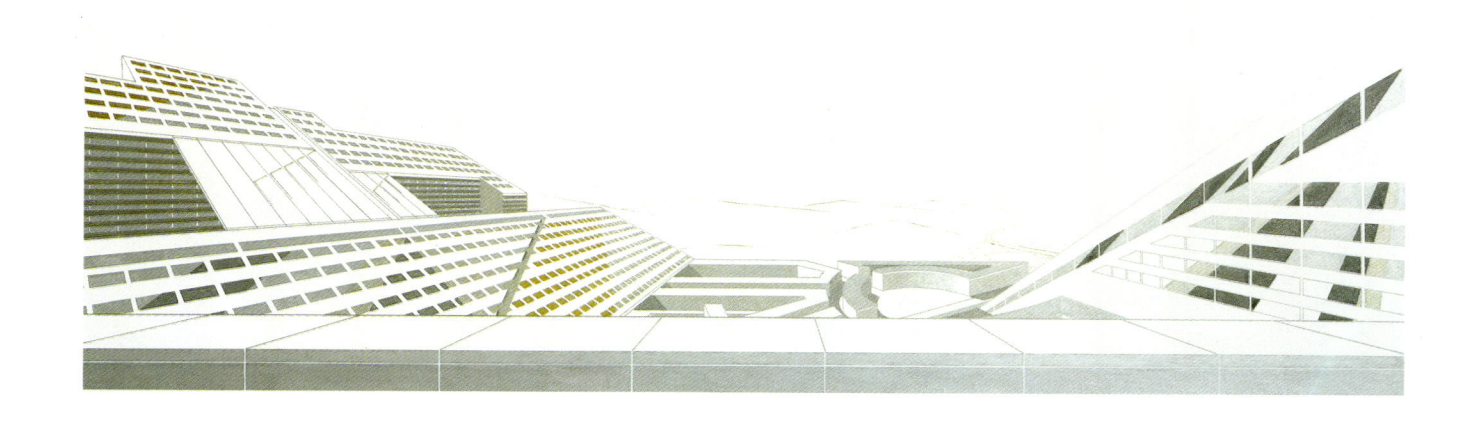

Top: Perspective view of the park as seen from under the museum, part of the Mega-Communications center, and view of the Polyhedric Community Center.

Bottom: Perspective view of Central Park with the Community Center facing the museum.

Aerospace

A museum with attached open theatre for more than 30,000 spectators to be built over a natural setting of wooded area.

This is a construction in direct, total contact with the sky from which it receives natural light filtering down into its exhibition rooms. The building gives the impression of flying over the ground, always visible from the windows of the exibition rooms on its underside.

The Mega Communications Centers and Aerospace, are facilities that can be visited during the day by up to 20,000 persons and used at night by tens of thousands of spectators in the theatre. During the day, a multifaceted exhibition museum area has a capacity of 2,000 visitors per hour through a continuous and precisely programmed flow over its 20,000 square meters of space. At night, the open theatre will use the stage and the supporting system of lighting and sound that is built on the overhang and in the prescenium. The necessary large parking facilities near the building can be utilized economically day and night.

Mega-Communications Centers can revitalize old areas and attract many visitors to new ones with well-programmed shows, while producing substantial revenues.

Top: Site plan of building at ground level.

Bottom: Bird's eye view of Aerospace - marble model mesuring approx. 4 x 5 feet.

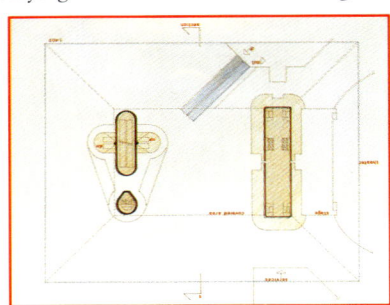

Top: Perspective drawing illustrating the design concept.

Bottom: Elevation of building on the stage side.

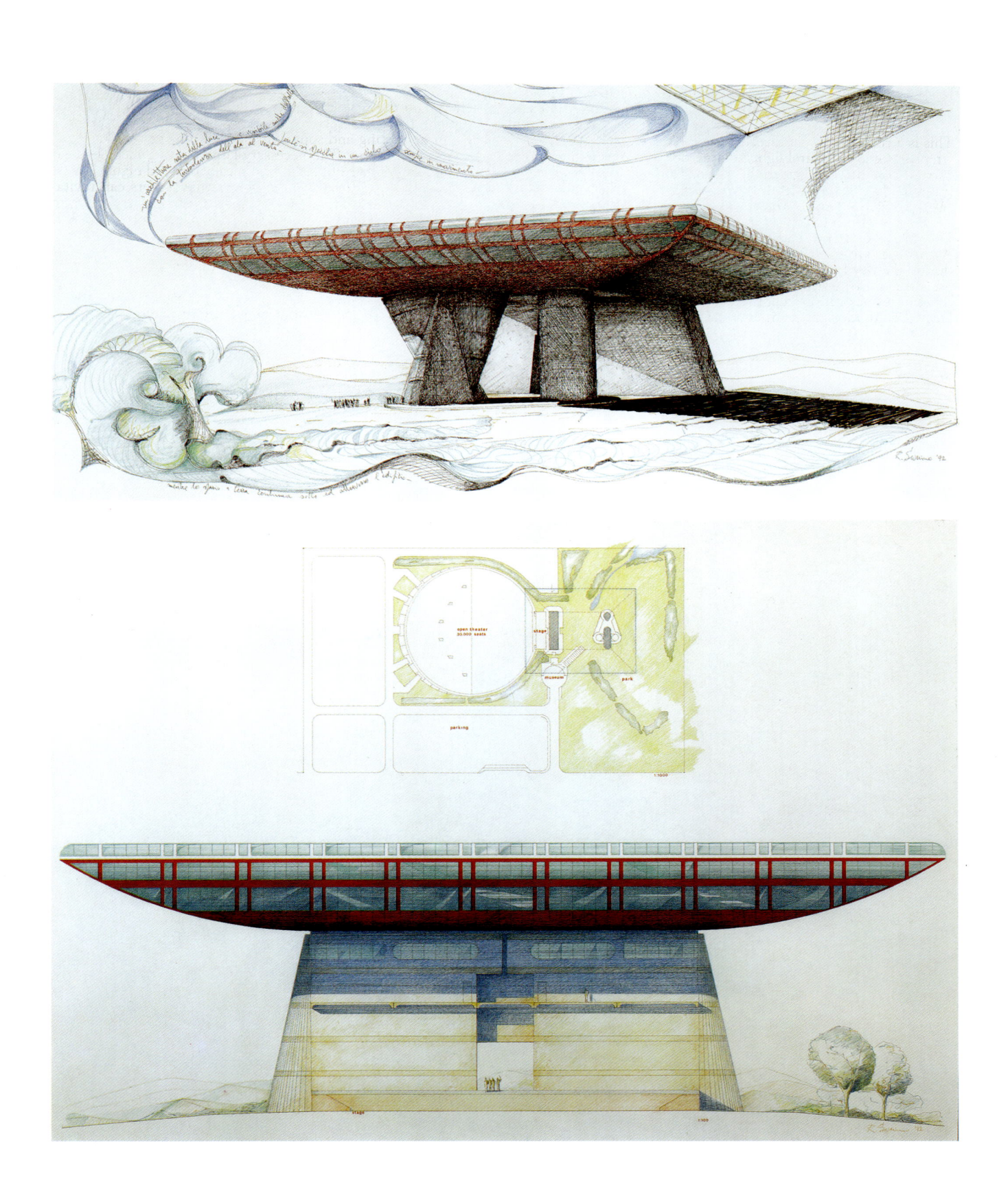

Top: Section of building.

Bottom: Perspective view of model.

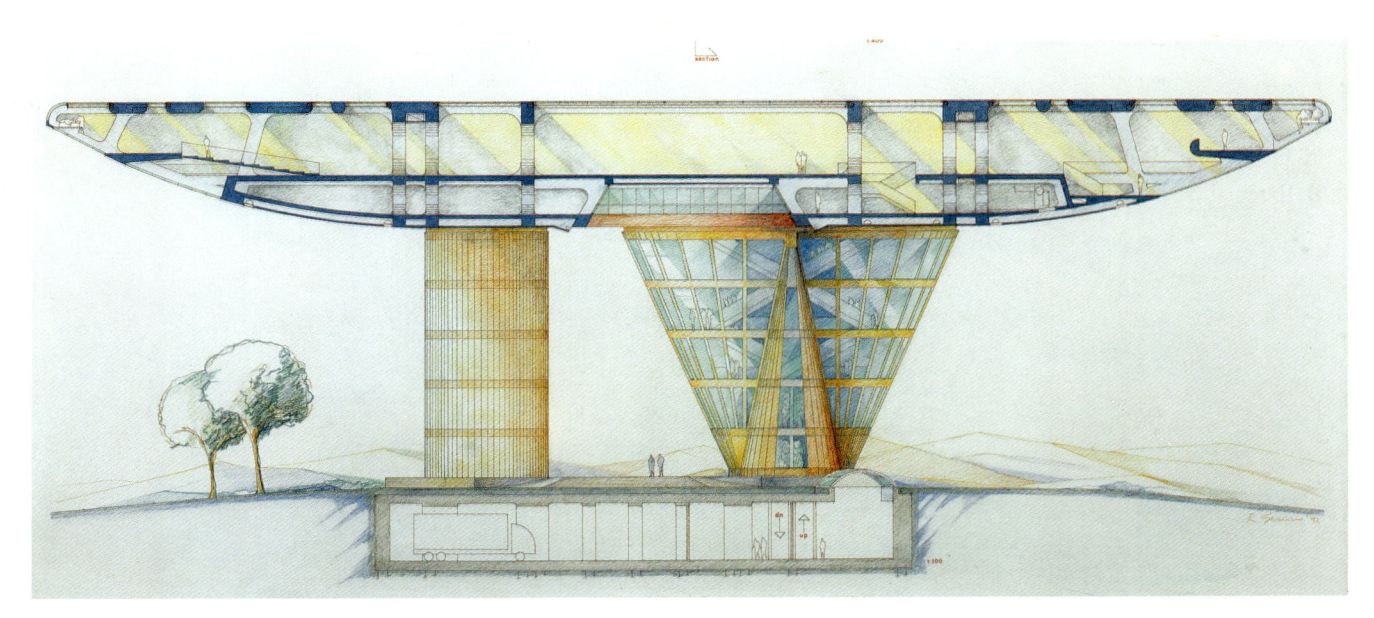

Top: Detail of typical skylights in the roof.

Bottom: Bird's eye view of roof. Model.

Pro-Uptech - Progressively Updated Technology

Timely planned replacement of all systems with advanced products.

1) External sun screens and insulation.
2) Fixed double glazing.
3) Internal sun screens for light control.
4) Lighting system for day and night.
5) Light diffuser system.
6) Spot lighting system.
7) Cell for skylight reading, connected to 8.
8) Controls for light monitoring.
9) Solar panel system.
10) Rainwater collection system.

The large area of solar panels can produce enough electricity to cover almost entirely the quantity needed by the HVAC and the lighting systems of the building.

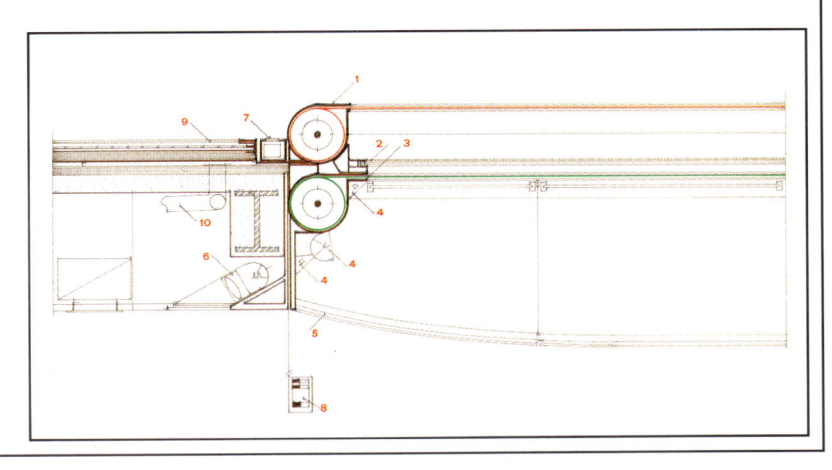

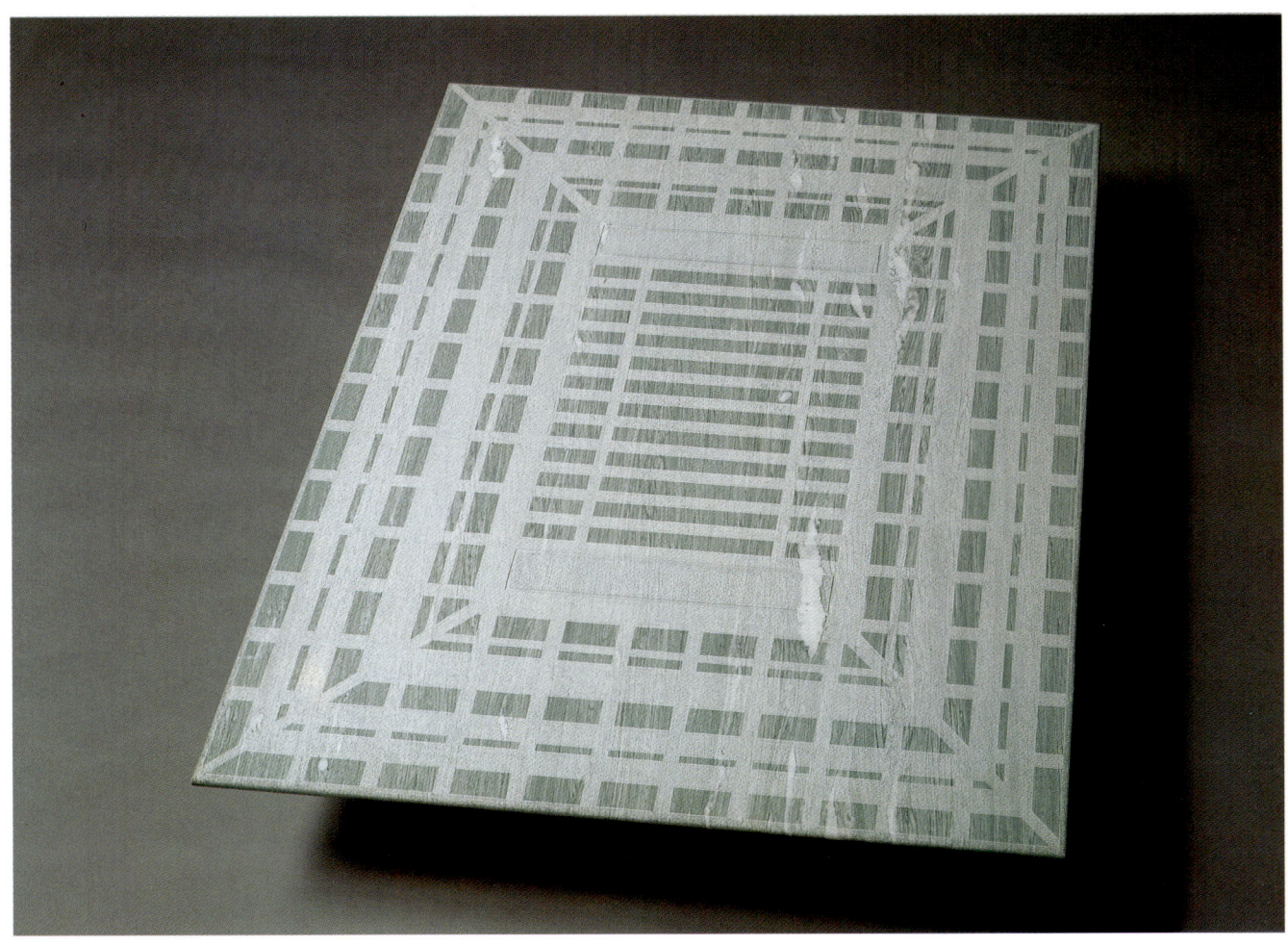

Polyhedric Community Center

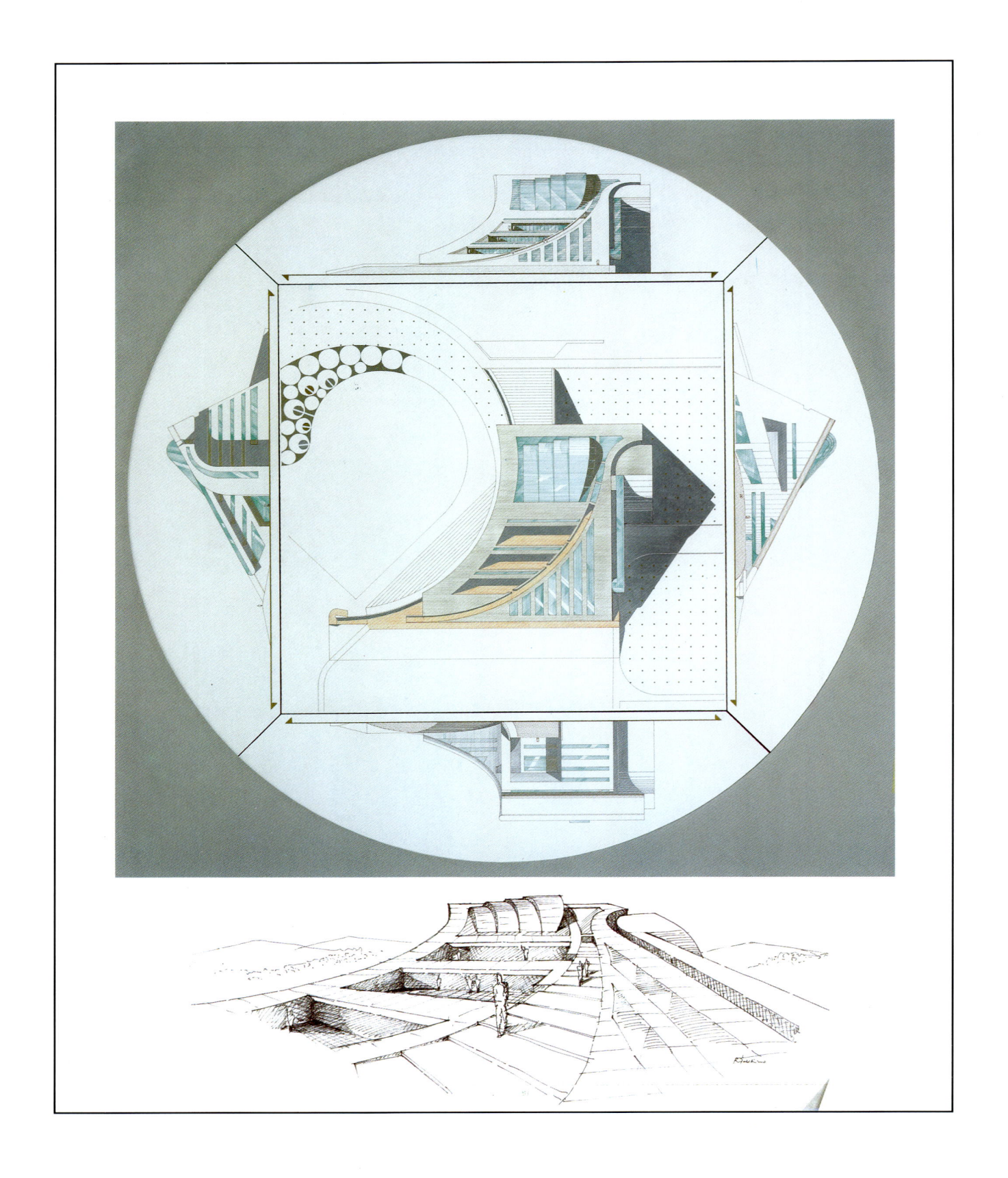

Next Page: Plan and elevations of the Polyhedric Community Center where a variety of activities can be carried out simultaneously: school activities, community meetings, conferences, and sports events.

It has been foreseen that the building will be frequented for up to 16 hours a day and users will be able to go from one activity to another without necessarily having to cross its interior, by walking on the inclined and terraced surface of the roof.

Next Page: Perspective drawing of the ramp on the roof connecting various panoramic terraces.

This Page: Longitudinal section and marble model of the Center.
The building faces different activities on each of its sides.

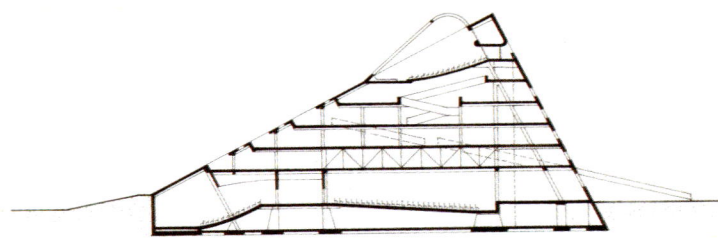

ECOLOGICAL BUILDINGS

An architecture conceived in symbiosis with nature to allow more direct participation in its beauty and order

A new design approach on all levels is necessary to achieve a fully ecological architecture. The application of eco-systems to unsuitable building schemes of the past has proven to be only a sterile and limited exercise, incapable of producing realistic results.

Scientific exactness is necessary in determining the appropriate solutions. A balanced artistic synthesis must include an entire spectrum of inputs coming from the spheres of knowledge, intuition and emotions.

The ecological buildings are volumetrically inconspicuous and adapt their shape to the characteristics of the terrain by following the contours of the site and assuming a shape that complements the surrounding nature. They do not have to compromise their personality and their form which are, instead, distinct and clearly perceivable.

L'Onda, the Wave
A small museum immersed in the nature that surrounds it

During the summer, the water of the pool is pumped over the roof to cool its glass surface and generates a waterfall cascading from the building. In winter the solar panels, inserted in the roof's structure, will provide a good percentage of the required energy.

Chameleon I

This page:
Model of the building constructed in marble and metacrilate.
Night view.

Below: Sketch of design concept.

Next page:
Model of the building, day view.

Section and other drawings describing Chameleon I.

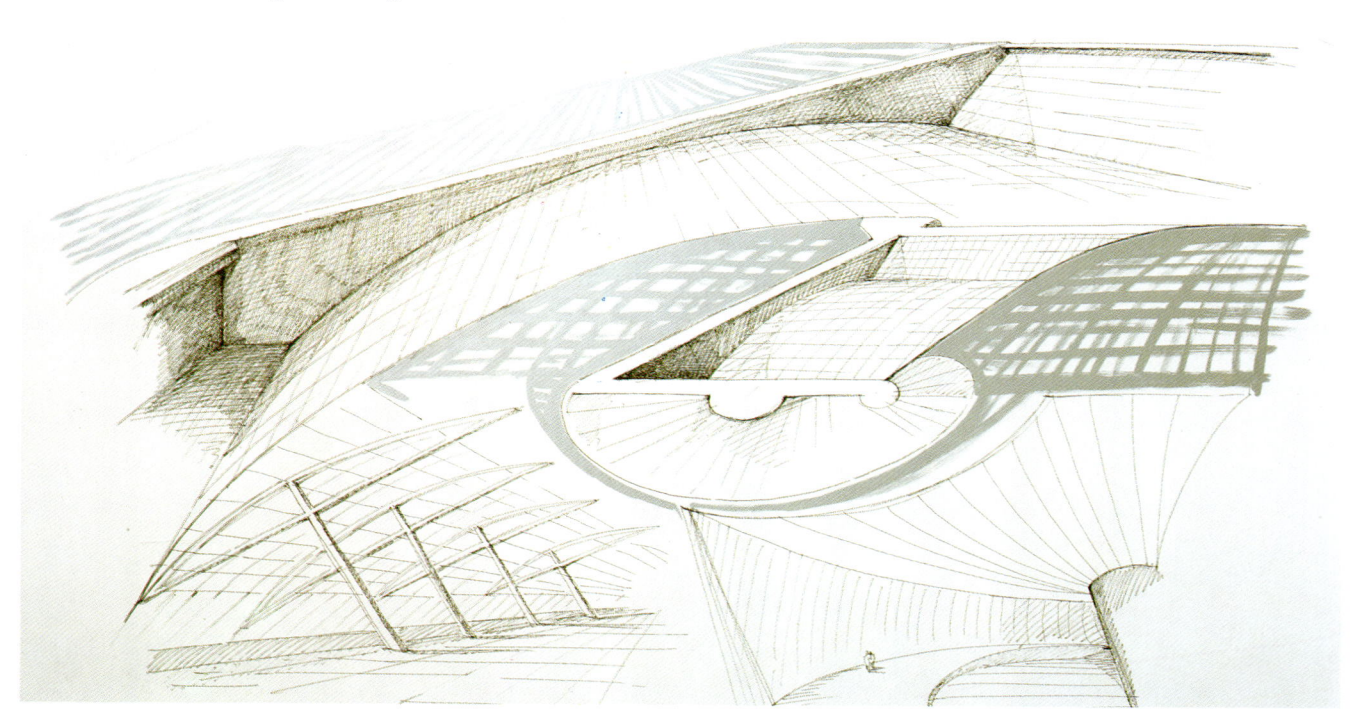

Chameleon I is a building conceived as a research center. It is built into a gully; the continuity of the terrain around it will be re-established after construction. The geographical area suitable for this type of building is one where very cold winters and very hot summers are common.

In winter, the solar collection will help greatly, while in summer the geo-physical low temperature combined with the exterior screening of the glass surfaces will be instrumental in saving a considerable amount of conventional energy.

The roof of the building is conceived as a panel that opens and closes to the sun and light using a sophisticated system of screens of various type. These screens roll out from two cylindrical containers and are supported by lightweight girders moving on tracks.

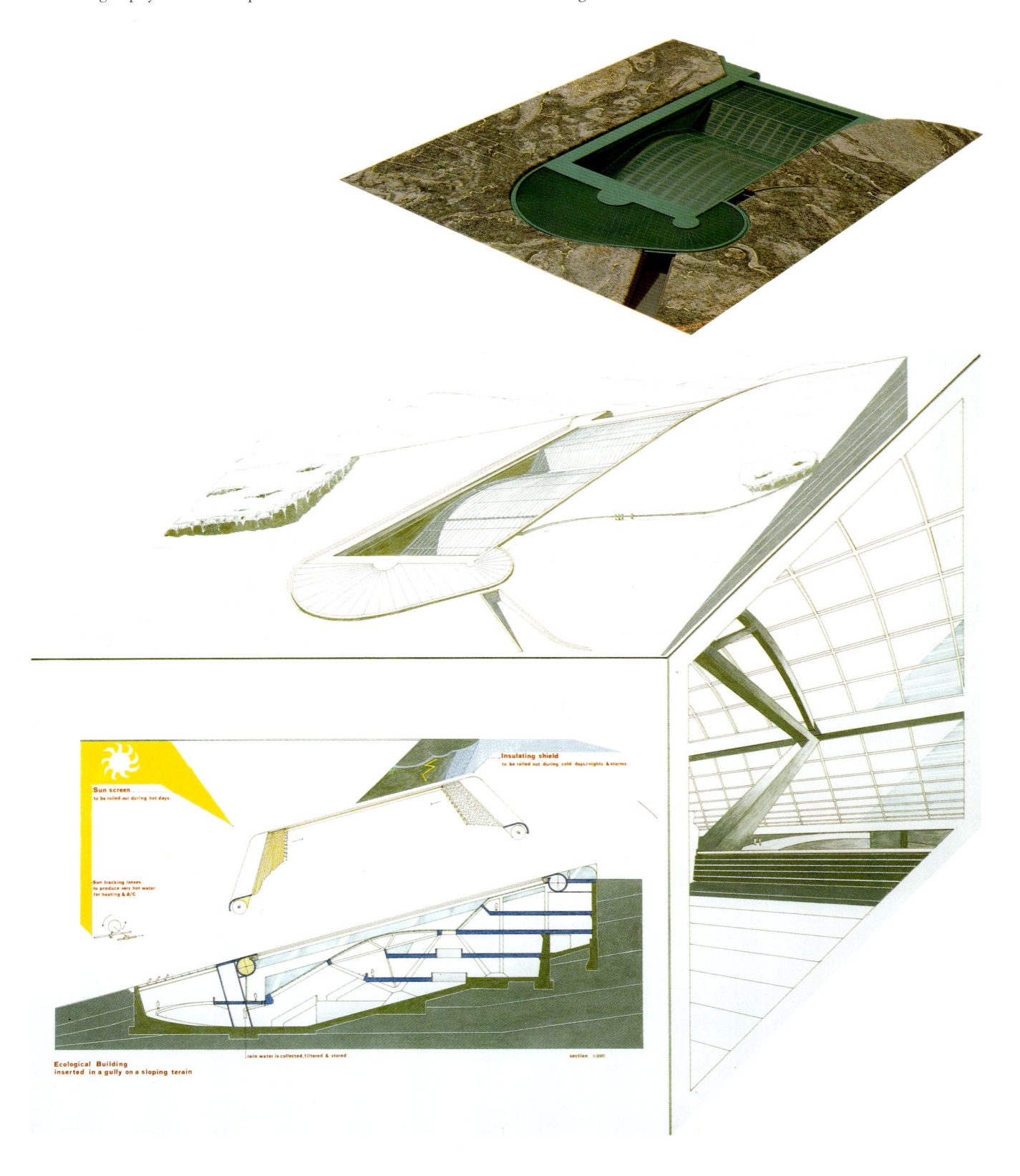

Chameleon II

This is a structure of large dimensions that adapts to the land configuration and due to its size must find in the terrain a compositional equilibrium on various planes of different inclination. Structured as a Convention Center, the building covers a large underground garage and includes exhibition halls, meeting areas and offices.

An open theatre for 20,000 spectators is attached to the building through a large stage connected to it.

This page: Model in marble and wood of Chameleon II and transverse section.

Opposite page: Bird's eye view and longitudinal section of the Center.

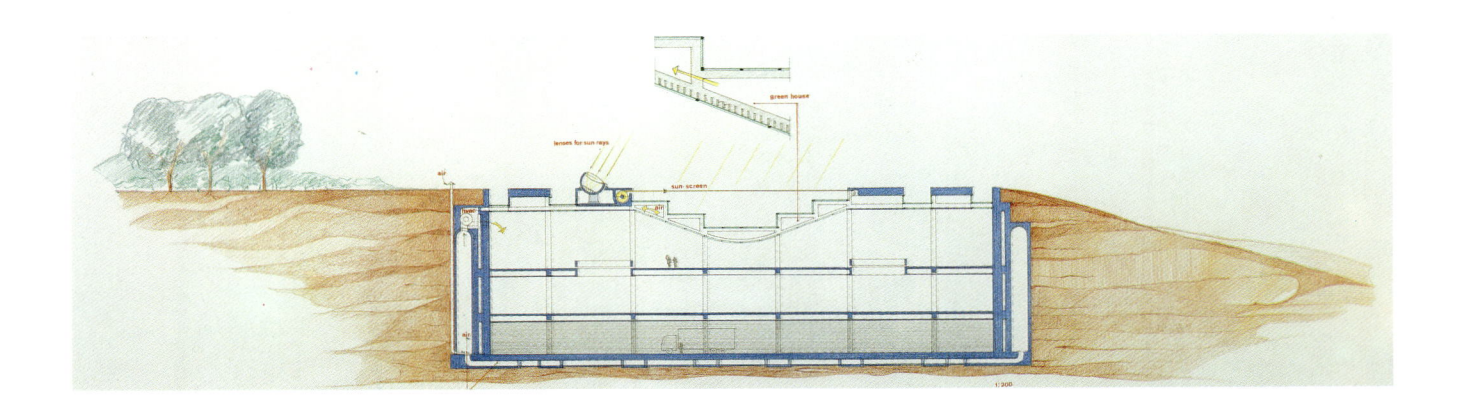

The ecological technology of this building features a "solar cavity" system that absorbs the sun's energy when necessary. Each cavity can be covered with various types of screens during hot days and cold nights. A lens system designed to concentrate the rays of the sun produces the high temperatures necessary for transformation into cool air for space conditioning. Moreover, air circulation at low temperature coming from the underground cavities below and from the sides of the building will also support the HVAC system during summer.

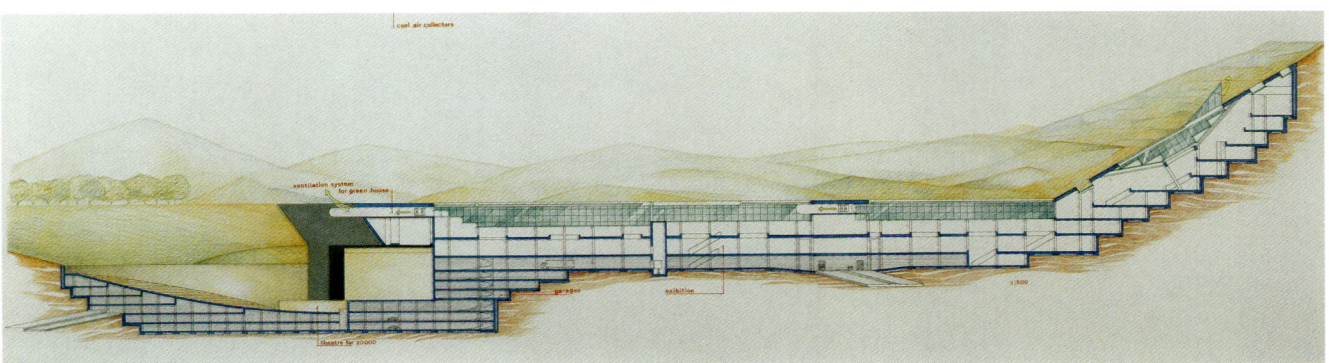

Crossbow

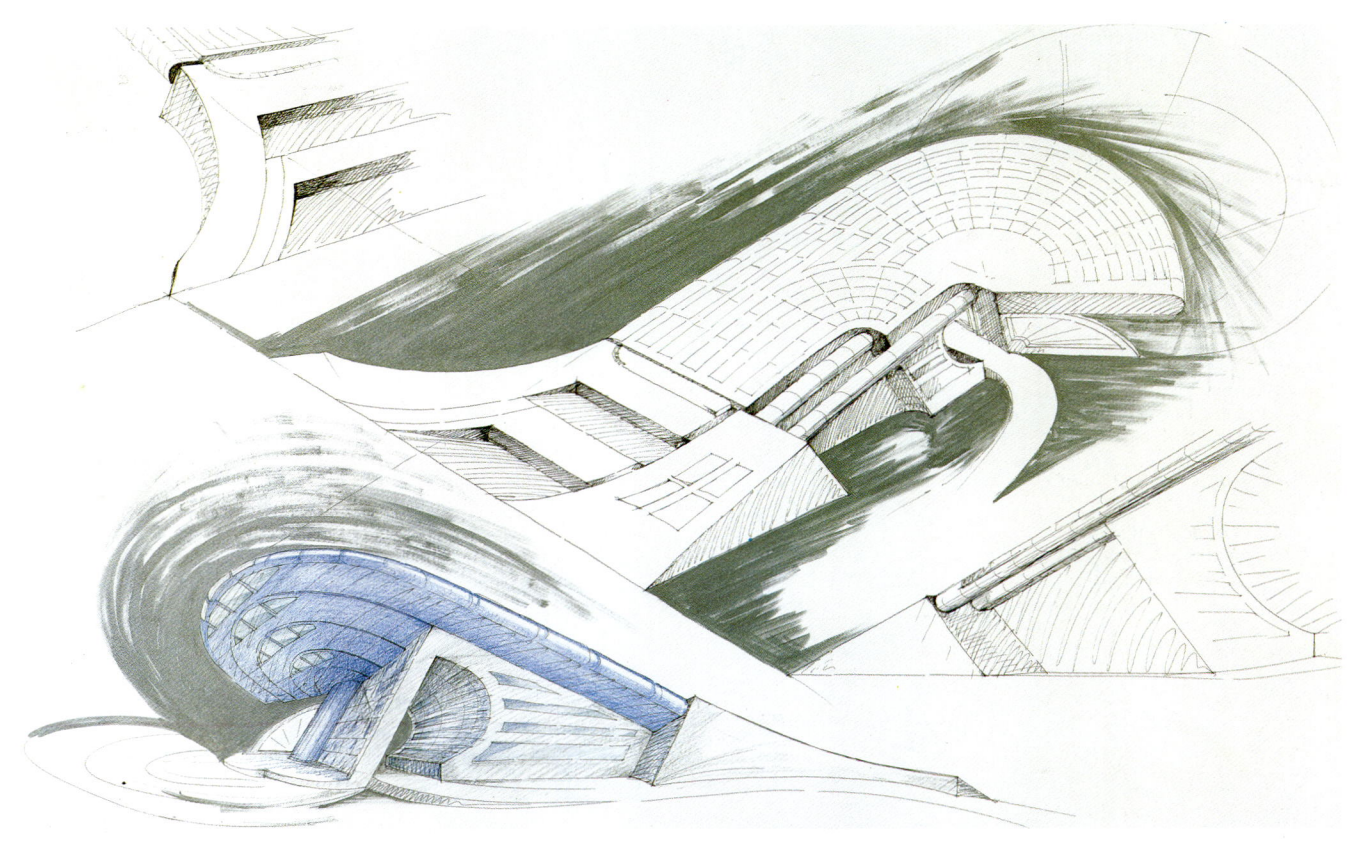

Crossbow is a **Mega-Communications Center** dynamically conceived as an inclined sculpture that rises up from the ground. This building includes exhibition space and a convention center with an open theatre for 30,000. From each floor there is an unobstructed view of the skies and the ground.

The characteristic design of the skylights built with goldtone reflecting glass which is noticeable during the day will retain the same visual pattern and color at night when the interior lights are on.

During the day, the intensity and color of the light coming in from the skylights is controlled by an interior screen system. On the surface of the roof a variety of heat collection systems are active, providing a large percentage of the energy needed for the building.

The visitors brought up by escalators will circulate through the exhibition space from the top downwards, from one floor to the next down.

Next page:
Above: Conceptual sketches of the building.
Below: Metacrilate model of Crossbow. Main Entrance view of the building.

This page:
Above: Roof plan of the building and plan of theatre on smaller scale.
Below: Lateral view of the model.

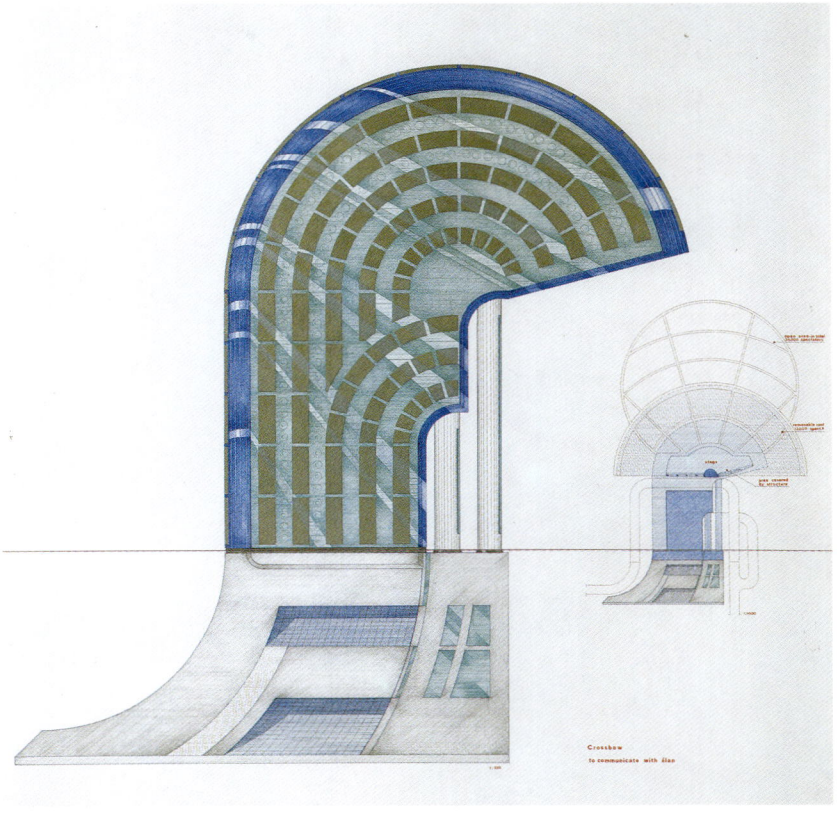

144

This page:
Top: Section and elevation of building drawn in various scales.
Below: Section of theatre with removable teflon tent.

Next Page:
Above: View of stage seen from the seating area.
Below: Lateral view of model.

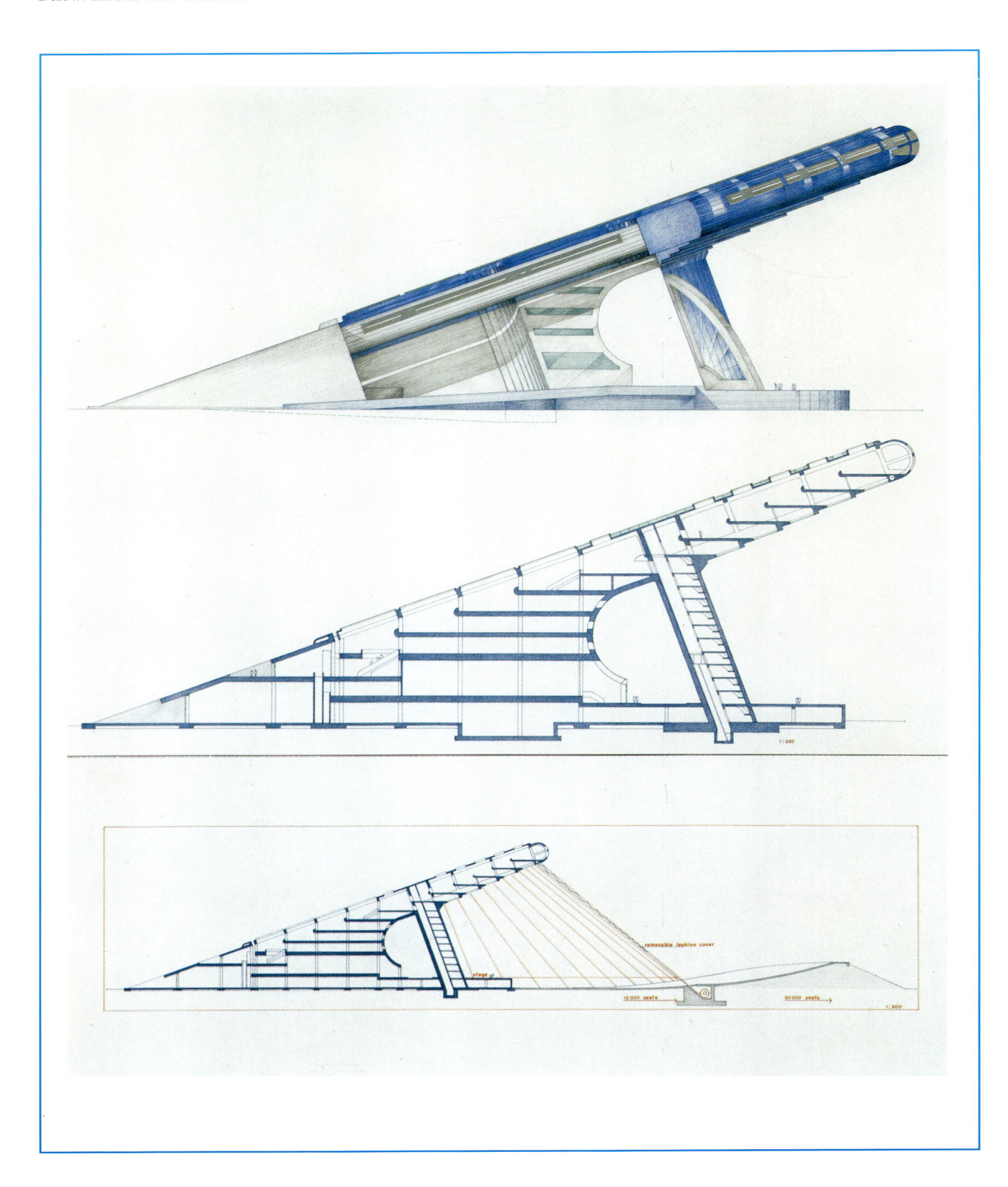

The stage of the open theatre is situated under the wing where the lighting and audio systems are located.

A number of cables that are housed in the structure and that spring from the edge of the overhang can, when needed, be connected to the ground to support a tent covering an area that will accommodate 12,000 spectators - see section.

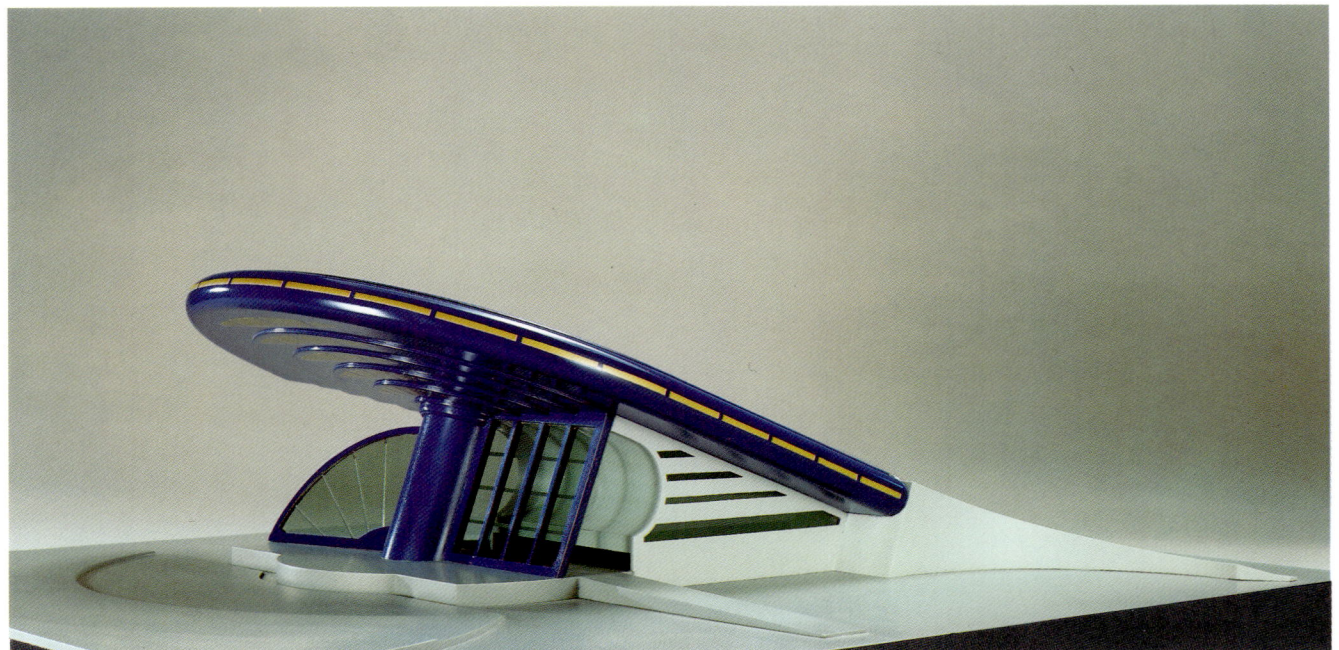

Multilink Township Pattern - MTP

A new concept of contemporary urban aggregation

A proposal for the growing suburban areas in the United States. Four major principles inspire this proposal:

1 - Tridimensional physical space of the Town Center.
2 - Low per capita costs while meeting all ecological demands.
3 - A new notion of functionality and economy.
4 - A new dimension of zoning ordinances.

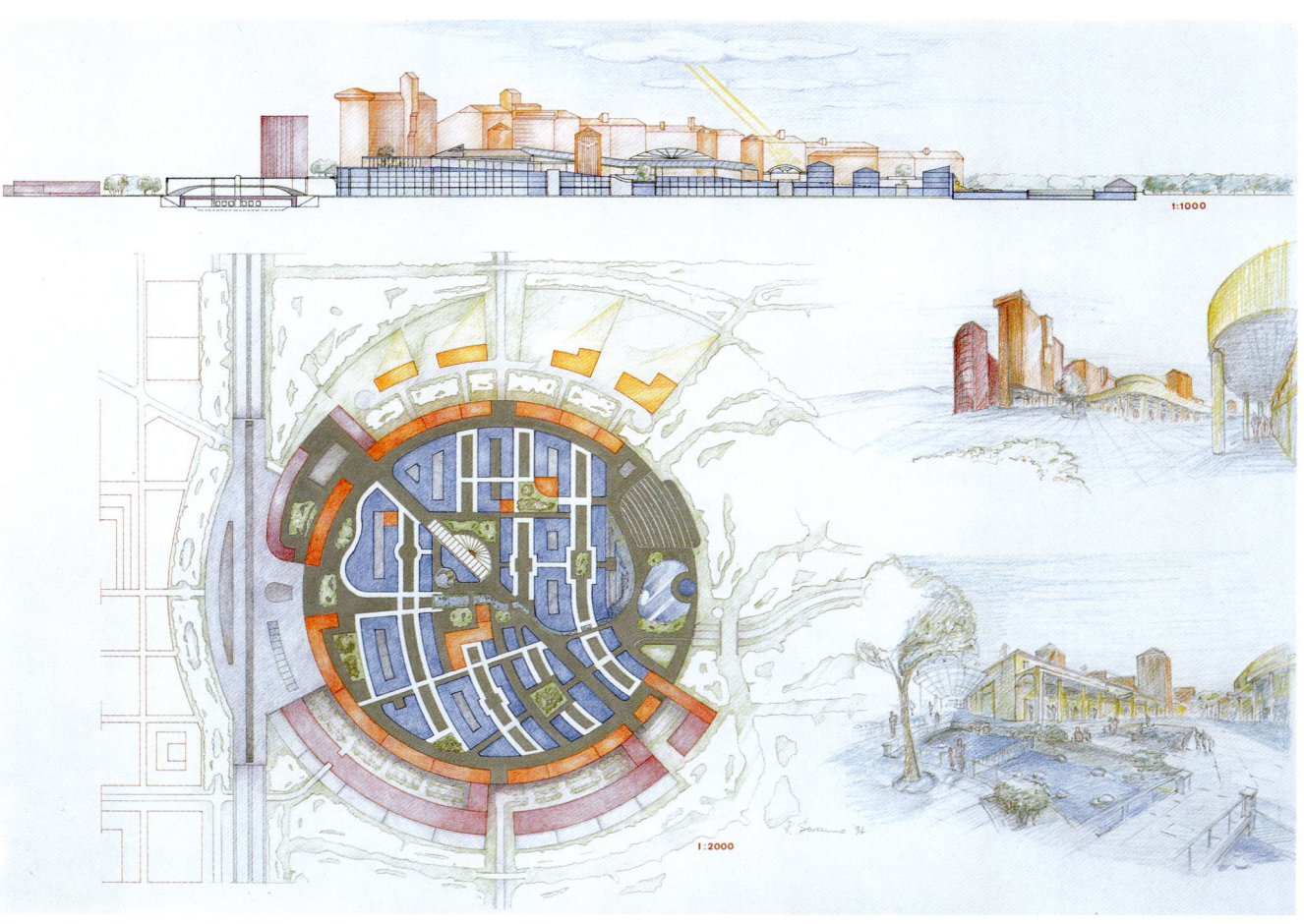

147

This page:
Top: A perspective of Town Center.

Bottom: Bird's eye view of the entire town.

Next page:
Top: Perspective of Town Center showing artificial stream.

Bottom: Plan and section of Town Center.

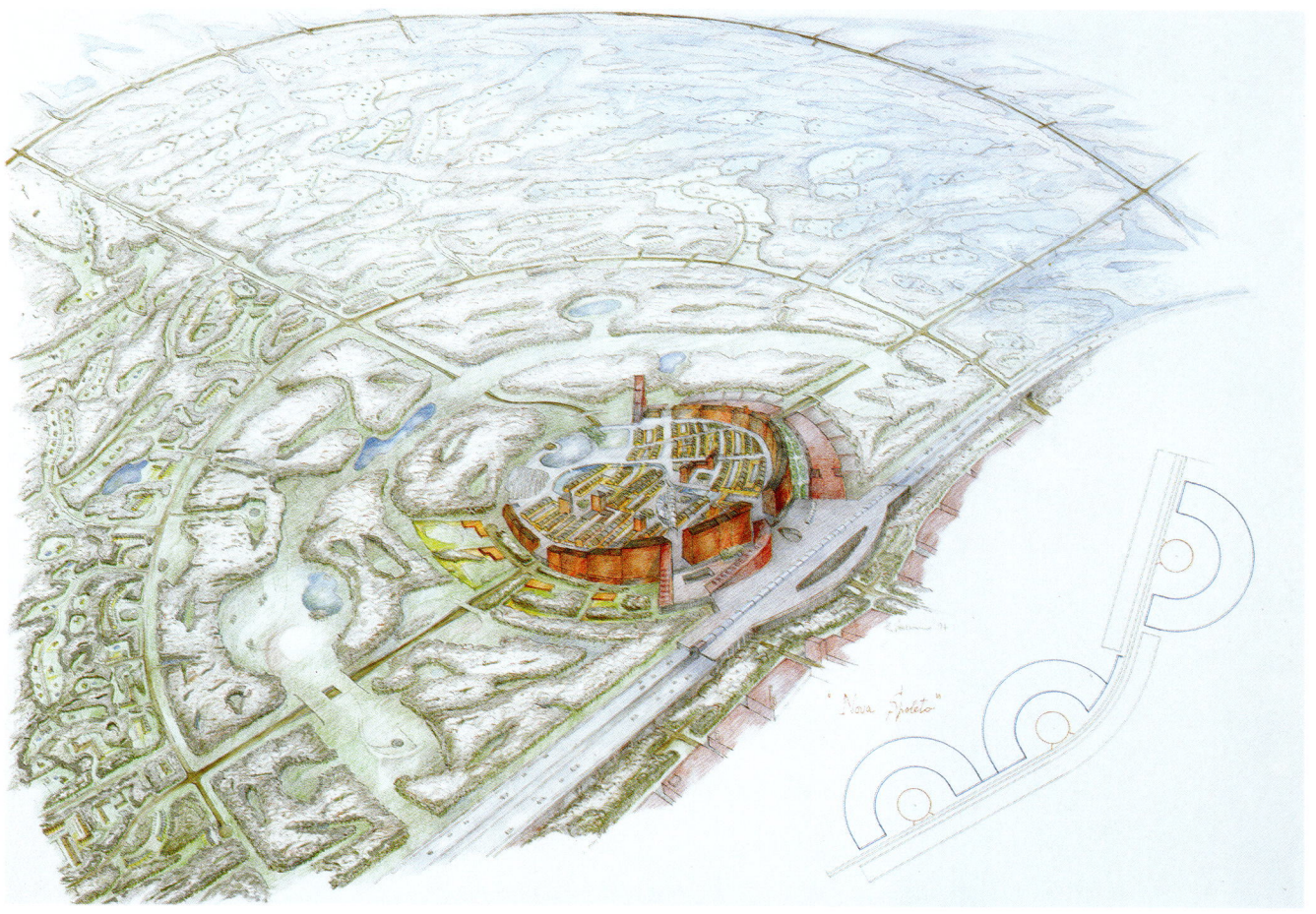

Skilab

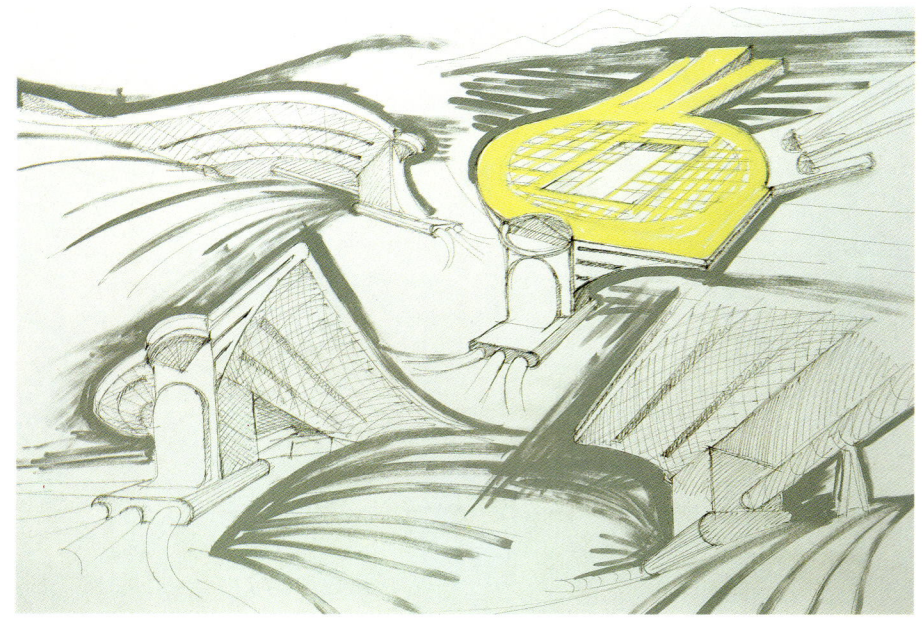

Sketches, elevations, sections and plan of a skiing facility in the mountains, conceived as a center for logistical and recreational activities.

Skiers reach Skilab from the valley by means of small tube trains.

Inside the building are restaurants, lounges, meeting rooms and protected sun terraces that can be covered by sliding skylights.

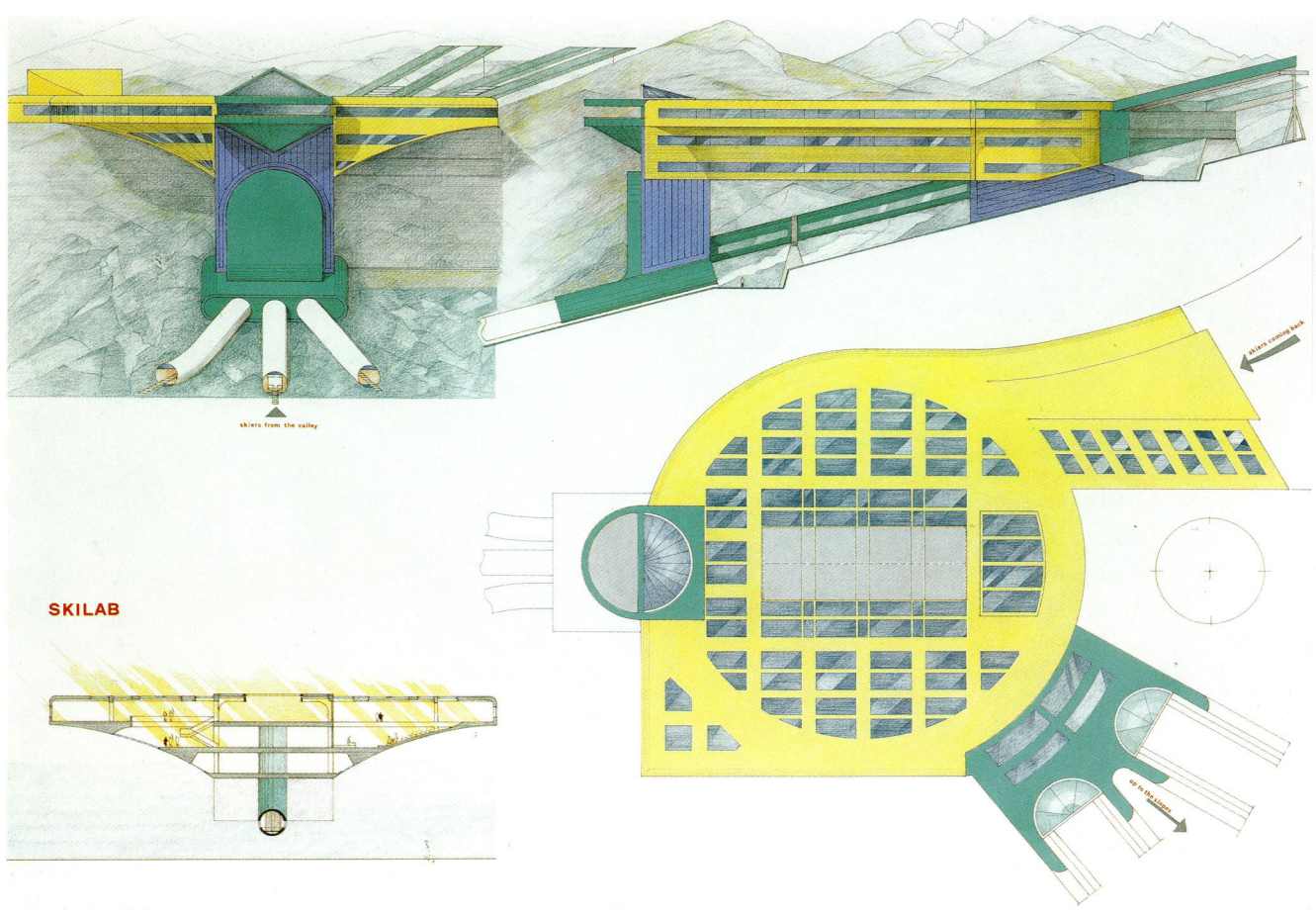

SKILAB

4 - A Possible Aesthetics for Meta-realism in a Future Projection

If neither traditional nor technological language is to find a place in the new architecture that is capable of silent communication, how are we to define the aesthetics of Meta-realism? Architectural languages are systems invented by man to establish relationships between concepts that can be expressed through conventional signs, using the same metaphors in different situations. Nature, on the other hand, although daily creating infinite examples in the animal, vegetable and mineral worlds, uses the reproductive mechanisms of each species or structure to place it within a well-defined system, where the same forms are always used. Moreover, Nature, although it produces an infinite variety of themes, with components deriving from various systems and species, uses expressions that cannot really be termed a language, insofar as they do not express complex ideas or emotions by means of conventional signs.

Nature basically shows only a system of construction that follows the most suitable technique for each scope, the right environment and the pre-determined function, conceived in its logical dimension, always in the most direct and economical mode. In analyzing natural form, moreover, the difficulty in judging certain intrinsic developments in each species and the reasons, either environmental or biological, that have produced them must be taken into consideration.

The aesthetics of Meta-realism will come in part from natural shapes derived from a mode of construction concerned with the appropriate use of materials and the right techniques for each context. Technical progress will of course take place, as it always has, but following a biomorphic theory of development conditioned by its functionality with the most logical, direct solutions required for each particular situation. The physical structure of the architectural installation will derive from this formulation and will determine the methodology of the development.

Each architect will find his or her own mode of expression, developing and refining it in the best and easiest way, to achieve an ever simpler and more logical construction, in the same way as Nature does, without having to adhere to principles that determine an aesthetics a priori based on pre-established symbols. This biomorphism must therefore be spontaneous, deriving from a form made natural through the absence of language.

Within this context, the problem of level of complexity and possible refinement of solutions of biomorphic derivation must be dealt with. Particularly in considering the future, there is of course the factor of financial limitation due to the complexity of the construction, since biomorphism tends to use curves and elaborate designs, which are potentially costly to create. The Modern Movement instead leaned towards economy, due to the schematic nature of its solutions. However, a certain number of architects belonging to this movement succeeded in creating notable works that, while remaining within the limits of Modernism, were of more complex origin based on a conception of biomorphic inspiration.

One of these architects was Pier Luigi Nervi, who between 1935 and 1965 used such an economical technology in the design and construction of his roofs, achieving aesthetically brilliant results and creating a refined biomorphism. These complex constructions could be built because the cost of labor in Italy at that time was relatively low, whereas the cost of materials was proportionately much higher. It was therefore logical to save on materials rather than on labor costs.

The tridimensional elements of Nervi's large constructions consisted of prefabricated parts, first made by hand and then assembled in sequence and linked together by a final concrete casting. The prefabricated elements, relatively light since they had a very thin structure, were made with great precision. It was in fact their lightness that determined the economic factor and simultaneously created a refined aesthetics, far removed from the crude directness of technological solutions, producing complex and detailed configurations deriving only from the logic of the distribution of forces within the structure. The specific construction process of this type of architecture was in itself organic because it was manual and slow, producing many small elements to be put together gradually in the creation of great volumes, just as coral reefs or beehives are created. This technique was diametrically opposed to the rapid mechanized technological process. Nervi, the engineer, was in fact, a sculptor of great internal spaces who used a technical medium to give shape to his fervent imagination. (10)

While Nervi's biophormism was directed toward resolving the structural problems of great roof spans, that of Alvar Aalto and Aero Saarinen was turned more towards solutions of organic derivation with a more three-dimensional tendency, involving both the structural and functional conception of the buildings. The naturalism of Saarinen in particular was inspired by a broader philosophy and a methodological and theoretical approach designed to solve more complex problems. Although it achieved important formal results, this approach tended to become a pure exercise in skill, exciting and original, but very uneconomical due to inefficient use of the spaces created and difficulties and cost of its construction. This philosophy, which produced some fine and still celebrated examples such as the TWA terminal at JFK Airport, New York, was destined to out-date itself since it was unable to attract a large following due to its insuperable economic limitations.

At the same time, the work of Frank Lloyd Wright, which developed along similar lines of organic origin, produced a philosophy that was to indirectly influence the whole of XX century architecture, with a series of works indicating a number of sure roads to the creation of spaces with a consistent personal form. Wright's organic starting point was to prove an important contribution and a lesson in balance, born of the genuine American tradition, which has not been lost even after the damage caused by the storms of rational Modernism and the traditional revival.

Even before Wright the Art Nouveau movement, prominent at the turn of the century, undoubtedly made a significant organic contribution, extending to all fields of art including furniture and other objects in search of new solutions unrestricted by the pressures of tradition and technology. The works produced by this movement, inspired by personalities such as Mackintosh, Hoffmann and Horta, clearly show the efforts made by these artists to free architecture from the excesses of either the Beaux Arts school or the purely technological one. It is not surprising that the Art Nouveau movement developed at the same time as the Chicago School and was contemporary with the construction of the Brooklyn Bridge in New York, in the last decade of the XIX century. These two schools emphasize the revolutionary spirit of architects of genius whose work was an attempt to find a new equilibrium capable of resisting the negative influences of the time.

In hypothesizing an architecture of the future, it will surely be impossible to create physical permanence and high artistic quality without taking account of the relevant financial costs. The subject of cost and relative durability of buildings must be faced as part of the meta-realistic synthesis in order to guarantee the stability and continuity of cities. Historically only high quality buildings are handed down to the future, because they were well built and thus can last longer.

In architecture the integrity of forms of biomorphic derivation is the major element supporting the logical structure of the composition. This integrity has two specific qualities. The first of these is formal equilibrium since Nature always completes its constructions within a pre-established sequence, where each element in a composition is expressed in a form deriving from its role. The stability and aesthetic durability of each composition will thus be guaranteed by the geometric equilibrium of the parts. The second consists of immediacy of communication of the spiritual image, which must appear distinctly at first sight without allusions. The sincerity and instinct of the composer make the music precise and perfectly structured but at the same time easy to listen to.

As far as integrity is concerned, the dilemma between simplicity and complexity does not really exist, when it is possible to achieve the clarity of immediate communication and the beauty dictated by just proportions. In terms of logical development, we may observe how Nature can turn back to the most direct road by a system of self-correction that produces a form more suited to the new need. It has been seen how Nature has made corrections where two programs are superimposed, thus preparing an evolution or change of direction. But it is obvious that human thought can only reach simplicity by the longest and most difficult path, through analyzing, decomposing and recomposing in a search for the solution judged to be right at that moment. The crucial factor in this research, more than the architect's self-control, is the time allowed by economic constraints for producing the design, which seems to be ever shorter.

As regards the proportions of parts in terms of the whole, Nature never errs, using its own measure based on the internal balance of the species. Thus each part of the composition takes on, according to its function and within the pre-established limits, the appropriate dimension, structure and weight. But this is not to say that nature always produces beautiful forms. Obviously, when the proportions are not decided by nature, it is up to the architect to produce the right synthesis. Here it should be noted that Meta-realism in art has always applied the same criteria in the search for compositional balance. This phenomenon is documented by all realistic works from different historical periods. The observation of art over the course of time shows us, in fact, that when the human mind achieves the realistic state it has always found the same proportions, within contingent limits, rejecting the distortions produced by the search for a new approach.

It is to be hoped that our society, already subjected to many conflicting pressures, will reject an architecture of self-deception derived from an ethical-aesthetical void that uses a symbolistic cover-up typical of the uncertain times of decadence. The further appearance of new "isms" on the art scene will only mean the resurgence of extremist ideologies which are certainly not conducive to a built environment of permanence. A meta-realistic architecture consisting instead of balanced organic solutions, free from distorted and preconceived ideas, will bring to our society a balanced way of life that we have been seeking for decades.

Another significant element in the aesthetics of biomorphism is its forms of expression, which can be read at different levels. The communicative power of the form of natural origin will prove once again to be substantial, influencing as it does all elements of human evaluation ranging from intellectual comprehension to the emotions and senses (11).

10) Since 1960 the construction techniques described here have become economically unfeasible, inasmuch as they require intensive labor, which by this time had become very expensive so that it only be used to obtain an exceptional architectural effect. Steel structures made of standardized elements became the most economic and rapid method of covering large spaces but they lacked the fascination of the aesthetic stability and richness typical of natural forms.

11) - See page 153 - The power of the senses stimulated by forms of pleasing proportions and great beauty, also to be seen in the physical attraction between the sexes, is inherent to an appreciation of the forms of the human body in general. Human aesthetic judgement instinctively reacts first to proportion, not mediated by any other considerations. This aesthetic judgement, which derives from the instinct of natural selection aiming toward improvement of the species, perceives instantaneously the difference between forms that are the most attractive and others that are less so. This fact has been exploited by experts in marketing, conditioning to a great extent all sectors of production, where a similar instant communication has been used to attract the consumer. Successful marketing either emphasized existing natural forms or created an image that would produce an attraction of sensorial origin, often based on human sexuality. All kinds of containers, from clothes to bottles, thus assumed a natural image as close as possible to the physical form of the human body, by the creation of pleasing proportions with sexual allusions. This appeal, particularly visible in all fields of fashion, tended to remain within the limits of direct transmission of a purely sensorial or fetishistic type of message. It was however clear to those who believed in the stability of the architectural presence above and beyond fashion that aesthetics born in the realm of the senses and used as a consumeristic attraction had obvious limitations, being unable to provide a stable intellectual or emotional equilibrium. Is this merely a purely aesthetic manifestation in which the elegance and sensuality of the form are signs of decadence?

A series of architectural experiments were made by the author, creating a organic design translated into sinuous lines recalling the human form. These forms were used successfully for office buildings located in the countryside of New York State, constructed using curtain walls. The appearance of fluidity was pleasing and fitted in well with the surrounding environment, being neither mechanical nor menacing.

Such architectural solutions follow the tradition of the nude sculpture or perhaps even more the painted nude. The allusions to the physical shape of the body in Cranach's "Eve" or the "Maja Desnuda" may appear excessive in this context if we consider the difference and level in the result: realistically clear in the painting but only indirect in architecture. But such a parallel may not be out of place as regards the inspiration of a building conceived as a form placed in a natural context, and thus seen as a reclining figure of classical inspiration. In parallel, this inspiration is very effective in the design of cars, whose shapes seem to suggest a much broader significance is apparent in the first visual impression of the object itself.

The human form is suggested in these buildings which represent an effort to give shape to an architectural container limited by its function, which is purely practical. In the absence of higher values, an attempt was made to design a building whose appeal would be instinctive and immediate.

Non meta-realistic architecture

Two buildings constructed in the Eighties in Westchester County, New York.
Renato Severino Associates, Architects and Planners.

Top: Mount Pleasant Corporate Center.
Center: Mr. Norman McGrath who photographed the two buildings is shown at work.
Bottom: Sandbank Studios.

These buildings are considered attractive and are also efficient containers for business activities, but their limited functional scope lacks that permanent social dimension capable of giving continuous long-term significance to architecture. Predominance of the utilitarian aspects shortens the life of a building.

5) Town and City in the XXI Century

a - URBAN VERSUS SUBURBAN

Since the Seventies the inhabitants of the western nations have become increasingly suburban. In the United States particularly, in 1990 over 65 percent of the total population was living in suburbs that had grown rapidly in the preceding twenty years.

This phenomenon of migration, visible on both sides of the ocean, has been attributed to the flight from the cities of the middle class in search of a better life in the countryside. Living in large cities had become increasingly difficult and expensive due mainly to the large influx of the poorer sector of the population unable to contribute toward paying rising costs of operation and being, on the contrary, constantly in need of help. City life has thus lost its aura of glamor and seems no longer the source of regional or even national mental energy, while the cultural tension resulting from the continuous confrontation of ideas and power has been perceived as progressively diminishing. The countryside has thus begun to attract those families who dreamed of choosing their own environment with their own life-style in a bucolic setting. Industries and corporations also began moving outside the city boundaries, taking advantage of the newly built highways in the countryside. Their prevailing dream was to recreate the campus life with the subdued tones of a protected and secluded enclave.

In the United States the exodus to the country was so massive that in a few years the old problems of the inner cities were almost entirely recreated there, first among them the traffic problem due to the rapid increase in the number of cars and their daily mileage. The longed-for freedom led to the creation of a great number of green belts, buffers and large private parking lots in the attempt to find isolation and privacy. The distances between buildings increased exponentially along with the extension of the road systems. As a consequence, the operative costs of all municipalities increased immensely in proportion to the size of the services network, spread out over larger territories, while leisure time was drastically slashed by the hours taken up in commuting to work and driving in general. In addition to the quantifiable negative factors, there are other more subtle aspects of suburban life that are equally disturbing. Too often an unappealing built environment and the pervading sensation of an amorphous bidimensional chaotic sequence of structures negates that necessary sense of place which is basic to the human civilized spirit. While longing to create their own world, many individuals in moving to the countryside have too often produced an incoherent assembly of solitudes and incommunicative personal domains. Many refugees of the old cities with a glorious cultural history find themselves citizens of a non-descriptive town made up of the same chain stores, gas station and autodealers to be seen everywhere in the nation. In those communities the feeling of having become an anonymous citizen of the XX century buried alive in suburban America suddenly becomes pervasive.

Peter G. Rowe, professor of architecture and urban planning, Dean of the Graduate School of Design of Harvard University, has put forth in several books and articles a very coherent and brilliant overall view of the growth of the american suburbs. Refering to various proposals and strategies of other authors on this subject, Peter Rowe writes:

"It is not at all clear, for example, where the constant reconfiguration and despecializing of America metropolitan areas is leading in broad social terms. Finally, much more speculation is required around contemporary urban-architectural themes including district making, viable suburban infill, and redesign of sprawling mixed-use realms which form so much of the current context for urban life. The American metropolitan landscape is still very underdeveloped in both a physical and cultural sense. Like the city and country beforehand, which were constantly being made and remade, the initial outlines of this domain are now in need of thoughtful elaboration".

b - WHERE THE NEW URBAN ENTITIES ARE DEVELOPING

All over the world, not only in Europe and the United States, a relentless migration of people and industries is taking place due to impelling economic motives generated by growing international competition in all fields of production of goods and services for the global market. The necessity for cutting labor and related costs generates a relentless search among entrepreneurs and multinationals for areas that can offer a better economic package with a cheaper labor force and an existing network of services and transportation. These areas are not situated in the classic industrial regions of the past half century that became so crowded and consequently very expensive, making it necessary for companies to pay employees high salaries. These new developments are instead cropping up far from the large cities of the northeast and west coasts of the United States and the high-cost areas of Europe. The development of electronics, moreover, has made communication with every point in the world extremely easy. There is no longer any reason for the major companies to keep their large clerical staffs in regions that require high salaries to match the cost of living. The new areas offer labor, office space and housing at lower costs. Employees are guaranteed a satisfactory life style without constantly being confronted by the temptation of luxuries beyond their reach, fuelling discontent, as was the case in the fashionable big cities.

The industrial dislocation that produces local unemployment in the abandoned districts has generated strong political disputes. Those who believe in the economic defense of their territory and want to keep alive local industries to protect local jobs forcefully oppose those who believe instead in the free market doctrine that defends the right to produce goods and services anywhere in the world. Will this new territorialism which embraces all aspects of traditionalism be able to successfully oppose the globalism of the free market ideology? Certainly, the results of this opposition could have a major influence on the pace of development of the new industrial areas or on the salvation of the old ones. The final years of this century will be critical in deciding this matter.

Our prevailing concern for the new areas of development has to do their growth, which on the average is taking place without any precise and all-encompassing plans, and merely with the goal of quickly providing basic accommodations for new communities. The common belief seems to be that, despite the dramatic growth in world population, no new cities will be built in the future; there will be simply the unchecked growth of the existing ones, spreading out into ever larger suburbs.

In many regions of the western nations the volume of construction has more than doubled in the last thirty years, but in a disorderly and incoherent manner. This situation explains why the classic cities such as Paris, London, New York and San Francisco, with their distinct personalities, are increasingly flooded with tourists eager to experience the sculptural values of their architecture and the feeling of permanence deriving from the secular historical heredity.

The new communities of the western countries are taking on a major responsibility in disregarding the cultural element of urban space and opting for mere functionalism. By using the territory simply ad hoc, like warehouse space to be abandoned when it is no longer useful, they are compromising their future. The essential characteristic of a stable society is the planning in all its details of long-term action to prevent the loss of initial investments and to protect the future of the built environment. The nomad society, which numbers millions within the boundaries of the United States, constantly dislocates from one place to another leaving behind discarded shells of buildings, ultimately leading to the demise of many areas. The architecture of the XX century has, in fact, mirrored a rapidly changing and dramatically growing society that has not only demolished constrictive social and psychological barriers, but also wreaked incalculable damage on our planet. The planning activity and the architectural process of the first part of the XXI century will, instead, have to represent a more balanced society, ecologically concerned and closer to the ideals of Meta-realism

It is to be hoped that constant, responsible and coherent action will be taken by citizens to obtain a high-quality built environment for the growing number of new communities now are being established. Valid guide lines for debating and voting on all items should be set up to evaluate detailed proposals coming directly from the community, rather than seeking rapid public consensus on preconceived alternative plans. The contribution of creative ideas coming from citizens is essential in shaping the new urban fabric, while proposals of unconcerned commercial developers can be disruptive for the equilibrium of the town. It is essential that the residents know in advance the cost of each and every alternative project as well as its advantages since they are the ones who will have to pay. It will also be advisable to construct theoretical models to be translated into a system of exploratory virtual reality for testing before any final decision is taken to implement the approved plan.

c - TWO OPPOSED CONCEPTS OF URBAN FABRIC: STRUCTURED PLANNING OF RENAISSANCE HERITAGE VERSUS EPISODIC SUBURBAN SPRAWL.

A structured planning activity totally programmed in three dimensions and in all details calls for a decisive, precise course of continuous action. Consequently, the intelligent direction of a team of capable, talented planners and architects is required to lead this activity and to implement this decisive course of action but, above all, it is essential that the consensus of the community be consistent over a considerable length of time. Such a consensus is difficult to obtain because there is at present a trend toward rapid shifts in the priorities of the electorate. Voters frequently endanger the coherence of a sequential decision-making process in projects that require some time to implement.

An episodic system of suburban planning, on the other hand, is much easier to direct because it is more flexible and receptive to diverse inputs and is ready to accept, at different times, various changes of course. Such a system has a potential for great freedom to implement the most diverse concepts. Los Angeles is an example of this type as it represents a chaotic yet often attractive environment that, while plagued by all sorts of problems including traffic and pollution, is considered by the followers of the episodic suburban planning a successful solution free from constrictions.

Individual freedom in planning has a marked tendency to become uncontrolled license, as can be seen in many suburbs where disorder reigns supreme. On the other hand, as has been only too often experienced in the last fifty years, a plan implemented with rigour and decisional ability that is however an unbalanced one can damage both the individuals and the community.

To obtain positive results, it is certainly easier to successfully plan, totally and tridimensionally, a limited area of urban space that becomes the hinge on which the whole architectural composition rotates. Therefore, it is necessary to design urban spaces able to create elements of cohesion, with a distinctive personality, recognizable at a distance, that become meeting areas for the public and serve as centers of gravity of communitary cultural interest. The dynamic idea of this search is in the ability of finding creative solutions capable of avoiding the limiting and uncreative zoning syndromes, while outlining a new strict system of controls supported by the community. A new concept of contemporary urban aggregation with many of the features of the old city centers should be proposed, within the constraints of the existing situation. It will then be necessary to try to reinstate, with an appropriate architecture, the sense of belonging of the community to one specific place of its own, as a first step towards a constructed entity able to last well into the future.

d - A NEW CONCEPT OF CONTEMPORARY URBAN AGGREGATION: **MULTILINK TOWNSHIP PATTERN - MTP.**
AN OUTLINE OF A REALISTIC SOLUTION: **NOVA SPOLETO.**

A new dimension in a wider perspective must be found for the growing suburban environment and for the new urban fabric of the XXI century.

Four principles should direct the planning activity:

1 - A new degree of freedom should be offered each individual in assembling his or her built environment in a common framework, while projecting towards the future the certainty of a stable cultural relationship between the community and the tridimensional physical space of the town center.

2 - The per capita costs of construction, maintenance and operation of each planning solution, of which the ecological aspects are a most important element, will be made clear to all.

3 - A new notion of functionality will have to be offered, updated to the current socio-economical situation, that considers the allocation of time necessary for each task performed by each inhabitant, a major component in the evaluation process.

4 - A wider awareness will have to be encouraged for cultural, socio-political and ethical choices in relation to the administration of the built environment. This should be conceived as an entity beyond the limits and the prejudices of the zoning ordinances, which are now mainly derived from engineering standards.

The new urban aggregation conceived as a systematic approach which we call **MULTILINK TOWNSHIP PATTERN - MTP** can be structured on the territory as a series of contiguous entities that are psychologically and economically self-sufficient from the point of view of basic services. Each Township, part of the Pattern, will be designed for a fixed maximum number of inhabitants with very precise rules of development that will limit the size and number of buildings in each area. Any growth beyond the established limits will be transferred over to the next town if this is still not complete, or to a new one to be initiated. The Townships are connected by a highway system and by rail, in addition to slower internal roads of the countryside. A mass transit corridor will develop along the industrial-commercial areas and corporate office parks will be built on the other side of the Town Centers, along the highways and the railroads. All areas of the same zoning aggregation in each town of the Pattern will be linked and will be in direct contact with one another. In each fascia of diverse building types there will be a consistency of activities and similar type of traffic. The final result is an urban pattern made up of a series of nuclei, each with its own shape and function in a continuous chain. This pattern can become an integral and complete city, with a personality of its own, if the relationship among all its parts is unitarian and visually appealing as a whole entity.

NOVA SPOLETO, a township of 20 - 30,000 inhabitants, can be described as follows:

The design concept rotates around the Town Center which is visually and functionally the focus of the composition. The Center is built over a multi-traffic Platform penetrated on one side by the highway and by the railway. The transportation center is conceived as one multi-faceted facility that includes train and bus stations connected to the highway exits and a large poly-functional garage and truck loading areas. All these buildings are covered and, therefore, easily usable in any climate.

The Platform is designed to contain a series of multi-storey garages and pedestrian corridors to connect all buildings of the Center. A service of small electrical busses will operate within the Platform while a number of bus lines will connect all areas of the town. A series of courtyards and skylights give air and natural light to the areas underneath the Platform. The surface of this structure consists of a series of pedestrian plazas, surrounded by porticos, on which are located the shops, restaurants and cafes, banks and professional offices, the post office, some churches and temples and entrance foyers of theaters. The truck unloading areas are underneath these buildings. Apartment buildings of various heights and density will be built around the edges of the Platform, which also includes their garages.

The Town Center in consideration of all its different activities will be animated and in use day and night. From an architectural point of view, it is visualized as a tridimensional entity similar to an old European town, offering an attractive environment in which to live and work. From such a state of intimacy and trust derives affection for the physical space and long-lasting attachment to it. Appreciation of the proportions of a space is very similar to a respect for ethical principles. On this sense of values is founded the permanence of classical architecture; the old cities, in fact, were defended and have survived throughout the centuries because of such values and their monuments are the symbols of their continuity. The design and quality of the materials of an architecture is therefore essential to assure the permanence of a city. Buildings can be constructed using various materials and design approaches, giving greater freedom to users and developers.

On one side of the Town Center, several areas with lower density will be designated for schools, churches and museums while the opposite side will be allocated to commercial and large retail buildings. All these structures will use the multi-storey parking garage under the Platform designed with advanced safety and security features; they will thus be fully utilized at all times and their spaces allocated according to routine use for special events. One of the most important aspects of this proposed plan is its avoidance of the large visible parking lots that are usually located around buildings and are unattractive and not conducive to contemporary economical solutions. Parking lots, in fact, destroy the continuity of architectural space and increase the road systems and the costs and time of transportation, both public and private. A spread-out town also needs a larger network of utilities and larger police and fire-fighter forces. In the proposed solution instead, high school students need not drive to school but can use the bus system which is very efficient over short distances.

The Town Center is accessible from the residential areas, through the park and visible gates that underline its significance and are instrumental in delineating and controlling the defensible space. The residential areas are accessible from the radial roads departing from the Center and from those linked to the internal and external circular boulevards. From this major road system will depart the secondary roads that follow the terrain in an episodic way and lead to individual family houses built on lots ranging in size from a quarter acre to a maximum of one acre. Lots larger than one acre will be allowed only on the area outside the external circular boulevard. Town houses and small apartment buildings will be built on the internal circular boulevard, but only on the side away from the park.